AF228374

DRANESVILLE

A Northern Virginia Town in the Crossfire
of a Forgotten Battle, December 20, 1861

Ryan T. Quint

Savas Beatie
California

First edition, first printing

ISBN-13: 978-1-61121-693-6 (hardcover)
ISBN-13: 978-1-61121-694-3 (ebook)

Library of Congress Cataloging-in-Publication Data

Names: Quint, Ryan T., author.
Title: Dranesville : A Northern Virginia Town in the Crossfire of a Forgotten Battle, Dec. 20, 1861 / by Ryan T. Quint.
Other titles: Town in the crossfire of a forgotten battle, Dec. 20, 1861
Description: El Dorado Hills, CA : Savas Beatie, [2024] | Includes bibliographical references and index. | Summary: "The fall and early winter of 1861 was a hotbed of activity that culminated in the December combat at Dranesville. A host of characters and commands that would become household names cut their teeth during these months. Though soon eclipsed by larger and bloodier battles, Dranesville remained a defining moment for many of its participants--soldiers and civilians alike--for the rest of their lives"-- Provided by publisher.
Identifiers: LCCN 2023052926 | ISBN 9781611216936 (hardcover) | ISBN 9781611216943 (ebook)
Subjects: LCSH: Dranesville, Battle of, Dranesville, Va., 1861. | Virginia--History--Civil War, 1861-1865. | Dranesville (Va.)--History--19th century.
Classification: LCC E472.6 .Q56 2024 | DDC 975.5/03--dc23/eng/20231213
LC record available at https://lccn.loc.gov/2023052926

SB

Savas Beatie
989 Governor Drive, Suite 102
El Dorado Hills, CA 95762
916-941-6896 / sales@savasbeatie.com / www.savasbeatie.com

All of our titles are available at special discount rates for bulk purchases in the United States. Contact us for information.

Printed and bound in the United Kingdom

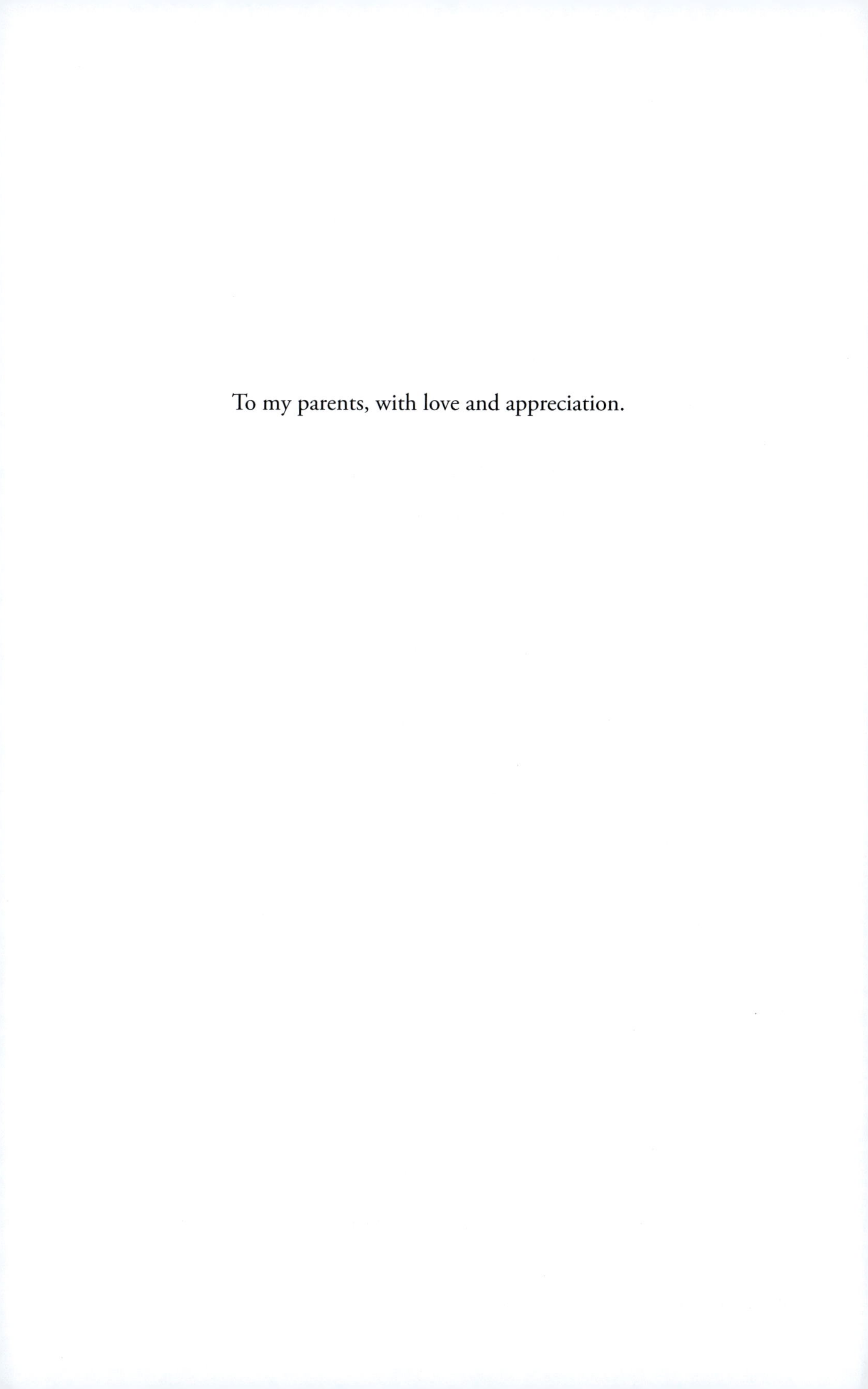

To my parents, with love and appreciation.

LIST OF MAPS

ABBREVIATIONS

BYU: Brigham Young University

CSR: Compiled Service Record

FRSP: Fredericksburg & Spotsylvania National Military Park

Frank English Letters: "Letters and Genealogy of the Means-English Families, 1828-1950"

LOC: Library of Congress

NARA: National Archives and Records Administration

OR: Official Records of the Union and Confederate Armies

JCCW: Report of the Joint Committee on the Conduct of the War

USAHEC: United States Army Heritage and Education Center

USC: University of South Carolina

VMHC: Virginia Museum of History & Culture

WCU: Western Carolina University

Photos have been placed throughout the text for the convenience of the reader.

Introduction

The following pages are proof as to how a project can take on a life of its own, twisting and turning into something entirely unexpected. I came to the battle of Dranesville in a rather roundabout way. The story starts with the wounding of Thomas "Stonewall" Jackson at the battle of Chancellorsville.

When Jackson went down from a volley fired by his own troops, command of the Army of Northern Virginia's Second Corps lay in flux. Major General A. P. Hill at first took charge of the corps, but he was soon wounded himself, the victim of Federal artillery fire. The other division commanders in Jackson's corps were not yet experienced enough, nor did they have the appropriate rank, to lead almost 28,000 men and officers. So, Robert E. Lee turned to Maj. Gen. James Ewell Brown (J. E. B.) Stuart.

Commanding the Confederate army's cavalry, Stuart reached the scene around midnight on May 3. He inherited a command expected to continue Jackson's attack from the evening before, though it was badly fragmented by the thick confines of Spotsylvania's Wilderness. In a matter of hours, Stuart organized the corps and launched a series of devastating attacks against the Union lines around Chancellorsville. By 10:00 a.m., Maj. Gen. Joseph Hooker's Army of the Potomac was in full retreat from Chancellorsville. The Army of Northern Virginia had won another victory, however impractical it seemed on paper.

This was a story I told as I worked for the National Park Service at the Fredericksburg & Spotsylvania National Military Park. On programs that focused on Jackson's wounding and its aftermath, I always mentioned the arrival of J. E. B. Stuart early in the morning to assume responsibility for the action. Up to that point, I explained, Stuart had only commanded infantry once before in the war, at the battle of Dranesville—where Stuart had led some 2,000 soldiers.

Now he was expected to command 28,000 in his second infantry command. The battle of Dranesville hadn't gone so well for Stuart, but at Chancellorsville, his leadership played a large role in the eventual Confederate victory. In those retellings I gave for visitors at the National Park, many people had never heard of the December 20, 1861, engagement, and that's not very surprising, considering the dearth of material about it. There are certainly articles about the battle, or chapters set amongst larger works, but this is the first monograph dedicated solely to the actions around Dranesville in the fall and winter of 1861.

In those articles and summaries of the battle, Dranesville is usually classified as a meeting engagement of two opposing foraging parties that bumped into each other and started the battle. That is partially true, but as I began to research, I realized there was an undercurrent of events that never seemed to get any mention. And that is where the project began to develop in its own direction. My original intention was to write a tactical narrative and analysis of the battle of Dranesville—something that I believe I have still accomplished—but I quickly realized telling that story required coming at it from another angle that up until now others had overlooked. That angle involved the very active role that the civilians of Dranesville played in their own story. White and Black, free and enslaved, Unionist and Confederate, the people of the tiny town threw themselves into the conflict that began to tear at the country's seams in April 1861. Dranesville's civilian activity eventually produced responses from both armies in the fall of 1861. That led to the persecution of Unionists, ambushes of Federal soldiers, and raids into town in the days and weeks before the formal battle of Dranesville. The events of this cat-and-mouse game have never been discussed to any serious length until now, and readers will find the whole story in the pages that follow.

Occurring in the winter of 1861, Dranesville has often been overshadowed by other, larger battles, including the war's first major engagement at First Manassas that summer. Smaller battles like Wilson's Creek and Ball's Bluff still held sway in the northern populace's consciousness in a line of Federal defeats. But Dranesville did have important ramifications. First, the Federal victory there, no matter how small it was, gave the sagging Union morale a badly needed boost. Second, it proved to be a baptism of fire and chance to command large numbers of troops for officers who would go on to become some of the war's most famous leaders. Edward Ord, for example, commanded a brigade of Pennsylvania Reserves in its first fight. He finished the war commanding the Army of the James; the Reserves became one of the finest divisions in the Army of the Potomac. For the Confederates, J. E. B. Stuart's defeat at Dranesville proved to be a blackmark against his record that drew criticism both by fellow officers and newspaper editorialists, with some even calling for his removal from command. It was criticism that he would weather and overcome—rising to prominence as commander of the Army of Northern Virginia's cavalry until his death in 1864. I wanted to dive into and flesh out these stories, of which I only had a bare understanding. With that, the project morphed into a story about a town, its people, and a battle that transformed the lives of everyone involved.

Acknowledgments

This project has taken nearly seven years to complete, and it would not have been possible to finish without the help of the numerous people below. I hope each one of them knows they have my ultimate thanks for the million ways they showed support and assisted during the course of writing this book.

The thanks start with the legions of librarians and archivists who helped in the search for materials. That includes the staff of the Central Rappahannock Regional Library, the Virginia Museum of History & Culture, the City of Alexandria Library, the Library of Congress, the University of Virginia, Minnesota Historical Society, the New York State Library, Winthrop University, and the Public Library of Anniston-Calhoun County. The staff at the University of South Carolina, especially McKenzie Lemhouse, helped find Frank English's correspondence and the wartime photo of John Bratton, reprinted below. Because of my repeated visits to the Virginia Room at the Fairfax County Library, Christopher Barbuschak, Michele Bernocco, Suzanne LaPierre, and Elaine McRey all deserve special thanks. Victoria Thompson at the Fairfax County Court House helped track down the Coroner's Inquest for Henry St. Clair.

Early in the phases of research that led to this book, Ron Baumgarten graciously fielded questions about Dranesville, and Jim Gandy at the New York State Military Museum pointed me to resources for the 34th New York Infantry. Becky Ryer sent me the writings of her ancestor, Cordello Collins, a Bucktail with the 1st Pennsylvania Rifles, and Maureen Lavelle saved me a trip all the way out to Utah when she scanned the papers of Thomas Kane for me. Becca Toy likewise scanned material from the College of William & Mary. Brandi Oswald, a friend and archivist at the National Archives, saved the day when they helped track down the proceedings and case files of Dranesville's accused men, which had been misplaced on the shelves at College Park. All the way out in California friend David Dixon scanned documents from the collections of the esteemed Huntington Library. Pittsburgher Jim DiNucci, one of the kindest people I've ever met and worked with, sought out the grave of Alexander Smith and sent me photos. Rich Condon, another proud Pittsburgher, sent along information about Capt. Robert Galway.

Just as I seemed to be coming to the end of the research for this book the outbreak of COVID-19 brought everything to a screeching halt. Some of the research I still needed was housed in the papers of Edward Ord, at Stanford University—obviously a vital piece of the puzzle. The staff at Stanford's special collections, led by Tim Noakes, sent nearly 100 scans of Ord's letters in what amounted to a game-saver.

Closer to home, friend and co-worker at the Fredericksburg & Spotsylvania National Military Park, Noel Harrison, found out about my Dranesville project and was more than happy to share his veritable wealth of knowledge from his days as a graduate student. He graciously shared an article that he wrote about the Fairfax civilian experience, which tipped me off to the much larger story of persecution of Unionists in 1861 in communities like Dranesville.

Help also came from the now retired Chief Historian at Fredericksburg, John Hennessy, who kindheartedly fielded questions that I had regarding Joseph Johnston's headquarters following the battle of First Manassas.

As the manuscript came along, I set out to compile a total list of casualties from the battle. One of my best friends, Sean Redmiles, helped in a project that proved mutually beneficial, as he worked at the Frying Pan Farm at the time. He scoured the compiled service records even more than I did. Then came John Moyle and his son, Matthew. Matthew's Eagle Scout Project was to establish a sign commemorating the battle. John joined the effort of totaling up the losses, not an easy task due to the multitude of newspapers with different names and spellings, and some names not reported. John also became a sounding board as I shared my interpretive ideas of the battle with him. I believe the list of names that is appended to this book is the end result of a lot of hard work by the likes of Sean, John, and Matthew. They deserve the credit and my thanks.

Once the rough draft of this manuscript was finished, many people read it over and sent back feedback that made what exists now a much better result. Chris Mackowski, a great historian and greater friend, read the entire thing and provided line edits. Jim Morgan, expert on the battle of Ball's Bluff, read my chapter on that engagement and saved me from some embarrassing hiccups. Jake Wynn, another person I'm privileged to call a friend, provided feedback and suggestions regarding Andrew Curtin's mobilization of Pennsylvania volunteers. Keith Poulter line edited the rough draft and caught several errors that would have otherwise gone unnoticed. His knowledge of the English language is a delight to behold, and our conversations sometimes made my head spin, but he was right every time. David Snyder likewise copyedited the manuscript and caught numerous mistakes that I thought I had earlier corrected. Shannon Doherty took a clunky and bloated manuscript and made it much more readable—she has since become my Civil War travel companion and my best friend. I am eternally grateful for all their efforts in making this a better book.

Edward Alexander masterfully created the maps, taking my sometimes rough and unclear directions and turning them into wonderful pieces of cartography that makes this a much more readable manuscript.

The staff at Savas Beatie, especially Ted Savas, Sarah Keeney, Lisa Murphy, and Veronica Kane were all extremely helpful in shepherding the project along. It has been a long time coming, and they helped to turn a series of disjointed Word documents into the book you hold today.

I must close by also thanking the congregation of the Church of the Brethren in Dranesville for welcoming me to their annual remembrance of the battle. I was an outsider looking to tell a story—their story—that they've known for so long and have kept alive. Their words of encouragement, especially from John Waggoner and Craig Stutzman, greatly aided me over the years, and their somber ceremony each December proved a continual reminder that this story is about people who breathed, lived, loved, and—ultimately—died at Dranesville.

Thank you all, sincerely, from the depths of my heart.

Prologue

"You Have Killed Him"

The Murder of Henry St. Clair

December 30, 1854, was a busy day in the small community of Dranesville, Virginia, 20 miles to the west from the District of Columbia. It started with the annual hiring out of enslaved people. A common practice throughout the institution of slavery, the hiring occurred on or around New Year's Day when enslavers auctioned off people for a year's worth of work to the highest bidder. Dranesville's hiring was no different. The town's small populace turned out at this public occasion to watch and place bids. Bidders looked up at the platform, considering the choices of human chattel up for auction. Neighbors vied against one another, competing for the best available bids as the day went on. They examined the people standing on the platform, checking for anything they could consider deficiencies in order to lower the asking price that the masters had set.[1] Lewis Clarke, formerly enslaved, later reminisced on the dread that accompanied the season: "If anybody is going to sell a slave, that's the time they do it; and if anybody's going to give away a slave, that's the time they do it; and the slave never knows where he'll be sent to. Oh, New-Year's a heart-breaking time."[2]

It's not known where exactly the bidding took place, but "local tradition in Dranesville is that slave hiring was conducted on a platform near the Drane

---

1 Jonathan Martin, *Divided Mastery: Slave Hiring in the American South* (Cambridge, 2004), 47.

2 Lewis Clarke, "Leaves from a Slave's Journal of Life," *The Anti-Slavery Standard, 20 and 27 October, 1842,* accessed Jan. 4, 2020. https://docsouth.unc.edu/neh/clarke/support1.html#menu_links.

Tavern."[3] When the hiring was finished, the crowds began to break up to look for food and drink to pass the evening. Many of them moved west down the Leesburg Pike, headed for another of the town's taverns owned by Henry Bicksler. One of those people, twenty-one-year-old Henry St. Clair, had just hours to live.

*   *   *

The September 8, 1818, edition of the Leesburg newspaper *Genius of Liberty* carried a brief advertisement. "Washington Drane respectfully informs his friends & the public in general, that he has opened a house of entertainment at his new building on the road leading from Georgetown to Leesburg—15 miles from the former and 16 miles from the latter." Drane's advert continued, "The house and furniture are new and elegant and every requisite attendance has been provided for the genteel accommodation of either parties of pleasure or persons on business." Drane came to call his establishment the Mountain View Hotel. Guests could stay for twelve and a half cents per night and get breakfast the following morning for another twenty-five cents.[4]

Washington Drane had come from the District of Columbia to set up his new hotel. His entire business plan hinged on location. As he was constructing his hotel, the Leesburg Pike was almost completed, opening travel between Georgetown and Leesburg. Drane figured his hotel would be a natural half-way stopping point for wagon traffic traveling between Washington and Leesburg. Nestled at the intersection between the Leesburg and Georgetown Turnpikes, Drane hoped to get business from both.[5]

The idea paid off handsomely. Historian Charles Poland writes, "From 1815 to 1830 it was commonplace for 40 or 50 wagons pulled by four and six horse teams to daily traverse the small town." That much business traveling down the turnpikes soon enticed others to open their own taverns and way stations so that, at one time, there were no fewer than five taverns operating within the immediate area.[6]

Even as others came to the growing community, they respected Washington Drane as the unofficial town leader. He was a toll collector on the turnpike and served as the community's postmaster.[7] Drane died in 1832; eight years later, the

---

3 Janet Hofer, "A Most Foul Murder," *Great Falls Historical Society Reflections*, 1984-1985, 17.

4 *Genius of Liberty*, Sep. 8, 1818; *Genius of Liberty*, Jul. 4, 1820; *Genius of Liberty*, Jun. 7, 1825.

5 *The Sixth, Seventh, and Eighth Annual Reports of the Board of Public Works to the General Assembly of Virginia: Volume 3* (Richmond, 1824), 79.

6 Charles Preston Poland Jr., *Dunbarton, Dranesville, Virginia* (Fairfax, VA, 1974), 17.

7 Gina McNeely, "Dranesville Tavern: The History of a Roadside Inn," *Virginia Cavalcade*, 43, No. 2, Autumn 1993, 74; *List of Post Offices in the United States, with the Names of the Post-Masters* (Washington, D.C., 1828), 30.

Virginia General Assembly set aside thirty acres of land to "be laid off into lots with convenient streets and alleys." This new town was to "go by the name of *'Dranesville.'"*[8]

Though the town was well established by the mid-1850s, it was still small enough that everyone seemed to be related to one another. For example, Drane's widow, Ann M. Dade, remarried the same year her husband died, this time to a man named John B. Farr. Farr assumed Drane's responsibilities as postmaster and Justice of the County Clerk.[9] The taverns continued to flourish—especially Drane's old Mountain View, which hosted the slave hirings every year at the eastern end of town.

By the 1850s, daily traffic through Dranesville kept the town afloat, though change lurked on the horizon. Just to the south, the Alexandria, Loudoun, & Hampshire Railroad Company was laying tracks through the town of Herndon. Soon, iron rails would siphon traffic away from mules and oxen, and from Dranesville.

On the evening of December 30, 1854, after the slave-hiring ended, Farr was joined by the soon-to-be-dead Henry St. Clair. The two ate dinner together, Farr recounted later. St. Clair finished his food first and left for Henry Bicksler's tavern. Farr followed soon after "smoking a segar." When he got to the tavern, Farr "heard a fuss and supposed there was a fight."[10]

Others were already clearing out of Bicksler's Tavern because of the growing tension. Doctor William B. Day, one of those who left, towered over most men, weighing nearly 275 pounds, with piercing blue eyes. Usually, he was affable and in good humor—those eyes of his closed "so tightly when he laughed that you could not see them."[11] Yet Day was far from jovial that night. "Twenty minutes before the fracas," he later said, "I was afraid there would be someone killed." Not wanting anything to do with the goings-on, Day made his way home, just a few hundred yards from the tavern.[12]

---

8 Daniel A. Willis, *Legends, Half-Truths, and Cherished Myths of the Drane Family* (Privately Published, 2016), 70; *Acts of the General Assembly of Virginia Passed at the Session Commencing 2nd December 1839, and Ending 19th March 1840* (Richmond, 1840), 128. Emphasis in original.

9 Edith A. Sprouse, ed., *Fairfax County in 1860: A Collective Biography*, Vol. 2 (Fairfax, VA, 1996), 633.

10 John B. Farr Deposition, Henry St. Clair Coroner's Inquest, Historical Records Room, Fairfax County Courthouse.

11 Elisabeth Alice Gibbens Cole, *An Account of Our Day Family of Calvert County, Maryland* (Lettsworth, MD, 1982), 73.

12 William B. Day Testimony, St. Clair Coroner's Inquest; Fairfax Commission Maps, 1860, 6-4, Historical Records Room, Fairfax County Circuit Courthouse.

Dr. William B. Day
in a poor original image.
*Courtesy of the Fairfax County Public
Library Photographic Archive*

Back inside Bicksler's, St. Clair began to antagonize a man named Thomas Dickey, picking the fight that would kill him. St. Clair and his friends grabbed Dickey, who "begged them to let him go," according to one witness. Bartender James Waldren remembered others crying out, "Let's have a fair fight!" Waldren and others jumped forward, trying to separate the men, and the melee was on.[13]

Dickey soon got reinforcements: his brothers John and Robert. John tried to enter the tavern but was stopped at the door. Shouting, "Let me git in, God Damn, let me git in," John Dickey started his assault, trying to get to his besieged brother while throwing punches in every direction. John B. Farr, recently arrived with his cigar, tried to stop Dickey, but soon "the crowd came rushing out," pushing both men out of the way.[14]

Finally, the bartender Waldren successfully cleared the room. Waldren grabbed St. Clair's collar and half-dragged, half-shoved the young man out of the door. Thomas Dickey, finally freed from St. Clair's grasp, decided to enact his revenge, and swung out with his fist, landing "several blows" on his attacker.[15]

As the masses of people tumbled out of the tavern and into the darkness, St. Clair had no idea who had hit him. But he had his suspicions. He lunged off the porch, shouting, "God damn your soul Bob Dickey. What did you hit me for."[16]

---

13 Townsend T. Milstead Testimony, St. Clair Coroner's Inquest; Deposition of James F. Waldren, St. Clair Coroner's Inquest.

14 Moses Williams Testimony, St. Clair Coroner's Inquest; John B. Farr Testimony, St. Clair Coroner's Inquest.

15 Deposition of James F. Waldren, St. Clair Coroner's Inquest; Henry Bicksler Testimony, St. Clair Coroner's Inquest.

16 William Walker Testimony, St. Clair Coroner's Inquest.

Robert Dickey, nine years older than St. Clair, had saved his brother, Thomas, and now found himself in the front yard of the tavern, standing in the darkness. It should have been nothing more than a standard bar brawl with a few punches and curses passed back and forth. But Robert Dickey, before he left the barroom, made a spur of the moment decision. He reached into his left pocket and pulled out a small knife. Many around Dickey, including Waldren, tried to convince him to put the knife away, but when St. Clair jumped from the porch, Dickey was still holding the weapon.[17]

A crowd gathered in front of the tavern, drawn to the commotion. In the darkness they now saw two figures start to fight and trade blows, but no one could tell who exactly was continuing to fight. Neither did they see Dickey's knife doing its deadly work. Minor Crippen, a resident of Dranesville, saw "a few blows lapsed" before he finally saw St. Clair's face clearly.[18]

St. Clair collapsed to the ground. The throng of onlookers, finally realizing something was wrong, surged forward. A small fire was burning nearby, and in those flames the people saw Robert Dickey stagger back. Witnesses saw his hand covered "as if he had dip'd it up to [the] elbow in a tub of blood."[19] They looked down at St. Clair, who was either already dead or very close to it. With adrenaline coursing through his body, it did not appear to have dawned on Robert Dickey what he had just done. Someone in the crowd said, aghast, "Robert you have killed him." Dickey snapped back into reality and sprinted off into the night.[20]

Farr's brother sent for Dr. Day, the same man who had left the tavern not a half hour before. Day investigated St. Clair's body inside the tavern and his deposition left a grisly picture. Day found seven stab wounds and pronounced, "I think the three on the breast would have caused death or even any of the wounds in the stomach or thigh."[21]

While Day performed the autopsy, others hunted Dickey. He did not make it far, getting captured about a quarter of a mile from the tavern. His captors dragged him back to the tavern, while others found Dickey's bloody knife, thrown into a nearby field.[22]

---

17 Moses Williams Testimony, St. Clair Coroner's Inquest; James Waldren Testimony, St. Clair Coroner's Inquest.

18 Minor Crippen Testimony, St. Clair Coroner's Inquest.

19 John B. Farr Testimony, St. Clair Coroner's Inquest.

20 Moses William Testimony, St. Clair Coroner's Inquest.

21 William B. Day Testimony, St. Clair Coroner's Inquest.

22 Moses William Testimony, St. Clair Coroner's Inquest.

In his capacity as Justice of the Peace, John B. Farr called on Robert Drane, town constable (and Washington Drane's son), to convene an inquiry of 12 men to go back to Bicksler's and sort out the details of the death. By 10:00 p.m., three hours after the murder, the twelve men reported as directed. Their investigation did not take long. In lieu of a jail, which Dranesville lacked, Dickey was imprisoned "all night in the room where the corpse of his mangled victim lay." The next morning, he was transported to the Fairfax County jail.[23]

Dickey had to wait several months for the next court session to begin. When it opened in June, his case took four days to prosecute. He was found guilty on charges of second-degree murder and sentenced to 18 years imprisonment.[24]

Life went back to normal in Dranesville. Wagons kept traveling down the turnpikes, and the yearly slave hirings continued. But a storm was coming, one that would bring far more death and destruction than just one knifing. And amid that same storm, John Farr, William Day, and many others who were present at Bicksler's would know what it meant to face their own charges of murder.

23 *The Daily Express*, Jan. 6, 1855.

24 Hofer, 4.

Chapter One

"The Union Is Dissolved"

South Carolina's Secession and Fort Sumter

Seconds seemed like hours in the deathly quiet room. One at a time the 169 delegates answered the question posed to them. They sat awaiting their turn and, "As name by name fell upon the ear of the silent assembly, the brief sound was echoed back, without a solitary exception in that whole grave body—Aye!" The roll call started seven minutes past 1:00 p.m. and finished when the last delegate affirmed his decision eight minutes later.[1] It was December 20, 1860, and the delegates in St. Andrew's Hall had just voted for South Carolina's secession.

Word soon raced out into Charleston's streets. "The enthusiasm was unsurpassed," a newspaper column read. "Old men went shouting down the streets. Cannon were fired, and bright triumph was depicted on every countenance."[2]

The whirlwind of celebrations reminded a visiting schoolteacher of a "double-distilled Fourth of July." Shops closed for the day, and the bells of the famed, white-spired St. Michael's rang continuously. To add to the din, fire companies raced down the streets "noisily jingling their bells." Bands played "La Marseillaise," and the "ground fairly shook beneath the double-quick of all the young men of the city under arms and apparently eager for duty." Elsewhere, groups of African Americans "stood . . . at every passageway," watching the events unfold before

---

1 *Charleston Mercury*, Dec. 21, 1860.

2 Ibid.; Maury Klein, *Days of Defiance: Sumter, Secession, and the Coming of the Civil War* (New York, 1997), 145.

them. Printers at the *Charleston Mercury* jumped to their presses and published an extra edition of the paper that boldly declared, "THE UNION IS DISSOLVED!"[3]

But for all the celebrating, the actual Ordinance of Secession had yet to be signed. For that, the delegates reconvened at St. Andrew's Hall at 6:30 p.m. Meanwhile, the city continued its festivities throughout the entire afternoon, and it was decided to move the affair to a larger venue, Institute Hall, down the street. The column "formed in procession and moved forward in silence" towards Institute Hall. The route "was ablaze with burning tar, which overflowed so that some-times the whole width of the street was aflame."[4]

It took the delegates about fifteen minutes to get to the Hall, an imposing Italianate building constructed in 1854. Designed to hold 3,000 people, that night the Hall overflowed with spectators, and many more crowded Meeting Street. Taking the whole event in was Edmund Ruffin, whose long, snowy white hair drooped down to his shoulders. An acerbic, fierce secessionist, Ruffin had come from his home in Virginia to witness the Secession Convention. He followed the delegates from their initial meetings in the state's capital at Columbia and now, in the evening hours, ticked down the seconds to the moment for which he had waited so long—the dissolution of the Union. Watching the crowd, Ruffin later wrote in his diary, "In the rear & on the sides of the hall, & in very spacious galleries above, there were places for an immense audience—& every seat was filled."[5] The massive crowd waited eagerly for the delegates to arrive.

Delegates entered the building in pairs of twos, arm in arm. They were among the wealthiest men in South Carolina, including John L. Manning, who enslaved 648 people. Mary Chesnut, whose husband James was a delegate, wrote, "South Carolina was never more splendidly represented."[6] The spectators drowned the delegates with applause as they walked into Institute Hall.

Senators and representatives from South Carolina's state government accompanied the secessionist delegates. A stage in the center of the hall held the key dignitaries, including the state's governor, Francis Pickens, and the President of

---

3 Anna C. Brackett, "Charleston, South Carolina (1861)," in *Harper's New Monthly Magazine*, Volume 88, December 1893 to May 1894 (New York, 1894), 946; W. F. G. Peck, "Four Years Under Fire in Charleston," in *Harper's New Monthly Magazine*, Volume 31, June to November 1865 (New York, 1894), 358; *Charleston Mercury*, Dec. 20, 1860. Emphasis in original.

4 *Charleston Mercury*, Dec. 21, 1860; Brackett, "Charleston, South Carolina," 946.

5 William C. Davis, *Rhett: The Turbulent Life and Times of a Fire-Eater* (Columbia, SC, 2001), 411; Edmund Ruffin, *The Diary of Edmund Ruffin: Volume 1*, ed., William Kauffman Scarborough (Baton Rouge, 1972), 512.

6 Ralph Wooster, "Membership of the South Carolina Secession Convention," in *The South Carolina Historical Magazine*, Vol. 55, No. 4 (Oct. 1954): 193; Mary B. Chesnut, *A Diary from Dixie*, eds., Isabella D. Martin and Myrta Lockett Avary (New York, 1906), 4.

the Secession Convention, David F. Jamison. To begin the evening, Jamison stood and read to the crowd the secession ordinance. It would not have taken him very long; the whole document was only 108 words long. The 3,000 people in front of Jamison listened as quietly as they could as he read. At the end of the document, Jamison finished "The union now subsisting between South Carolina and other States, under the name of 'The United States of America,' is hereby dissolved."[7]

As the word "dissolved" left Jamison's lips the crowd "could contain themselves no longer, and a shout that shook the very building, reverberating, long-continued, rose to Heaven, and ceased only with the loss of breath." The cheering continued in waves for the next two hours, as the delegates were called to sign their names to the parchment.[8]

Someone ran outside and read the document to the throngs of waiting people. In the tumult that followed "the two palmetto-trees which stood on either side of the platform were despoiled of their leaves by the audience as mementos of the occasion, and the meeting slowly dispersed."[9] It had been a day that few would ever forget. And in exactly a year—December 20, 1861—South Carolina's sons would be fighting and dying at Dranesville. Almost no one could have foretold the sacrifice and suffering that lay in the future.

*   *   *

Even before the signatures dried on the parchment, it became clear that South Carolina was not fully prepared to be its own independent nation. A correspondent from the *New York Tribune*, who found himself suddenly in enemy territory in Charleston wrote, "There is neither an army nor navy to protect her."[10]

But that was not wholly accurate, either. Charleston was filled nearly to bursting with militia companies. They kept wary eyes on the United States soldiers, under the command of Major Robert Anderson, who were stationed at Fort Moultrie and Castle Pinckney. Robert Rhett, one of South Carolina's most fiery secessionists, called those garrisons "the great and most threatening

---

7 *Journal of the Convention of the People of South Carolina, Held in 1860, 1861 and 1862, Together with the Ordinances, Reports, Resolutions, etc.* (Columbia, 1862), 48; *The War of the Rebellion: A Compilation of the Official Records of the Union and Confederate Armies* (Washington, D.C.: U.S. Government Printing Office, 128 volumes), Series 4, Volume 1, 1. Hereafter cited as *OR*. All references are to Series 1 unless otherwise noted.

8 *Charleston Mercury*, Dec. 21, 1860.

9 Ibid.

10 *New York Tribune*, Dec. 24, 1860.

difficulty," to South Carolina.[11] For all their enthusiasm, the militia companies lacked any centralized command, and before anyone in the city understood what was happening, Anderson whisked his command out of Moultrie and Pinckney. By the time Charlestonians woke up on December 27, the Federal soldiers were safely ensconced within Fort Sumter, a bastion in the center of Charleston's harbor. Members of the secession convention, livid that Anderson had slipped past their patrols, responded by passing resolutions condemning the major's move as overtly hostile.[12] It soon became apparent that there would be a showdown over the fate of Fort Sumter, and for that, South Carolina needed more troops.

Wheels were already in motion. Three days before the formalization of secession, South Carolina passed "An Act to Provide an Armed Military Force," which directly led to the organization of the first ten regiments of South Carolinian infantry. One of those ten, the 6th South Carolina Infantry, would, in a year's time, see action at Dranesville.[13]

Zealous calls for volunteers flooded the countryside. One of the most eager was young Frank English. Sixteen years old, English lived with his parents and siblings on a plantation outside of Columbia. His father, who was worth nearly $90,000, enslaved 87 people on the plantation, and was referred to as "Colonel" throughout the county.[14] Frank wrote to a friend in Virginia supporting secession and looking forward to war. His friend replied, "I hope you may be gratified and come home as scatheless as the ducks we used to shoot at last winter." Saying goodbye to his family, and bringing along an enslaved man named Lewis, Frank raced off to enlist.[15]

He joined the Fairfield Fencibles, a company led by his cousin, John Bratton, a well-respected planter and doctor in Winnsboro. Bratton's personal wealth totaled $21,000 and included 76 enslaved people. His peers called him "quiet,

---

11 Robert B. Rhett, *A Fire-Eater Remembers: The Confederate Memoir of Robert Barnwell Rhett*, ed., William C. Davis (Columbia, SC, 2000), 18-19; *OR* 1, 2-3.

12 *OR* 1, 2-3; See Davis Detzer, *Allegiance: Fort Sumter, Charleston, and the Beginning of the Civil War* (Orlando, 2001), 116-132; *Journal of the Convention of the people of South Carolina, held in 1860, 1861 and 1862, together with the ordinances, reports, resolutions, etc.*, 115.

13 *The Statutes at Large of South Carolina*, Vol. 12 (Columbia, SC, 1874), 726.

14 Frank English 1860 Census Info found in Richland County, South Carolina 1860 Census; Information on John English's slave ownership in 1860 South Carolina, Richland County Slave Schedule; "History of the Means Family," Vol. 3, T52, South Caroliniana Library, University of South Carolina.

15 Charles R. Venable to Frank English, Jan. 19, 1861, "Letters and Genealogy of the Means-English Families, 1828-1950," Volume 1, South Caroliniana Library, University of South Carolina (hereafter referred to as Frank English Letters); Frank English to his mother, Apr. 15, 1861, Frank English Letters.

cultured, self-possessed, ostentatious, efficient, without fear and without reproach, not self-seeking."[16] The company of soldiers, under Bratton's leadership, soon got to drilling.[17]

On a calm spring day in March, the Fencibles marched into Winnsboro. The women of the town bequeathed a newly sewn flag to the soldiers in an elaborate ceremony. Handing the flag to the volunteers, one of the women said, "Take this banner and under the guidance of our gallant and experienced commander, may it ever lead you on to honor and victory." With their new flag, and alongside the other companies that soon made up the 6th South Carolina, the soldiers kept at their drill in the weeks to come.[18]

As the days passed and the 6th South Carolina trained, events continued at a breakneck speed. Following the Palmetto State's lead, six more states passed their own secession legislation. Those states sent their own delegates to Montgomery, Alabama, the provisional capital of the new Confederate States of America. Working out the details of their new government, the delegates picked Senator Jefferson Davis from Mississippi to be their president.[19] In early March, Davis focused his attention on Charleston, and sent newly commissioned Brig. Gen. P. G. T. Beauregard to oversee operations against Fort Sumter.[20]

As Beauregard's positions around Charleston Harbor became more and more fortified, the 6th South Carolina was finishing its own preparations. On March 20, its colonel wrote directly to Jefferson Davis, "The same spirit of patriotism which actuated this Regiment to volunteer in the defence of their State has caused them to authorize me to tender their services in defence of our common country, the Confederate States," the regiment's colonel pledged. All of Winnsboro was astir on April 9, three weeks later, when news came that the regiment was ordered to

---

16 John Bratton 1860 Census Info found in Fairfield County, South Carolina 1860 Census; John Bratton, *General John Bratton, Sumter to Appomattox: In Letters to his Wife*, ed., J. Luke Austin (Sewanee, TN, 2003), 1-3; John Bratton Compiled Service Record (hereafter cited as CSR), National Archives and Records Administration, (hereafter NARA).

17 John Bratton, *Letters of John Bratton to his Wife*, ed., Elizabeth Porcher Bratton (privately published, 1942), 3-4.

18 *The News and Herald*, Memorial Edition, May 25, 1910.

19 William C. Davis, *A Government of Our Own: The Making of the Confederacy* (New York, 1994), 120, 128.

20 *OR* 1, 25. Though born as Pierre Gustave Toutant Beauregard, and thus usually referred to by historians as P. G. T. Beauregard, he had in fact dropped the usage of his first name by the Civil War, and signed his correspondence using only "G. T." T. Harry Williams, *P. G. T. Beauregard: Napoleon in Gray* (Baton Rouge, 2d ed., 1995), 6; *OR* 1, 27.

Charleston.[21] The infantry, including John Bratton and Frank English, boarded trains that rattled down the tracks towards Charleston. The regiment arrived in Charleston on the evening of April 11.[22]

Meanwhile, Beauregard prepared for the confrontation with Fort Sumter, towards which all his batteries were pointed. By the time the 6th South Carolina arrived, Beauregard's correspondence with Anderson was nearing an end. Beauregard had tried to coax Anderson's command out of Sumter to no avail, and time was running out.

In early April, President Abraham Lincoln ordered Gustavus Fox to mount a relief expedition for Fort Sumter. Fox had urged Lincoln's predecessor, James Buchanan, to allow him to sail to Sumter's relief, but the lame-duck president did nothing. With Lincoln in power, Fox again suggested the idea, which was quickly greenlighted. Fox's goal was to deliver supplies that were loaded onto his steamer, the *Baltic*. If Confederates in the harbor prevented Fox from resupplying Sumter, however, he was to blast his way through and relieve the fort.[23]

After ordering Fox's armada to set sail, Lincoln followed up with a message to South Carolina's governor, Francis Pickens, that told him of the relief expedition on its way. Pickens quickly alerted Beauregard that Fox's ships were coming. Continuing the chain reaction, Beauregard wired back to Montgomery to alert the Confederate secretary of war, LeRoy Walker, of the recent developments. Walker telegraphed back bluntly, "Under no circumstances are you to allow provisions to be sent to Fort Sumter." With his orders, Beauregard redoubled his efforts to force Anderson to capitulate.[24]

Those efforts ended early on April 12. Knowing Anderson would not give in, Beauregard sent his final message: the Federals had an hour to surrender, or he would open fire. At 4:30 a.m., an officer pulled the lanyard on a 10-inch mortar. The shell arced high into the predawn air before exploding in a great fireball. From all over the harbor other guns, mortars, and howitzers opened fire, following the signal.[25]

The 6th South Carolina heard gunfire for the first time in those early morning hours. The regiment's major, Thomas Woodward, recalled in a speech years later, "How you rushed out, formed your companies, and clamored for your arms,

---

21 Thomas W. Woodward, *Address of Maj. Thomas W. Woodward: From Fort Sumter to Dranesville* (Columbia, SC, 1883), 4; *The News and Herald*, Memorial Edition, May 25, 1910.

22 Woodward, *Fort Sumter to Dranesville*, 5.

23 *OR* 1, 235-236; Samuel W. Crawford, *The Genesis of War: The Story of Sumter, 1860-1861* (New York, 1887), 405.

24 Abraham Lincoln, *Collected Works of Abraham Lincoln*: Vol. 4, eds., Roy P. Basler, Marion Dolores Pratt, and Lloyd A. Dunlap (New Brunswick, NJ, 1953), 323; *OR* 1, 289.

25 *OR* 1, 1, 14; Detzer, *Allegiance*, 269.

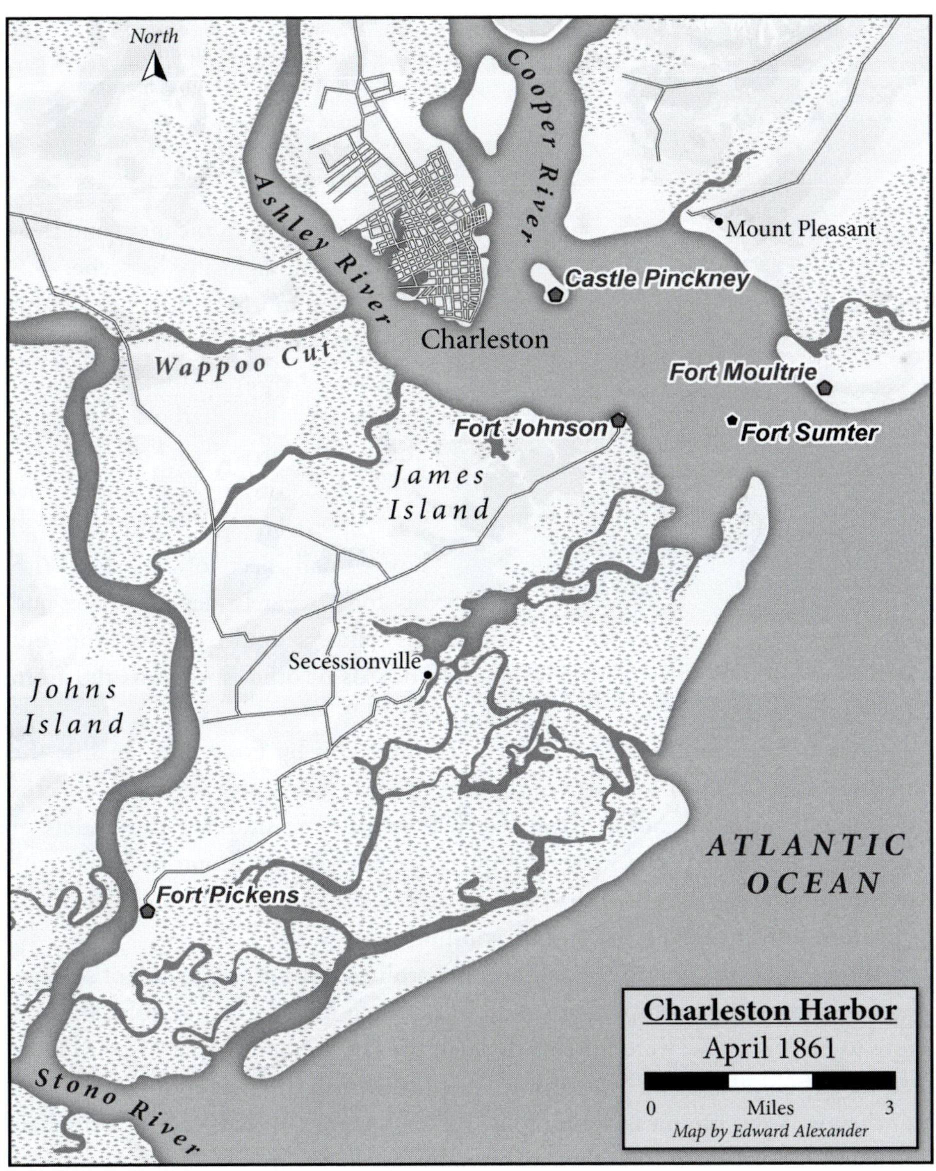

which were here for the first time issued to the command." With muskets in hand, the regiment made its way "to the battery, where we remained silent but eager spectators of the conflict which was going on around the harbor." They were far from the only ones watching the bombardment. Mary Chesnut scribbled in her diary, "The women were wild, there on the housetop. Prayers from the women and

John Bratton
6th South Carolina Infantry
Courtesy of South Caroliniana Library, University of South Carolina, Columbia, SC

imprecations from the men, and then a shell would light up the scene."[26]

As the morning hours ticked by, the Confederate artillery continued to hammer away at the fort. At the mouth of the harbor, observers noticed the arrival of Fox's armada. What those observers did not know was that strong gales had scattered Fox's small fleet of vessels. With his force severely depleted, Fox and his officers could do nothing but watch Fort Sumter get pummeled, just as hundreds of other spectators did from Charleston's rooftops.[27]

Confederate officers feared, though, an incursion by Fox's ships against the underside of Charleston, via any of its inlets or side rivers. Beauregard's concerns lay primarily with the Stono River. He had spent time studying the outlets of the river and realized that Federal ships could sail up the Stono to bypass the batteries ringing the mouth of the Harbor. Beauregard ordered reinforcements sent to garrison outposts along the Stono's winding route.[28]

Those orders made it to the 6th South Carolina and the companies of soldiers were soon scurrying to ships that would bring them into the Stono. John Bratton wrote to his wife, "We were hurried through the city so rapidly that I had to leave everything behind, among other things, that little brush bag that your mother gave me when we went on our wedding tour." Bratton regretted that, "My favorite hair brush and indeed everything that it contained are lost with it." The companies of the 6th were divided up and dropped off at the various outposts along the Stono. Now without his hairbrush, Bratton and his Fairfield Fencibles were stationed on

---

26 Woodward, *From Fort Sumter to Dranesville*, 5; Chesnut, *Diary from Dixie*, 36.

27 *OR* 1, 1, 11.

28 Ibid., 194, 274.

General P. G. T. Beauregard

NARA

Battery Island at Fort Pickens. Young Frank English finally had his war.[29]

But Fox's ships never came. They stayed out of range of the Confederate guns and waited for the inevitable. Too far away to take part in the bombardment, Bratton and the other soldiers of the 6th watched and listened as Beauregard's guns continued to fire. Just shy of 2:00 p.m. on April 13 those guns began to fall silent. Over the preceding 34 hours 2,361 shot and 983 shells had been fired at the fort, and much of the interior was on fire. It was useless to resist anymore. Anderson surrendered his garrison.[30]

The battered garrison boarded Fox's steamship, and the small armada turned for New York. Thus ended the bombardment and began the war. In the opening shots of the conflict the 6th South Carolina had not suffered any casualties. But eight months from then, on a battlefield outside Dranesville, the regiment would not be so fortunate.

29 Woodward, *From Fort Sumter to Dranesville*, 5-6; Bratton, *General John Bratton*, 9.

30 H. W. Hubbell, "The Organization and Use of Artillery in the War of the Rebellion," in *Journal of the Military Service Institution of the United States, Volume 11* (Governor's Island, 1890), 398; *OR* 1, 12; Abner Doubleday, *Reminiscences of Forts Sumter and Moultrie in 1860-'61* (New York, 1876), 158.

Chapter Two

"You Have Chosen to Inaugurate Civil War"

Virginia Secedes

*O*n a cool March afternoon Abraham Lincoln stood on a platform outside the Capitol Building, overlooking thousands of people. He spoke carefully to the crowd, before delivering his conclusion. "In your hands, my dissatisfied fellow-countrymen, and not in mine, is the momentous issue of civil war." After his address Lincoln made his way to the White House. It was March 4, 1861, Inauguration Day, and one of the first items waiting for the new president was a letter from Maj. Robert Anderson.[1]

The major wrote to explain to Lincoln the unfolding situation at besieged Fort Sumter. Anderson warned his commander-in-chief of "the limited supply of our provisions," and suggested that it would prove difficult to relieve the garrison "with a force of less than twenty thousand good and well-disciplined men." That, however, would prove impossible. In 1860, the entire strength of the United States Army numbered only 16,367, scattered throughout 197 companies. Only 18 of those 197 companies were east of the Mississippi River.[2]

But it was not just the army pressing Lincoln to act. Newspaper editorialists screamed for Lincoln to do *something,* and letters arrived daily from the Northern public. One letter from New York read, "Give up Sumpter, Sir, & you are as

1 Lincoln, *Collected Works of Abraham Lincoln*: Vol. 4, 271.

2 Abraham Lincoln Papers, Series 1. General Correspondence. 1833-1916. Robert Anderson to Lincoln, Feb. 28, 1861, Library of Congress (hereafter LOC); Clayton R. Newell, *The Regular Army Before the Civil War, 1845-1860* (Washington, D.C., 2014), 50-51.

dead politically as John Brown is physically. You have got to fight."[3] Then the Confederates opened fire.

The North came alive with patriotism. Flags appeared atop poles and lamp posts, and with them came fiery speeches defending Old Glory. But Lincoln needed soldiers more than he needed flag-wavers. On April 15, Lincoln called for 75,000 volunteers to put down the rebellion.[4]

That same day, Lincoln ordered Secretary of State William Seward to telegraph the governor of each state that had not seceded, calling up their militia units to Federal service. Each state had a quota expected of it, including the number of regiments, and numbers of officers and men. As the North's most populous state, New York was asked to provide 17 regiments, totaling 13,280 men. Pennsylvania followed, with initial requests for 16 regiments and 12,500 men. State governors throughout the North pledged their support.[5]

Lincoln's proclamation and quota met a decidedly cooler reception in the South. Beriah Magoffin, governor of Kentucky, bluntly wrote to the Lincoln Administration, "I say emphatically Kentucky will furnish no troops for the wicked purpose of subduing her sister Southern States." John Ellis, governor of the Old North State, told Lincoln, "You can get no troops from North Carolina."[6]

It was John Letcher, though, from the Old Dominion, who lashed out at the new president with the most vitriol. On April 16, a day after Lincoln's proclamation, Letcher replied: "I have only to say that the militia of Virginia will not be furnished to the powers at Washington for any such use or purpose as they have in view. Your object is to subjugate the Southern States, and a requisition made upon me for such an object . . . will not be complied with." Letcher ended with a bone-chilling threat: "You have chosen to inaugurate civil war, and having done so, we will meet it in a spirit as determined as the Administration has exhibited toward the South." Words soon turned to action, and everything was about to change.[7]

Until Lincoln's proclamation, Virginia's reaction to secession had been lukewarm at best. Indeed, there were people like Edmund Ruffin who screamed loudly and often for disunion, but for every Ruffin there were legions of others who were not convinced secession was the answer. In 1860, when the country went to the polls to elect its new president, the race in Virginia was neck-and-neck between Southern Democrat John C. Breckinridge and Constitutional Unionist John Bell.

---

3 Harold Holzer, ed., *Dear Mr. Lincoln: Letters to the President* (Carbondale, IL, 1993), 144.

4 *OR* 1, Series 3, 67.

5 Ibid., 68-75.

6 Ibid., 70, 72.

7 Ibid., 76.

It came down to the wire; in the end, Bell got 74,491 votes to Breckinridge's 74,325—a difference of just 166. Bell's attempt to have it both ways—leaving slavery intact and keeping the Union together, resonated with Virginia's voters. Among all the uncertainty of the Secession Winter heading into 1861, one of the biggest questions remained: What would Virginia decide as the rest of the South embraced disunion?[8]

On January 7, 1861, Governor Letcher spoke to Virginia's Senate and House of Delegates. "Is it not monstrous to see a government like ours destroyed merely because men cannot agree about a domestic institution, which existed at the formation of the government," Letcher asked. The domestic institution to which he referred, of course, was slavery—especially important to the Old Dominion. Virginia contained the most enslaved people of any state, totaling nearly half a million in bondage.[9]

The House of Delegates voted a week after Letcher's address to assemble a special convention of 152 delegates to discuss secession. Commissioners to this special convention were elected on February 4. In the words of historian James I. Robertson, Jr., "Three weeks of local but intense campaigning followed. Candidates ran as secessionists, unionists, or moderates."[10] On the day of the election, though, it was clear that of the roughly 145,000 Virginians who went to the polls, many of them still opposed secession. Unionist delegates won 30 seats to the convention.[11]

The convention began on February 13. For the next two months, the delegates did what delegates do best: they talked in circles. Resolutions, amendments, and committee meeting notes flew in all directions of both chambers of the House of Delegates. Richmond newspapers followed the action carefully, but the most ardent on both sides grew restless at the delegates' lack of progress.[12]

Meanwhile, a hundred miles away in Washington another conference was already underway. As a last attempt to stave off war, commissioners from both free and slave states met in Willard's Hotel. Led by former president John Tyler—who had also been elected to Virginia's secession convention—the commissioners in

---

8 Michael F. Holt, *The Election of 1860: A Campaign Fraught with Consequences* (Lawrence, KS, 2017), 195.

9 *Message of the Governor of Virginia and Accompanying Documents* (Richmond, 1861), viii; United States 1860 Federal Census.

10 James Elliott Walmsley, "The Change of Secession Sentiment in Virginia in 1861," in *The American Historical Review* 31, No. 1. (Oct. 1925): 85; James I. Robertson, Jr. "The Virginia State Convention of 1861," in *Virginia at War, 1861*, ed., William C. Davis and James I. Robertson, Jr. (Lexington, KY, 2005), 3.

11 Henry T. Shanks, *The Secession Movement in Virginia, 1847-1861* (Richmond, 1934), 153.

12 Robertson, "The Virginia State Convention of 1861," 5.

Washington tried to hash out details that would spare bloodshed. Predictably, it went nowhere. Delegates from the South, including Tyler, wanted promises that slavery would be allowed to expand into new territories. Republicans, who had won the 1860 election with a platform diametrically opposed to slavery's expansion, adamantly refused. "These two points," an Ohioan at the conference wrote, "are all that is material." As with so many other negotiations, the commissioners' failure to meet a resolution regarding slavery meant the conference's failure. In late February, Tyler and James Seddon, another Virginia delegate, returned to Richmond, with the latter saying, "the Conference was a delusion and a sham, as well as an insult and an offence to the South."[13]

In Richmond, the sentiments of the delegates started to move towards secession. John S. Preston from South Carolina, Henry L. Benning from Georgia, and Fulton Anderson from Mississippi all arrived in Richmond with speeches to persuade Virginians to join their states in secession—that secession was in fact the only way forward. Speaking first, Anderson stroked the egos of his Virginian audience, praising the Old Dominion's prominent place "in the first great struggle for independence." He then went on to blame the recent strife on the Republicans and ratcheted up the fear that they would stop the expansion of slavery with the ultimate aim of abolishing it. In the following days, Benning and Preston gave similar speeches continuing to highlight the importance of slavery to secession. The Deep South knew it needed Virginia's manpower and industry, and the three speakers desperately tried to sway the 152 delegates.[14]

Political persuasion, however, was not enough. On April 4, the delegates voted for the first time. The resolution for secession failed, with only 45 voting in the affirmative and 88 voting against. When Edmund Ruffin heard of the failure he wrote, "This is worse than I supposed possible even of that submissive & mean body."[15]

But then South Carolinians bombarded Fort Sumter. Lincoln called for 75,000 volunteers, and Governor Letcher replied. Public opinion in the streets of Richmond swung wildly away from moderation. John Jones, who would soon become a clerk in the Confederate government, wrote, "Business is generally

13 Robert Gray Gunderson, "Letters from the Washington Peace Conference of 1861," in *The Journal of Southern History* 17, No. 3. (Aug. 1951): 387; *New York Times*, Mar. 1, 1861; The best book regarding the Peace Conference is Robert G. Gunderson, *Old Gentlemen's Convention: The Washington Peace Conference of 1861* (Madison, WI, 1961).

14 Charles Dew, *Apostles of Disunion* (Charlottesville, 2001), 62. See Chapter Five, "The Mission to Virginia" for a full description of the three and their speeches to the Virginia Convention.

15 Robertson, "The Virginia State Convention of 1861," 14. The pairings and abstentions explain why the vote does not equal 152; Ruffin, *Diary*, 578.

suspended, and men run together in great crowds. . . . These crowds are addressed by the most inflamed members of the Convention, and never did I hear more hearty responses from the people."[16] The roaring tension reached its crescendo on April 17, when the delegates went into a secret session to hold a second vote regarding secession.

The session lasted for ten and a half hours, and by the end of it the Virginians had voted to leave the Union. Virginia's Ordinance of Secession mirrored other secession ordinances. It was above all succinct, claiming the Federal government had "perverted" the powers granted by the Constitution, "not only to the injury of the people of Virginia, but to the oppression of the Southern slaveholding States." The Convention called for the Ordinance to be "ratified by a majority of the votes of the people of this State, cast at a poll" to be held on May 23.[17]

As news of Virginia's secession spread, politicians like Letcher came to the same conclusion that South Carolina's leaders had the previous winter. If the Old Dominion was to become part of the Confederacy, separated from the United States only by the Potomac River, it would need more troops, and officers to lead them. A three-person council convened by Letcher recommended that "that the Governor tender to Col. Robert E. Lee the office of commander of the military and naval forces of Virginia."[18]

On the evening of April 21, a rider came to the Lee homestead, Arlington, and presented him with a letter from Governor Letcher offering command of Virginia's forces. The following morning, Lee left Arlington for the last time. On April 23, in Richmond, he officially accepted the position as commander of all of Virginia's forces. The onlookers, including recently arrived Confederate Vice President Alexander Stephens, raucously applauded.[19]

Virginia had its general, but it needed more men. There was no shortage of volunteers.

*   *   *

The man who would command the Confederate forces at Dranesville resigned his commission from the United States Army on May 3, 1861. James Ewell Brown

---

16 John B. Jones, *A Rebel War Clerk's Diary at the Confederate States Capital*: Vol. 1 (Philadelphia, 1866), 20.

17 Robertson, "The Virginia State Convention of 1861," 18; Virginia Convention (1861: Richmond), Records, 1861–1961 (bulk 1861), Accession 40586, State Government Records Collection, Library of Virginia, Richmond, Virginia.

18 *OR* 51, pt. 2, 21.

19 Douglas S. Freeman, *R. E. Lee: A Biography*, Vol. 1 (New York, 1934), 447, 465-468.

(J. E. B.) Stuart came from Patrick County, Virginia, the seventh of ten children. He had turned 28 that February.[20]

With ancestors who fought in the American Revolution and the War of 1812 it is unsurprising that Stuart followed in his family's martial footsteps. In the spring of 1850, 17-year-old J. E. B. made his way to the Military Academy at West Point. In a letter home, the young cadet wrote, "I know of no profession more desirable than that of the soldier."[21]

Stuart became fast friends with fellow Virginian G. Custis Lee, and Mainer O. O. Howard. The friendship with Custis, the son of Robert E. Lee and a fellow Virginian, made sense. Howard, though, seemed like an odd bond. In fact, the Mainer remembered Stuart as "My best friend," and recalled that Stuart "spoke to me, visited me, and we became warm friends, often . . . visiting the young ladies of the post together."[22]

Stuart graduated in 1854, ranked 13th in a class of 46. In his final exams, Stuart ranked 10th in cavalry tactics, 13th in artillery, and 14th in infantry.[23] For the next year and a half, Stuart's home was Texas, serving in a regiment of Mounted Rifles. In 1855, Stuart received a promotion to the 1st U.S. Cavalry, which saw service against American Indians and a deployment to "Bleeding Kansas." While in Kansas, Stuart met Flora Cooke, the daughter of a superior officer. They married in November of 1855. The newlyweds had just enough time for a brief leave of absence before Stuart returned to his regiment's service.[24]

Having served in the saddle for four years, Stuart had an idea for an invention that made it easier for cavalrymen to attach and detach sword scabbards from their belts. To patent it, Stuart made his way to Washington, D.C. in October 1859. By happenstance he overheard rumors, "whispered very cautiously through the different bureaux of the War Department," of an insurrection taking place at Harpers Ferry. He quickly volunteered his services and was assigned to Robert E. Lee, who had been told to quell the insurrection at the arsenal. With "barely

---

20 Burke Davis, *Jeb Stuart: The Last Cavalier* (New York, 1957), 17.

21 J. E. B. Stuart, *The Letters of Major General James E. B. Stuart*, ed., Adele H. Mitchell (Stuart-Mosby Historical Society, 1990), 23.

22 William B. Styple, ed., *Generals in Bronze: Interviewing the Commanders of the Civil War* (Kearny, NE, 2005), 176; O. O. Howard, *Autobiography of Oliver Otis Howard*, Vol. 1 (New York, 1907), 53. Stuart and Howard also bonded over their religious tenets—both belonged to the extra-curricular bible study group. Thomas, *Bold Dragoon*, 25.

23 George W. Cullum, *Biographical Register of the Officers and Graduates of the U.S. Military Academy at West Point, Volume 2* (New York, 1868), 375; *Official Register of the Officers and Cadets of the U.S. Military Academy, 1818-1872* (Washington, D.C., 1854), Class Rankings for 1854.

24 Thomas, *Bold Dragoon*, 43.

J. E. B. Stuart
LOC

time to borrow a un'f. coat and a sabre" Stuart found himself aboard a train that brought him and Lee to Harpers Ferry.[25]

The plan to retake Harpers Ferry was haphazardly thrown together, as Stuart soon realized. He was a volunteer aide to Lee, a lieutenant colonel of cavalry, who had at his command a company of U.S. Marines. On October 18, Lee sent Stuart to knock on the front doors of the firehouse, in which the raiders had barricaded themselves. When the door cracked open, Stuart "immediately recognized Old Ossawattomie Brown—who had given us so much trouble out here in Kansas." When John Brown refused to surrender, Stuart took a step back, waved a small handkerchief, and dodged aside as the Marines stormed in. Within minutes it was over, and Brown's men were all killed or captured. Stuart bragged to his mother, "If I had commanded the stormers my sabre would have saved Va the expense of B[rown]'s trial."[26]

In the wake of Brown's raid, and as the sectional divide grew, Stuart made it no secret where his allegiance lay. Writing to a friend in January 1861, he wrote, "I have had no hesitancy from the first that, right or wrong, *alone* or otherwise, *I go with Virginia.*" He wrote another letter directly to Jefferson Davis, still a Mississippi Senator: "In view . . . of the probable dismemberment of the Army, and of your prominence as one likely to exercise a large control in the organization of the Army of the South, I beg leave respectfully to ask you to secure for me a position in that

---

25 J. E. B. Stuart, "'The Greatest Service I Rendered the State': J. E. B. Stuart's Account of the Capture of John Brown," ed. Emory M. Thomas, in *The Virginia Magazine of History and Biography* 94, No. 3, *Virginians at War, 1607-1865* (July 1986): 352.

26 Ibid., 355-356.

army." If that had not been enough, unbeknownst to him, Stuart's mother wrote directly to Lee, requesting, "Can you save a place for him?"[27]

Stuart, his wife, and his two children were at Fort Riley, Kansas, when he heard of Fort Sumter's bombardment, Lincoln's call for troops, and the Virginia Convention's vote for secession. He immediately made his way east and wrote his resignation at Cairo, Illinois. In Washington, the resignation was received and processed by May 14.[28]

When Stuart got to Richmond, a commission was waiting for him. On May 10, he received orders to set out for Harpers Ferry and report to Col. Thomas Jackson, most recently a professor at the Virginia Military Institute. The professor placed the cavalier in command of the few mounted companies on hand. It was Stuart's job to fashion them into some semblance of a fighting force.[29]

*　　*　　*

While Stuart acclimated to his command in Harpers Ferry, the day arrived for Virginia's voters to have their say on the Ordinance of Secession. By the end of the day, May 23, nearly 150,000 people had cast their ballots.[30]

The result was never in doubt. Historian Henry T. Shanks later called the vote a "farce," since, "To all points and purposes, Virginia was out of the Union after April 17." As an indication that the final vote was already a done deal, the Confederacy had even moved its capital from Montgomery, Alabama, to Richmond on May 8—a full two weeks before the people of Virginia could have, theoretically, rejected the Ordinance. Thousands of men had already poured into Richmond, ready to fight the Federals.[31]

The events of May 23 also ignited the persecution of Unionists that eventually brought the U.S. Army to Dranesville. As early as February, when the townspeople debated who they should send to the Convention in Richmond, the imposing doctor William B. Day announced he "meant to have every Yankee driven out of the

<hr>

27 Stuart, *The Letters of Major General James E. B. Stuart*, 193; Stuart quoted in Davis, *Jeb Stuart: The Last Cavalier*, 46. Emphasis in original; Elizabeth Stuart letter to Robert E. Lee quoted in Davis, *Jeb Stuart: The Last Cavalier*, 49.

28 Letters Received by the Office of the Adjutant General, Main Series, 1861-1870, NARA; Letter of J. E. B. Stuart, May 3, 1861.

29 Thomas, *Bold Dragoon*, 67; James I. Robertson, Jr. *Stonewall Jackson: The Man, the Soldier, the Legend* (New York, 1997), 235.

30 Robertson, "The Virginia State Convention of 1861," 19.

31 Henry T. Shanks, *The Secession Movement in Virginia, 1847-1861* (Richmond, 1934), 204; See Jerrell H. Shofner and William Warren Rogers, "Montgomery to Richmond: The Confederacy Selects a Capital," in *Civil War History* 10, Number 2, Jun. 1964, for a full description of the decision to move the capital; Jones, *A Rebel War Clerk's Diary*, 33.

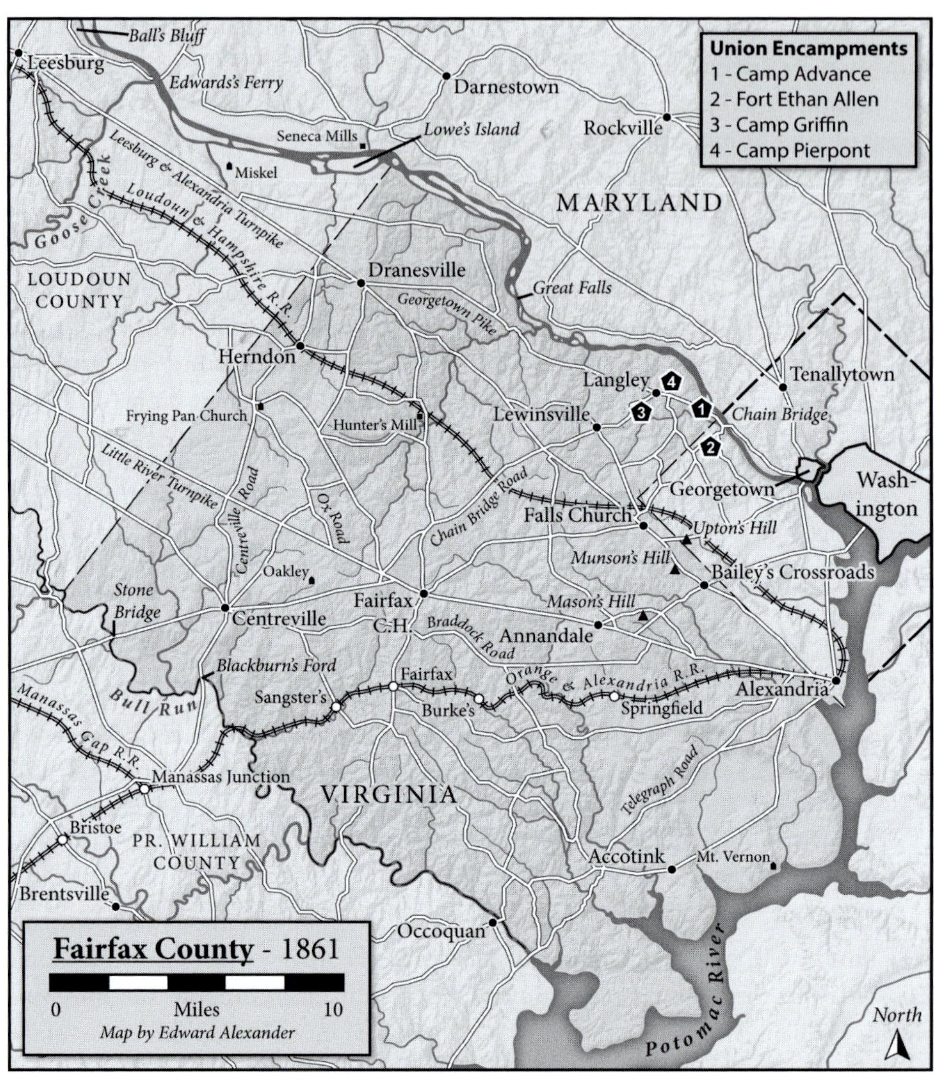

country," as anxious Unionists later remembered. Day "expressed the bitterest kind of sentiments against the Union cause." In one of his more grandiose outbursts, Day said, "that he would have walked in blood and brains before Lincoln would have taken his seat." Day, who had fled Henry Bicksler's tavern in 1854 for fear of violence, now seemed wholeheartedly in support of it.[32]

---

32 *Proceedings of the Commission Relating to State Prisoners*, 1862, Vol. 1, William B. Day Case File, Testimony of James H. Davis, (RG 59, NARA), 40 (hereafter cited as William B. Day Case File); William B. Day Case File, Testimony of Charles E. Johnson, 20.

A cartoon from the June 15, 1861, edition of *Harper's Weekly* alluding to violence against Unionist voters in Virginia. *LOC*

Dranesville was one of 14 polling locations scattered throughout Fairfax County.[33] After over a month of talking and waiting, the day to vote came, and the people of Fairfax County turned out. From Dranesville a visiting minister, Reverend W. G. Hammond, wrote, "The day was unusually quiet at this place."[34] That may have been true for those who voted for secession, but for Unionists, it was a day to tread carefully.

Voting was a very public occasion, and it was no secret on May 23 who supported the Ordinance of Secession and who did not. Over the course of the day 107 people in Dranesville voted to support leaving the Union. This included both William and John Day, John B. Farr, the acting Justice of the Peace back in 1854 when Henry St. Clair was killed, and various members of the prominent Coleman family. All these men would play bigger roles in the months to come.[35]

Opposing the secessionists, a grand total of four men voted to remain.[36] William Day and his half-brother John, not wanting to take any chances, continued to promote their secessionist ideals, even to the point of threats. The first two men to vote for Union were Benjamin Brady and Howard Lasher; Lasher later recalled to a committee that after he and Brady voted, William Day scowled that "he would mark us."[37] For some Unionists in town, like Nelson Voorhees and Minor Crippen, the threats of violence were enough to keep them away from the polls altogether.[38]

A different story unfolded just shy of 12 miles east of Dranesville at the small village of Lewinsville. Another of the polling locations in Fairfax County, Lewinsville was a reversal of Dranesville: 37 men voted for Secession while 86

---

33 See Brian A. Conley, *Fractured Land: Fairfax County's Role in the Vote for Secession, May 23, 1861* (Fairfax, VA, 2001) for the fourteen polling locations.

34 William G. Hammond diary quoted in Charles Preston Poland, Jr. *Dunbarton, Dranesville, Virginia* (Fairfax, 1974), 35.

35 Conley, *Fractured Land*, 75-78.

36 Ibid.

37 William B. Day Case File, Testimony of Howard Lasher, 23.

38 Nelson Voorhees Southern Claims File (NARA); Minor Crippen Southern Claims File (NARA).

others cast their vote for the Union.[39] Some Unionists came armed, refusing to be deterred from voting. One of those men was Lott Crocker who escorted his 71-year-old father "armed and equipped to protect him in his right to vote."[40] The stark contrast in the two towns' voting foreshadowed the violent political turmoil that was to come.

Though dramatic, the Unionists' votes at places like Dranesville and Lewinsville were not enough; by day's end the Ordinance officially passed. Virginia was now formally out of the Union and part of the Confederacy. In response, Federal forces moved immediately, crossing the Potomac and occupying Alexandria on May 24. Far more soldiers in blue soon came, and in time, a division of Pennsylvanians would make its way to Dranesville itself.

39 Conley, *Fractured Land*, 71.

40 Lott W. Crocker, Southern Claims File (NARA), 22.

Chapter Three

"What Will Pennsylvania Do?"

The Keystone State Responds

 G. Curtin, Governor of Pennsylvania, stood in a room of the White House, drumming his fingers on a pane of glass. Men were speaking around him, including the President, and General of the Army Winfield Scott, but Curtin said nothing. He was apparently so engrossed by his drumming that he did not realize the room had gone quiet. Finally, Lincoln looked at Curtin and said, "Andy, what will Pennsylvania do if I issue my proclamation?"[1]

Curtin did not answer, still drumming. He had helped secure the nomination for Lincoln, and he himself had only been governor of Pennsylvania for about four months. This was new ground for both, but the two politicians would have to learn on the fly.[2]

Snapping back to reality, Curtin looked at Lincoln and repeated the question. "What will Pennsylvania do?"

"Do!" Lincoln shouted, searching for an answer.

"Why, sir," Curtin began, "If you issue your proclamation, Pennsylvania will furnish you a hundred thousand men in a week."

"Give me your hand, Andy," Lincoln said, taking Curtin's in his own. "Thank God for that noble reply."[3]

Curtin, in Washington on business, had rushed to the White House when summoned by Lincoln, who was in the midst of preparing his April 15 proclamation

---

1 *The Agitator*, Sep. 9, 1863.

2 William H. Egle, ed., *Andrew Gregg Curtin: His Life and Services* (Philadelphia, 1895), 37.

3 *The Agitator*, Sep. 9, 1863.

calling for 75,000 volunteers. Curtin expedited troops to the capital in response, and the first soldiers arrived in Washington on April 18.[4]

Pennsylvania was required to provide 16 regiments of infantry, totaling 12,500 men. Men streamed from every hollow and hamlet pore of Pennsylvania to enlist.[5]

Pennsylvania's shared border with Virginia and Maryland made the necessity for troops even more dire. In the spring of 1861, no one knew what Maryland, a border state, would decide regarding secession. Baltimore especially remained a virulent den of hostility, with mobs haranguing or attacking Federal troops on both April 18 and April 19. Pennsylvania newspapers printed rumors of secessionist attacks and in Pittsburgh a "Committee of Public Safety" was created, harkening back to the days of the American Revolution.[6]

Volunteers came by the tens of thousands. They gathered in the east at Philadelphia, in the center at Harrisburg, and in the west at Pittsburgh. The men showed up faster than the mustering officers could process them. Harrisburg, the state capital, only had 16,000 residents at the beginning of the war, but within just nine days after Lincoln's proclamation, nearly 7,000 volunteers had descended on the city. It was impossible to adequately prepare for their arrival, and some of the new soldiers were billeted in churches until proper arrangements could be made. In response, authorities established Camp Curtin, a training camp on the outskirts of Harrisburg.[7]

In the blink of an eye, Pennsylvania filled its quota. Would-be officers were still offering their services to Curtin more than a week after the president's proclamation. Curtin had to deny them. "I cannot receive your company," he wrote to one officer, "Our quota is full. It will not do for you to come down; [I] have no place for you."[8] Yet for all of Curtin's denials, men kept volunteering with nowhere to go.

---

4 Stephen D. Engle, *Gathering to Save a Nation: Lincoln & the Union's War Governors* (Chapel Hill, 2016), 39; Charles Lockwood and John Lockwood, *The Siege of Washington: The Untold Story of the Twelve Days that Shook the Union* (Oxford, 2011), 101.

5 *OR* 1, Series 3, 69, 77.

6 *Centre Democrat*, Apr. 26, 1861; On Baltimore and violence see Lockwood and Lockwood, *The Siege of Washington*, Chapters 4 and 5; Edward G. Everett, "Contraband and Rebel Sympathizers in Pennsylvania in 1861," in *Western Pennsylvania Magazine of History* 41, Number 1, (Spring 1958): 31-33.

7 Edward G. Everett, "Pennsylvania Raises an Army, 1861," in *Western Pennsylvania Historical Magazine* 39, Number 2, (Summer 1956): 88. For a full treatment of Camp Curtin and its role, see William J. Miller, *The Training of an Army: Camp Curtin and the North's Civil War* (Shippensburg, PA, 1990).

8 Egle, *Andrew Gregg Curtin*, 222.

Andrew Curtin

Governor of Pennsylvania

LOC

Then, on April 26, Curtin received a telegram from Maj. Gen. Robert Patterson, commander of Pennsylvania's state forces. Patterson asked for another 25 regiments of infantry and one regiment of cavalry.[9] Reading Patterson's telegram, Curtin thought he had a solution to the volunteer companies he had turned away.[10]

Curtin raced to fulfill Patterson's wishes and pled his case to the state legislature. Speaking to the state senators and representatives, Curtin asked for funding for 15 more regiments, separate from those being raised to meet Lincoln's quota. The state politicians agreed and got to work on the legislation.[11]

But then the War Department got involved. On May 3, Secretary of War Simon Cameron dropped a bombshell on Curtin's plans. Cameron wrote, "General Patterson had no authority to make any requisition on you for twenty additional regiments, and you will understand me to say distinctly they cannot be mustered into service."[12] Curtin was embarrassed by the setback but refused to back down. He kept working behind the scenes to raise volunteers.

---

9 *OR* 1, Series 3, 139.

10 Edward G. Longacre, *The Early Morning of War: Bull Run, 1861* (Norman, OK, 2014), 40-43, 57; Robert Patterson, *A Narrative of the Campaign in the Valley of the Shenandoah in 1861* (Philadelphia, 1865), 26. The other major general appointed from PA was William H. Keim, who died in 1862 from typhus.

11 Egle, *Andrew Gregg Curtin*, 260-261.

12 *OR* 1, Series 3, 151. Simon Cameron and Andrew Curtin had a complicated political legacy— in 1855 both had run for a PA senate seat. The campaign got especially vicious "over a drunken insinuation that Curtin had fathered an illegitimate child." By 1861, both men absolutely hated each other; Jack Furniss, "Andrew Curtin and the Politics of Union," in *The Pennsylvania Magazine of History and Biography* 141, Number 2, (Apr. 2017): 153-154.

Curtin's work proved fruitful on May 15. Based on his earlier recommendation to raise troops separate from service in the U.S. Army, the legislature passed a bill agreeing to those regiments. The new body of soldiers, totaling 13 regiments of infantry, one regiment of cavalry, and one regiment of artillery, was to be armed, equipped, and paid for by Pennsylvania. As history would come to know it, the Pennsylvania Volunteer Reserve Corps was created.[13]

Governor Curtin had his soldiers; now he needed a commander. His first choice was George Brinton McClellan, the son of a prominent Philadelphia family and former captain in the United States Army. McClellan had resigned in 1857 but now sought a way back into service. Multiple governors, including Curtin, wanted McClellan to command their state's forces.[14]

In mid-April McClellan wrote to a close friend, "I have been proposed as the Cmdr of the Penna Reserves, & asked if I would accept—replied yes!" But then days passed. McClellan did not hear from Curtin and grew impatient. He instead took a commission as a major general in Ohio's state forces. Curtin had in fact offered McClellan the command, but mistakenly sent his telegram to Chicago; McClellan lived in Cincinnati and never received it. An administrative error cost the governor his first choice for the Reserves' commander.[15]

Curtin's second choice had been retired for eight years and was 59 years old. Born in Philadelphia, George McCall graduated from West Point in 1822 and spent the 1830s fighting the Seminoles in Florida. He served in Mexico and earned three brevet promotions for courage under fire. He retired in 1853 as a colonel and spent retirement at his home "Belair" outside of Philadelphia, where he "devoted much of his time to scientific pursuits and made numerous valuable contributions to natural history." [16] But these pursuits would have to wait; **McCall accepted** Curtin's offer to command the Reserves on May 16, 1861. With a handful of officers cobbled together to create a staff, McCall set out for Camp Curtin.[17]

*   *   *

13 Journal of the House of Representatives of the Commonwealth of Pennsylvania of the Session Begun at Harrisburg, on the First Day of January, A.D. 1861 (Harrisburg, 1861), 91.

14 For an overview of McClellan's pre-war life, see Stephen W. Sears, *George B. McClellan: The Young Napoleon* (Cambridge, 1988). For the governors of states wanting McClellan, see Ibid., 68.

15 George B. McClellan, *The Civil War Papers of George B. McClellan: Selected Correspondence, 1860-1865*, ed., Stephen Sears (New York, 1989), 4-5; Sears, *George B. McClellan*, 69.

16 Cullum, Volume 1, 299; Ezra Warner, *Generals in Blue: Lives of the Union Commanders* (Baton Rouge, 1964), 289; Sypher, *Pennsylvania Reserve Corps*, 61.

17 Sypher, *Pennsylvania Reserve Corps*, 62.

Major General George McCall
Pennsylvania Volunteer Reserve Corps
LOC

Elizabeth Kane gave birth to a baby boy on April 6, 1861. Doctors were concerned for the baby and mother's health, and confined Elizabeth to bed. In the meantime, her husband informed her he must leave, for he had business in the mountains of northern Pennsylvania. She did not learn about that business until days later, when doctors allowed Elizabeth out of bed and gave her a newspaper. Reading the headline, she recoiled in shock, later writing in her diary, "The *first line* I read announced my darling's name as an accepted volunteer." She continued, "I might have at least had the satisfaction of bidding him farewell." Her husband had lied; he had no business in the mountains. He had instead raised two companies of volunteers.[18]

Thomas Leiper Kane is one of the oddest characters associated with the story of Dranesville. By 1861, he had lived out enough stories to fill the biographies of half a dozen men, and he was just getting started.

He was born in 1822, son of John and Jane Kane. John, an intense and at times "overbearing" father, presided as a judge in Philadelphia courts. Thomas's older brother Elisha gained fame in the 1850s as an Arctic explorer. Thomas later wrote, "I have been born with the gold spoon in my mouth, to station and influence and responsibility here."[19] That aristocratic background gave Thomas access to the upper echelons of education, and at 17-years-old, he went to France to study philosophy, which "fueled both [Kane's] humanitarian drive and his religious unorthodoxy." Kane became such a devout follower of some of the philosophers that French

---

18 Elizabeth Kane Diary, Apr. 28, 1861, Kane Family Papers, Brigham Young University (BYU). Emphasis in original; Matthew J. Grow, *"Liberty to the Downtrodden": Thomas L. Kane, Romantic Reformer* (New Haven, 2009), 213.

19 Grow, *"Liberty to the Downtrodden"*, 1; Matthew J. Grow and Ronald W. Walker, eds., *The Prophet and the Reformer: The Letters of Brigham Young and Thomas L. Kane* (Oxford, 2015), 89.

Lieutenant Colonel Thomas L. Kane
1st Pennsylvania Rifles
LOC

police raided his apartment in fear that he was fomenting radical ideas.[20]

His unorthodox approach to religion and his voracious curiosity led the 24-year-old Kane to attend a lecture in 1846 given by an Elder of the Church of Jesus Christ of Latter-day Saints. The Mormons were locked in juridical brawls with the U.S. Government as they sought a place to settle their religious community. It seemed that every place they went, angry mobs followed and kicked them out, leaving them continually traveling west. Kane became fascinated with the Mormons' tenets and wanted to help in their settlements. He used his familial connections to introduce a Mormon speaker to the Vice President of the United States.[21]

Eventually Kane himself traveled west and met Brigham Young, the Mormons' leader. The two men forged a bond that lasted the rest of their lives. Kane became, as one writer puts it, "Young's closest non-Mormon friend."[22]

The friendship paid dividends in the late 1850s when it seemed like the Mormons and the Government were about to wage open warfare. Young had grand visions of a territory called the State of Deseret, which would encompass almost all the western portion of the United States. Young's belligerence regarding

20 Grow, *"Liberty to the Downtrodden"*, 22; Albert L. Zobell, *Sentinel in the East: A Biography of Thomas L. Kane* (Salt Lake City, 1965), 10-11.

21 Leonard J. Arrington, "'In Honorable Remembrance': Thomas L. Kane's Services to the Mormons," in *Brigham Young University Studies* 21, No. 4 (Fall 1981): 389-390.

22 David J. Whittaker, "New Sources on Old Friends: The Thomas L. Kane and Elizabeth W. Kane Collection," in *Journal of Mormon History* 27, No. 1 (Spring 2001): 68.

Deseret irritated President James Buchanan, as did the open hostility Mormons had for Federal agents. By 1857, Buchanan had had enough and ordered 2,500 soldiers to march to Utah to put a stop to Young's intentions.[23]

Young appeared ready to meet force with force and readied his Mormon militias for conflict. Then Kane stepped in as mediator. He met with Young to talk him down from open confrontation. During a long winter in which the army was holed up in its quarters, Kane continued to mediate between Young and Federal officers. Kane broke through the political stalemate and prevented a massive bloodletting. He returned home to Philadelphia a physically weak man, the actions of the past year having sapped all his energy, but he was hailed a hero by many, including President Buchanan. In his annual address to Congress the president praised Kane, "who, from motives of pure benevolence and without any official character or pecuniary compensation, visited Utah . . . for the purpose of contributing to the pacification of the Territory."[24]

While his work with the Mormons made him famous across the nation, Kane had been busy with other work as well. He held deep animosity towards slavery, and as a lawyer in Philadelphia refused to enact the Fugitive Slave Act, for which his own father jailed him for contempt of court. Outside of the courts, Kane helped runaway enslaved people through Philadelphia's Underground Railroad network. His anti-slavery work made him pen pals with likeminded people, such as Horace Greeley and Wendell Phillips. Besides abolitionism, Kane believed in women's rights, opposed capital punishment, and was, in fact, a pacifist.[25]

Thus, the conflict's outbreak in 1861 "caused him to approach the Civil War with unease," his biographer writes. Kane soon realized, though, that war was the only alternative. He wrote, "Peace, Peace at any price, and everything for Peace is the teaching of the Master, but He also teaches to let the oppressed to go free and a number of other inconvenient inconsistent things."[26] Kane volunteered his services

23 Arrington, 395. For an excellent monograph detailing the lead-up to the Utah War and its causes, see David L. Bigler and Will Bagley, *The Mormon Rebellion: America's First Civil War, 1857–1858* (Norman, OK, 2012).

24 Space considerations mean this admittedly short explanation of Kane's involvement in the Utah War will have to suffice. See William P. MacKinnon, "'Full of Courage': Thomas L. Kane, the Utah War and BYU's Kane Collection as Lodestone," in *Brigham Young University Studies* 48, (No. 4, 2009), for an excellent overview. For Buchanan's quote, see James Buchanan Annual Address to Congress, Dec. 3, 1858, James Buchanan and Harriet Lane Johnston Papers: Series IV: Additions, 1842-1867; Addition III; State of the Union message, 1858, Dec. 3, LOC.

25 See Grow, *"Liberty to the Downtrodden"*, 115 for Kane being jailed for contempt, 127 for Kane's Underground Railroad work, 141-148 for his women's rights campaign, and 36-40 for his opinions on capital punishment and pacifism.

26 Ibid., 211, 212.

to Gov. Curtin, and raised two companies of soldiers, before eventually setting off for Harrisburg—all without telling his wife.[27]

The soldiers Kane raised in the spring of 1861 became some of the most famous soldiers to serve the Federal army during the Civil War. They came from Forest, McKean, and Elk Counties, in the far northern reaches of Pennsylvania in an area referred to as the "Wildcat District." These men lived hard lives and made most of their money rafting goods and supplies down the Susquehanna River.[28]

Kane's soldiers formed at Smethport and waited for orders that would bring them to Harrisburg. On one especially slow day, one of Kane's soldiers, James Landregan, spotted a deer hide hanging outside of a butcher's shop. Landregan "pulled out his penknife, cut off the tail and stuck it in his cap." As the soldier walked back to his camp, "Kane noticed his headgear, seized upon the idea suggested, and instantly announced that the force he was recruiting should be known as 'Bucktails.'"[29] With his Bucktails in tow, Kane made his way to Camp Curtin.

The Bucktails' arrival certainly made an impression. They were, noted one observer, "ragged, undisciplined, ununiformed save in the singular ornament that surmounts their head gear." Without uniforms, the soldiers wore whatever they brought with them, and many "carried their own hunting rifles." It did not take long for the Wildcat District soldiers to start trouble.[30]

Long hours of drill with little respite led to "a tedious monotony about camp life" only broken up by a "a fight, a guard house row, or 'the drumming out' of an unworthy soldier," as one recruit wrote from camp.[31] Company officers, still mastering the finer details of *commanding* their men, had little power over the recruits who largely did what they pleased. The biggest allure for the Bucktails remained the access to alcohol in Harrisburg.[32]

The Bucktails became well-known for their drunken adventures. One night, some of the inebriated soldiers got into fisticuffs with police constables in town and were only brought back to camp when the mayor of Harrisburg called out three companies of soldiers to return them under guard. Thomas Kane personally

---

27 William H. Rauch and O. R. Howard Thomson, *History of the "Bucktails"* (Philadelphia, 1906), 7-8.

28 Edwin A. Glover, *Bucktailed Wildcats: A Regiment of Civil War Volunteers* (New York, 1960), 15-16.

29 Rauch and Thomson, *"Bucktails"*, 11.

30 Glover, 26; Rauch and Thomson, *"Bucktails"*, 22.

31 *The Agitator*, Jun. 19, 1861.

32 Miller, *The Training of an Army*, 18.

got involved on at least one occasion, bringing back three delinquent soldiers from Harrisburg drinking holes.[33]

Then General McCall arrived. The no-nonsense general began to mold the ragtag bunch into a semblance of a fighting force. Under his guidance the numerous independent companies around Camp Curtin were organized into regiments, and the Pennsylvania Reserves transformed from an organization in name only into a tangible fighting force. McCall gave "special care" to the Bucktails, training them to "maneuver in wooded hills, swamps, and ravines."[34]

As the regiment transformed into a fighting unit, its commanders changed, too. Kane, though fame preceded him, had no military experience, and turned command over to Col. Charles Biddle, a Philadelphian who had served in Mexico. Though Kane now found himself a lieutenant colonel, he was proud when the regiment voted to change its name. He informed McCall, "At the request of the officers, non-commissioned officers, and privates of the Rifle Regiment of the Reserve Volunteer Corps, commanded by Col. Biddle, it will hereafter be known as 'The Kane Rifle Regiment' of the Reserve Volunteer Corps."[35]

The Bucktails' progress seemed to be going well, and an officer wrote home, "We shall certainly have the crack regiment of the service."[36]

On June 21, the Bucktails got a chance to test themselves when orders arrived at Camp Curtin to move out. The Bucktails and another regiment, the 5th Pennsylvania Reserves, accompanied by a battery of artillery, were instructed to head to Cumberland, Maryland. Located in the mountains of far-west Maryland, Cumberland sat near the border of Virginia, and the only Federal presence there was a regiment of Indiana Zouaves under the command of Col. Lew Wallace. The Indianans needed reinforcement, and the Pennsylvanians were ordered out. When the order arrived at Camp Curtin, it was "received with mingled surprise and delight by the Bucktails."[37]

Though the regiment was eager for action, the ensuing service proved to be a disappointment. The Bucktails did have some skirmishing with irregular Confederate forces and scouts, but it seemed the largest source of fighting came between Kane and Biddle.

33 Ibid., 25; Glover, *Bucktailed Wildcats*, 34.

34 Sypher, *Pennsylvania Reserve Corps*, 62.

35 Rauch and Thomson, *"Bucktails"*, 33-34; Thomas Kane Papers, Box 19, Box 6, Item 16, BYU.

36 Charles F. Hobson, et al., "Colonel of the Bucktails: Civil War Letters of Charles Frederick Taylor," in *The Pennsylvania Magazine of History and Biography* 97, No. 3 (Jul. 1973): 341.

37 Rauch and Thomson, *"Bucktails"*, 39; For more detail about Lew Wallace's Zouaves at Cumberland, see Chapter 2 in Gail Stephens, *Shadow of Shiloh: Major General Lew Wallace in the Civil War* (Indianapolis, 2010), 17-33.

Biddle was under strict orders to stay at Cumberland and support the Federal foothold there, while Kane adamantly supported bringing the fight to the rebels in Virginia. As Biddle continued to ignore Kane's pleas, the latter began to fume. In Kane's papers at Brigham Young University is an unpublished article detailing the Bucktails' service along the Maryland-Virginia border. It eviscerates the colonel's lack of action, noting "his masterly inactivity in Western Virginia." Kane complained that "Biddle was deaf to every entreaty or to every entreaty turned a Southern ear."[38]

Biddle had been nominated to Congress as a Democrat in a special election in early June, thus Kane's not so disguised insult accusing Biddle of having a "Southern ear." Although the election would not occur until the fall, Biddle made it no secret that he opposed the war, which continued to infuriate Kane. While the Bucktails' campaign in Virginia did not amount to much, it created a rift in its command structure that would last up to, and even past, Dranesville.[39]

Under Biddle's command the Bucktails remained in Virginia as the calendar flipped from June to July. The soldiers continued to keep their eyes peeled for rebel soldiers and prepare for the day they would fight more than just scattered patrols.

38 Kane Papers, Box 20, Folder 03, Item 01, BYU.

39 Kane Papers, Box 20, Folder 03, Item 01, BYU; For Charles J. Biddle's Copperhead political views, see Nicholas B. Wainwright, "The Loyal Opposition in Civil War Philadelphia," in *The Pennsylvania Magazine of History and Biography* 88, No. 3 (Jul. 1964): 295-296.

Chapter Four

"Kill All the Damned Yankee Sons of Bitches in the Country"

The Dranesville Home Guard

Daniel Borden hailed from New York. He moved to Fairfax County and settled just a few miles out of Dranesville, in or around 1846. By 1861, Borden had a wife and four children, two hogs, and three cattle, scratching out a living as a carpenter, wheelwright, and wagon maker. He did not go to the polls on May 23 during the secession vote, but he made no secrets about his Unionist sympathies.[1]

On May 25, two days after the secessionist vote, a gaggle of men showed up at the Borden household. They were not there to exchange pleasantries, and Borden later identified seven of them, especially singling out John T. Day. The younger Day brother threatened, Borden later recalled, that if he went to Washington "to join Lincoln's army they would burn my property and massacre my family." Months later, Day defended his actions, claiming he did in fact go to Borden's house, "but did not get off [my] horse." Borden found himself under arrest for the crime of being a Unionist.[2]

Borden was the first to be arrested by the men of the town who had fashioned themselves into a "Home Guard." That group included both Day brothers, as well

---

1 Daniel Borden 1860 Census, Fairfax County; livestock inventory in Edith A. Sprouse, *Fairfax County in 1860: A Collective Biography,* Vol. 1 (1996), 173; Borden lists himself as a wagon maker and carpenter in Minor Crippen Testimony, Southern Claims. In that testimony, taken in 1877, Borden said he had lived in Fairfax County "Thirty-one years this fall," which would be around 1846.

2 Daniel Borden testimony in *Proceedings of the Commission Relating to State Prisoners*, 1862, Vol. 1, John T. Day Case, 32, RG 59, NARA (hereafter John T. Day Case File). John T. Day quote from Ibid., 33.

Courtesy of the Fairfax County Public Library Photographic Archive

as John B. Farr. According to Henry Bishop, another of the targeted Unionists, the men of the Home Guard "made it their business to hunt up and prosecute Union men." Another Unionist, Dennis Ormsby, claimed that when the Home Guard came, William Day threatened to "hang him right up."[3]

Bishop explained that when the Home Guard arrested him, they brought him to the general store belonging to Charles W. Coleman. The store and public house that Coleman ran morphed into "a kind of headquarters for the Rebel troops." Confederate soldiers and officers, of both the Home Guard and volunteer units on their way to Manassas, stopped by Coleman's for meals and bedding.[4] Coleman later admitted that it was true that he fed Confederates at his store, but also asked rhetorically "What would have been the consequence had I refused?"[5]

While Charles Coleman's store and public house were used by Confederates and the Home Guard, it is not entirely clear how much further his personal support went, as he never joined the Confederate army. The same could not be said for other members of his family.

The Colemans were one of the leading families of Dranesville, having lived in the area for almost 140 years, long before the town even got its name. Charles's ancestor had opened a tavern west of what became Dranesville on a tributary of the Potomac River called Sugarland Run. By 1755, the tavern was prominent

3 Henry Bishop Testimony in *Proceedings of the Commission Relating to State Prisoners, 1862*, Vol. 1, John B. Farr Case File, RG 59, NARA (hereafter cited as John B. Farr Case File), 20; Timothy D. Johnson quoting Ormsby in William B. Day Case File, 30.

4 Henry Bishop Testimony in *Proceedings of the Commission Relating to State Prisoners, 1862*, Vol. 1, Charles W. Coleman Case File, RG 59, NARA (hereafter cited as Charles W. Coleman Case File), 56.

5 *OR* 2, Series 2, 1287; Charles W. Coleman Testimony, Charles Coleman Case File, 59.

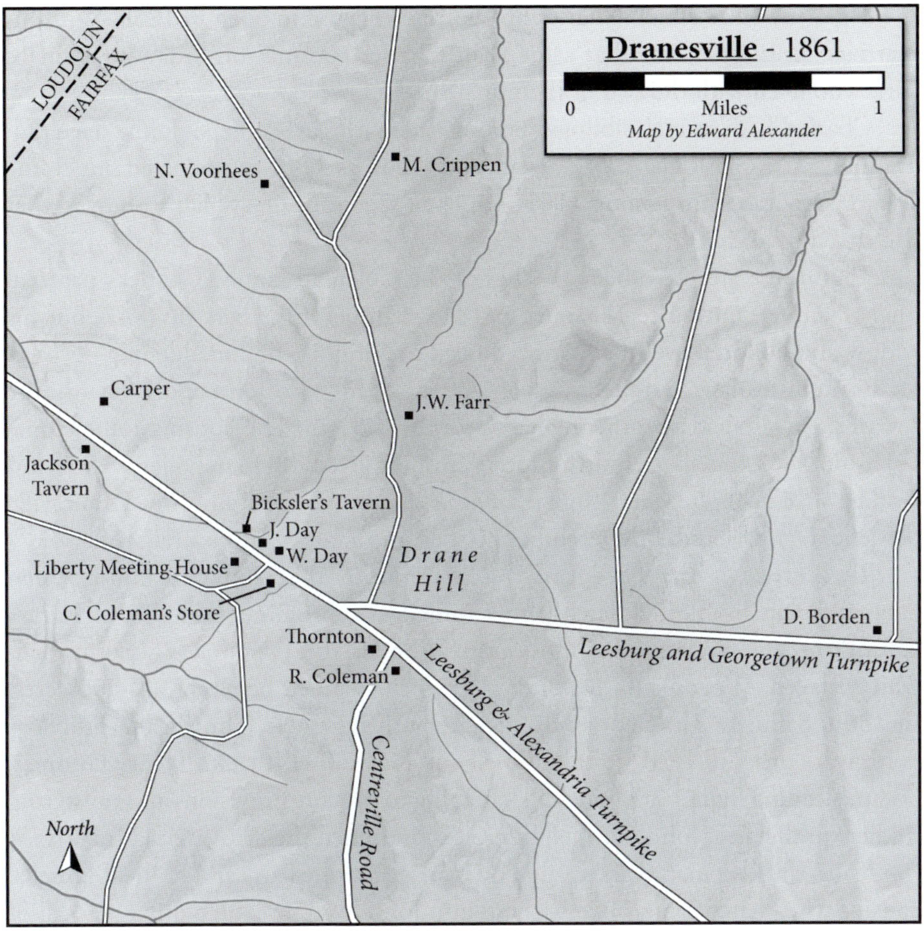

enough for British Gen. Edward Braddock's soldiers to stop at and gather supplies. George Washington's personal ledger noted at least ten stops at the tavern over a 15-year period.[6]

By the time Washington Drane came onto the scene in the 19th century, the Colemans were a fixture of the community, serving as trustees for one of the town's churches, the Liberty Methodist Meeting House.[7] Charles's father died in January 1861, leaving Charles, his eldest son, then 31-years old, to continue the family interests. Those included the Coleman tavern along Sugarland Run, as well

---

6 Poland, *Dunbarton, Dranesville*, 10; Norman L. Baker, *Braddock's Road: Mapping the British Expedition from Alexandria to the Monongahela* (Charleston, SC, 2013), 31; *The Papers of George Washington Digital Edition*, ed., Theodore J. Crackel (Charlottesville, VA, 2008); accessed May 7, 2017. http://financial.gwpapers.org/?q=content/colemans-ordinary-virginia.

7 Margaret Lail Hopkins, *Dranesville Methodism* (Stephens City, VA, 1984), 18.

as the general store which Charles had gotten a license to open in 1858. With his marriage to Lavinia Farr that same year, Charles became son-in-law to John B. Farr, who lived with the two of them in 1861.[8]

Charles had several siblings, among them three brothers: John, aged 24; Thomas, 21; and Richard, 17. John and Thomas both participated in Home Guard activities throughout 1861, while it seems from available sources that Richard did not.

Then there are the other branches of the Coleman family. Charles's paternal uncle, Samuel, moved to Missouri in 1843. Samuel died there in 1847, but his widow and children eventually moved back to Virginia. In a maddening decision for future historians, Samuel also named two of his sons John and Richard. The two of them also had a brother named George, who joined his cousins in the Home Guard in 1861. Finally, a fourth brother, Robert, lived in Dranesville in 1861 and worked as a schoolteacher. Robert's home sat on what became the Dranesville battlefield, and would, on December 20, become a target for Federal artillery.[9]

Then there is the Colemans' relationship to the Gunnell family. When Samuel Coleman married Sarah Ann Gunnell, two prominent families of Fairfax County became connected. John Gunnell, Sarah's brother, was a wealthy man who enslaved 23 people on his property, which spanned between 300-500 acres. In 1860, Samuel's son George, lived there with his uncle John on the property. With war's onset in 1861, John Gunnell and his brother Richard Henry Gunnell, became leading figures in Dranesville, helping to procure provisions and mustering soldiers in the area. John Gunnell himself soon joined the 8th Virginia Infantry.[10]

Thus, the Colemans were related by marriage to the Farrs and to the Gunnells; cousins who shared names like Richard and John lived near each other, and all of it would soon be thoroughly confusing to Federal officers who tried, sometimes unsuccessfully, to understand the convoluted family trees.

Of the entire family, Thomas Coleman was probably the most ardent supporter of the Confederacy. He eagerly joined the Home Guard and John Day sold Thomas a pistol "for half price because he . . . was going to fight the Yankees with it."[11]

8 Sprouse, *Fairfax County in 1860: Vol. 1*, 368; Poland, *Dunbarton, Dranesville*, 8-10, 73; *Alexandria Gazette*, Apr. 24, 1858; Testimony of Nelson Voorhees, Charles Coleman Case File, 53.

9 1850 Federal Census, Cooper MO; George's involvement in Home Guards found in John Jackson Testimony in *Proceedings of the Commission Relating to State Prisoners, 1862*, Vol. 1, George Coleman Case File, RG 59, NARA (hereafter cited as George Coleman Case File), 47; Robert Coleman being a schoolteacher found in Charles W. Butler Testimony, Ann Coleman Southern Claims File (NARA).

10 Sprouse, *Fairfax County in 1860: Vol. 2*, 814; John Gunnell CSR, Company G, 8th Virginia Infantry, NARA.

11 John C. Money Testimony, Charles W. Coleman Case File, 55; Timothy Johnson Testimony, John T. Day Case File, 29.

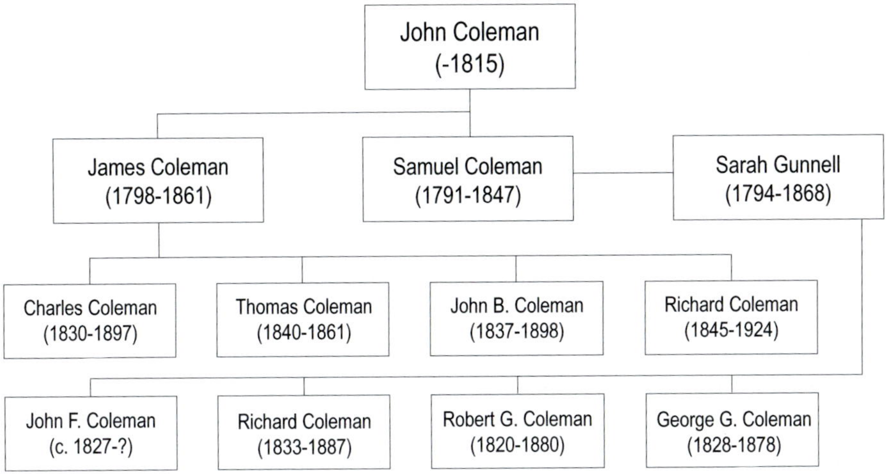

A sampling of the Coleman family tree shows how the duplicate names soon confused Federal officers—and historians generations later. *Author*

To especially intimidate his adversaries, Day had John Hurst, a blacksmith, make him a knife with an eighteen-inch blade. Day said, according to a Unionist, that he "got it to cut out the hearts of Union men."[12] Another Unionist, Nelson Voorhees, claimed he heard Day say, "if he had his way he would kill all the damned Yankee sons of bitches in the country, for they were all abolitionists."[13]

Day and Hurst's relationship went further than the latter just making a knife. Fairfax County local Henry Biggs claimed he was "threatened by Dr. Day and John Hurst," who "had a number of Confederate soldiers with them."[14]

By early June, many of the Unionists in and around Dranesville feared for their lives. There were rumors that at least one of the Home Guard "is now scouting about the woods with his gun" and seemed "to be watching Union men." That fear proved too much for many Unionists. When Daniel Borden was released from custody at Charles Coleman's store, he fled to Washington on June 10.[15]

12 Timothy Johnson Testimony, John T. Day Case File, 29.

13 Nelson Voorhees Testimony, John T. Day Case File, 28.

14 Henry Biggs Southern Claims File, Fairfax County, Virginia, 13.

15 Timothy J. Johnson Testimony in *Proceedings of the Commission Relating to State Prisoners, 1862*, Vol. 1, Dranesville Murder Cases, Mar. 27, 1862, RG 59, NARA (hereafter cited as Dranesville Murder Cases, Mar. 27, 1862), 7; Daniel Borden Testimony, Minor Crippen Southern Claims, Fairfax County, Virginia.

Others held on, bearing the violent rhetoric. Nathaniel Hanna, a Unionist who lived at Herndon, just south of Dranesville, joined the Home Guard out of peer pressure but promised his wife that "as soon as ever they ask me to fight, I'm off, 'cause I won't fight against the Union."[16]

The days passed as the Home Guard patrolled nearly every night, and more Confederate forces passed through the area on their way to Manassas Junction. The railroad hub south of Dranesville was becoming a central location for Confederate forces. By early July there were approximately 20,000 Confederates there, and the Dranesville Home Guard decided to join them.[17]

A call went out that every available man had to report the following morning with three days' rations. This was the line in the sand for the Unionists who refused to fight against their country. That same night, Nelson Voorhees and Minor Crippen made plans to head to Henry Bishop's, and together the three would make for the Potomac River. But, as Voorhees testified later, he and Crippen were delayed when "two officers came to my house about sundown." The two Unionists "didn't dare to go to Bishop's" for fear of Confederate patrols. Voorhees and Crippen could do nothing but stay in place.

They waited until they finally felt they could sneak out into the countryside. The two men made their way to the banks of the Potomac River, and "hunted for a boat but couldn't find any." Giving up their search, Voorhees and Crippen made their way to Bishop's home, where his father, Leverett, "told us Henry had left about an hour before to come to Washington." Accepting that they were on their own, the two started east, avoiding pickets and patrols as they walked the nearly fifteen miles to the small village of Langley. Daylight found them once again avoiding rebel pickets before finally they made their way to the Chain Bridge, about six miles northwest of Washington, D.C. The two exhausted men, and Henry Bishop before them, had reached safety.[18]

While the Unionists fled Dranesville, the two armies slithered towards each other around Manassas Junction. The Federal army left the environs of Washington on July 16, and two days later found itself on the opposite bank of the Bull Run near Centreville. Skirmishing on the 18th gave way three days later to the war's first major pitched battle. Though the Federal forces had an early advantage, the arrival of Confederate reinforcements late in the day tipped the scales, and

16 Virginia Carter Castleman, *Reminiscences of an Oldest Inhabitant* (Herndon, VA, 1976), 14.

17 Longacre, *Early Morning of War*, 84.

18 Nelson Voorhees Testimony, Nelson Voorhees Southern Claims, Fairfax County, Virginia.

the Union battle lines broke, retreating for the safety of Washington, D.C. The fighting left nearly 900 men dead, and another 4,000 wounded or captured.[19] A flurry of people and units arrived at Manassas Junction in time to witness the aftermath. Among them were two regiments that would fight at Dranesville: the 6th South Carolina and 10th Alabama. The Dranesville Home Guards showed up too, though they had little to do.

The 6th South Carolina had gone through an entire reorganization since its days at Fort Sumter. Stuck on the islands surrounding Charleston, the Carolinians grew bored and discipline became non-existent. Their colonel resigned, and the regiment elected new officers before it headed north. John Bratton, the planter from Winnsboro, lost his position as a captain, but soon after was elected as a second lieutenant.[20] While the officers quarreled, their soldiers killed time. Frank English, the young teenager from Columbia, routinely went "oyster and crab hunting."[21]

The regiment's drama delayed its departure to Virginia until the middle of July. It was a miserable trip in some stretches—the regiment rode in open flatcars on its way to Wilmington, North Carolina, and the skies opened, drenching the soldiers. One officer wrote that he "slept under a bench altho it rained on me as we had no shelter."[22]

The South Carolinians arrived at Manassas after a six-day trip, disembarking the cars on Sunday, July 21, around 2:00 p.m. In the distance they could hear the booming of the battle. They discovered that morale at the Junction was near bottom. Bratton wrote, "We heard along the way from the wounded and the rascally stragglers, who got enough and quit, that our S. C. Boys had been cut to pieces and that the enemy were surrounding with their overwhelming numbers our entire army." By the time the 6th got to the front, though, the battle had reversed course. Missing the fight, the Carolinians went into camp to wait for their next chance. Frank English wrote home and figured the army would soon "advance on Washington."[23]

The 10th Alabama arrived on July 23. The men had mustered at Montgomery a month earlier. Their own delay was caused by a train collision on the tracks, forcing the soldiers to march. They marched through the passes of the Shenandoah's

19 For complete treatments of the battle, see John H. Hennessy, *The First Battle of Manassas: An End to Innocence, July 18-21, 1861* (Mechanicsburg, PA, 2015) and Longacre, *Early Morning of War*.

20 Woodward, *From Fort Sumter to Dranesville*, 10; Bratton, *General John Bratton*, 19.

21 Frank English to his mother, Apr. 20, 1861, Frank English Letters.

22 Diary of Lieutenant Andrew McConnell During the Civil War, Valdosta State University Archives and Special Collections, 28.

23 Bratton, *General John Bratton*, 21; Frank English to his mother, Jul. 31, 1861, Frank English Letters.

mountains and jumped from train to train but were still too late for the combat. They, like other arrivals, were stuck in the pouring rain with nowhere to go.[24]

In the wake of the fighting, the gruesome work of attending to the wounded began. When the Dranesville Home Guard arrived on the battlefield in the wake of the action, William B. Day volunteered his medical services and, according to a letter he wrote months later, "rendered service" to wounded Federals as well.[25]

Besides tending to the wounded, Day and the others explored the battlefield, walking among the dead and collecting equipment, sometimes from corpses. A Unionist repeated that he heard that Day stripped the shoes off dead Federal soldiers. "When asked by [Charles] Coleman what he was doing that for, he, Day, replied that he was going to give the shoes to his negro man." He also got his hands on a "red Zouave dress" that he took to wearing around.[26]

Taking shoes and jackets was one thing, but the Home Guard's actions at Manassas also led to the birth of a particularly ghastly rumor. Appearing first in a testimony on Nov. 30, 1861, Nelson Voorhees, one of the Unionists who had fled prior to the battle, claimed he had heard from another Unionist, Nathaniel Hanna, that Day and Coleman cut the head off a dead Federal soldier. Supposedly, the story went, Coleman brought the head back with him to Dranesville, where he "stuck it on a pole in front of his house, where it remained for three or four weeks."[27]

Such a story had no foundation in fact. Not only was the story told by scared Unionists through second- and third-hand retellings, the story sometimes varied. A dismembered head remained a constant, but sometimes it was Charles Coleman who supposedly had it, and other times William Day. The doctor was sometimes even accused of having *two* heads at his house, which he used to adorn his front gate. In some retellings the head stayed outside "for three or four weeks," and other times supposedly stayed on a pole until at least October.[28] More embellished

---

24 Bailey George McClelen, *I Saw the Elephant: The Civil War Experiences of Bailey George McClelen Company D, 10th Alabama Infantry Regiment*, ed. Norman E. Rourke (Shippensburg, PA, 1994), 15; Ira Harrison Weissinger, Jr., "The Tenth Alabama Infantry Regiment in the Confederate States Army," Master's thesis (Auburn University, 1961), 34-35.

25 *OR* 2, Series 2, 1289.

26 Howard Lasher Testimony, William B. Day Case File, 23-24; Nathaniel Hanna Testimony in *Proceedings of the Commission Relating to State Prisoners*, 1862, Vol. 1, R. H. Gunnell Case File, RG 59, NARA (hereafter R. H. Gunnell Case File), 10.

27 Nelson Voorhees Testimony, Charles W. Coleman Case File, 52.

28 Nathaniel Hanna Testimony, R. H. Gunnell Case File, 9. Hanna claimed Coleman "brought a dead Yankee's head with them and placed it in front of his house and kept it there until Gen. McCall's division came there." McCall's PA Reserves first went to Dranesville on Oct. 19. The quote regarding William B. Day using the two heads to fill wooden balls come from Elisabeth Alice Gibbens Cole, *An Account of Our Day Family of Calvert County, Maryland* (Lettsworth, MD, 1982), 75. The author of the piece used strong sarcasm when she wrote, following the allegation of the bowls, "The two balls

rumors had Coleman also in possession of a "breast bone" that he kept in his general store and would take down and examine in conversation with patrons—but even that wasn't agreed upon, because other people swore it was a "shoulder bone."[29] Testifying in the winter of 1861, Richard H. Gunnell, John Gunnell's brother, professed he had heard the story of the decapitated head, but admitted he did not "know whether it was a joke or not."[30]

In a broader sense, the morbid story told among the local Unionists fits into a larger pattern. As historian John Hennessy writes, concerning the aftermath of Manassas, "Both sides tried to paint the other as barbaric practitioners of atrocities—accusations intended solely to confirm the virtue of one side and to inflame the populace to a more intense support of the war." The rumor that William B. Day had cut the head off a corpse fit among other unlikely stories, such as that Confederate soldiers fired into Federal hospitals on the battlefield, or that the Federal army planned to use rebel prisoners of war as human shields. Hennessy concludes, "Propagandists on neither side had much with which to work."[31]

The members of the Home Guard returned to Dranesville without a head or any other cut-off appendage belonging to Federal soldiers. They soon returned to their pre-battle business of hunting down Unionists and sought out one of their own who had deserted his post. Unionist Nathaniel Hanna, who had joined the Home Guards, promised his wife, Catherine, he would leave the unit as soon as he could. As they prepared to travel to Manassas, Nathaniel had a last dinner with his wife and bolted for Washington.[32]

While Nathaniel fled, Catherine stayed behind at the family home in Herndon with their four-year old son. Catherine, who went by the nickname Kitty, admitted later in life that her own loyalties were "so torn in twain," as her brother fought for the Confederacy. With Nathaniel back in Washington, Kitty's mother joined her at the family home.[33]

Kitty explained what happened when the Home Guard came looking for Nathaniel. Having put her son to bed, she sat up with her mother when she heard from the lane coming up to the house "the tramp of the horses' feet." From the

---

had been there for many years before the war started. They were solid wood all the way through, as were the heads of his accusers"; Cole, *Our Day Family*, 74.

29 Dranesville Murder Cases, Mar. 27, 1862, 6; *Proceedings of the Commission Relating to State Prisoners, 1862*, Vol. 1, Dranesville Murder Cases, Mar. 31, 1862, RG 59, NARA (hereafter cited as Dranesville Murder Cases, Mar. 31, 1862), 2.

30 R. H. Gunnell Testimony, R. H. Gunnell Case File, 12.

31 Hennessy, *The First Battle of Manassas*, 160.

32 Castleman, *Reminiscences of an Oldest Inhabitant*, 15.

33 Ibid.

Catherine "Kitty" Hanna, later in life.

Herndon Historical Society

darkness of the night someone called out, "This is where Nat Hanna lives," and Kitty then saw "the gleam of bayonets down by the front gate, showin' plain in the moonlight."[34]

Among the riders that night was the always present William B. Day. The men began "boomin' at the door," Kitty remembered. Her dog, Spice, began to bark at the men on the porch, and she grew terrified they would shoot him. After a few more minutes of back and forth, the Home Guards returned to their horses and rode back into the midnight darkness from where they came. Hanna also testified later that Day told his wife, "If they ever caught me they would riddle me with balls."[35] The entire ordeal left Kitty Hanna shaken so much that she packed "blankets an' pillows" and sought the comfort of nearby neighbors. She said decades later, "I've never forgot that night when death come near, and no news of our boys, which weighed heavy on my mind."[36] Such political fissures cutting through Dranesville would only worsen in time.

Two further examples demonstrate what kind of terror Dranesville Unionists faced. Seventy-one-year-old Francis Crocker had voted to remain in the Union when he went to the polls at Lewinsville. Devoted to the Union, he sometimes passed information to officials in Washington. Crocker's sons also joined Federal regiments from Pennsylvania and New York. Unable to get at the sons, Confederate authorities instead targeted Francis. Two days after the battle at Manassas, a contingent of soldiers arrested the old man at his home near Lewinsville. As they brought their captive to Culpeper, one of the Confederates hit Crocker with his musket, paralyzing the man. Never recovering, Crocker died in October. A Federal

---

34 Ibid.

35 Ibid.; Nathaniel Hanna, Testimony, R. H. Gunnell Case File, 10.

36 Castleman, *Reminiscences of an Oldest Inhabitant*, 16.

prisoner wrote, "Thus perished an old man of 70 years, whose only fault was being a Union man."[37]

Confederates also targeted another old man, 75-year-old Leverett Bishop. Henry Bishop's father, Leverett continued to live at his home near the Potomac River even after his son escaped to Washington. Unlike Crocker, there is no evidence that he spied or passed on information to Union authorities. The only crime Bishop could be found guilty of was that of being Henry's father. And just like Crocker, if the Confederates could not have the son, they'd have the father.

Confederates "took him from his bed at midnight, and without money or change of clothing . . . dragged him on to Richmond," Henry wrote later. Detained in Richmond for close to three months, Leverett was released without charges. Walking back home, Leverett made it as far as Warrenton, 95 miles from Richmond and still 40 miles from home. There, he was arrested again, and "worn out with privation and want, hope at an end, he died." All the grieving son's anger was poured like a funnel straight at William B. Day. "My father's blood is on his hands," Henry fumed. "God grant that the ghastly faces of the dead that he has stripped, and the groans of the dying who he has tormented and insulted . . . haunt him to his grave."[38]

Historian Noel Harrison writes "Between May 1861 and April 1862, at least seven of the counties' male citizens died in encounters with soldiers or while in their custody."[39] It was becoming readily apparent that the war would not be confined to the battlefield.

*   *   *

As the civilians fought their own war, the Federal army, beaten and humiliated, retreated towards Washington, D.C. The soldiers were soaked to the bone from constant rain. English diarist William H. Russell wrote how the men "were pouring irregularly, without any semblance of order, up Pennsylvania Avenue towards the Capitol."[40]

The news of the defeat preceded the Federal soldiers stumbling back into the capital. In a telegram that soon wound up in President Lincoln's hands, a Union officer wrote, "The day is lost. Save Washington and the remnants of this army."

---

37 Kenneth A. Link, "Courage and Betrayal: The Union Loyalists in Lewinsville," in the *Northern Virginia Heritage* VIII, No. 1, (Feb. 1986): 3; *New York Times*, Jun. 4, 1862.

38 *The Evening Star*, Washington, May 9, 1862.

39 Noel G. Harrison, "Atop an Anvil: The Civilians' War in Fairfax and Alexandria Counties, April 1861-April 1862," in *The Virginia Magazine of History and Biography* 106, No. 2. (Spring, 1998): 151.

40 William Howard Russell, *My Diary North and South: Vol. 1* (Boston, 1863), 467.

The president told a friend the news was "*damned bad*," and according to another source "sat with his head bent down upon his hand, and was evidently very much depressed." Standing beside him, though, Secretary of War Simon Cameron "was the coolest head in the Cabinet." Cameron "consulted with [General Winfield] Scott as to hurrying re-enforcements across the Potomac."[41]

Earlier that spring, Cameron had lorded his power over his political rival, Gov. Andrew Curtin, dismissing Curtin's efforts to raise more troops and refusing to accept any additional soldiers that the Governor gathered. Now, though, there were rumors and whispers that the victorious rebels would try to attack Washington, and the capital needed men to protect it. With the available forces in Virginia all but scattered for the time being, they could hardly be expected to stand up and fight if those Confederates did in fact march against Washington. Cameron swallowed his pride and telegrams began to flicker across the wires, headed north.

In a flurry, the messages arrived on Curtin's desk. "Get your regiments at Harrisburg . . . and other points ready for immediate shipment," the first telegram read. "Lose no time preparing." A second one, sent just a little later, read "Press forward all available forces." A third: "Start them before daylight in the morning." A fourth, written directly by Winfield Scott: "Send all the regiments at Harrisburg and elsewhere to Baltimore."[42]

Curtin reacted with the same gusto as he had when the war first began. The bulk of his available troops were the Pennsylvania Reserves under the command of George McCall. The same troops Cameron had initially refused to accept were now the ones he relied on to defend the capital. McCall wrote to Cameron on July 22 that his command "shall leave without delay for Washington."[43]

Curtin also recalled the Bucktails from Cumberland. The other regiments already in Harrisburg were immediately ordered to start their voyage to Washington via Baltimore. "Trains of cars—no palace or Pullman cars . . . but cattle, coal, and box cars, anything to get us aboard and off for Washington," wrote Charles Veil, a soldier in the 9th Reserves, recalling the frantic rush to mobilize.[44]

The Pennsylvanians headed for the capital—to save it, and to save their country.

41 *OR* 2, pt. , 747; Rodney O. Davis and Douglas L. Wilson, eds., *Herndon's Informants: Letters, Interviews, and Statements about Abraham Lincoln* (Urbana, IL, 1998), 207 (Emphasis in original); *The National Tribune*, Sep. 16, 1882.

42 *OR* 2, pt. , 749-751.

43 Egle, *Andrew Gregg Curtin*, 273.

44 Charles H. Veil, *The Memoirs of Charles Henry Veil: A Soldier's Recollections of the Civil War and the Arizona Territory*, ed. Herman J. Viola (Thorndike, ME, 1994), 9.

Chapter Five

"We Had a Little Fight"

The Battle of Lewinsville

Colonel J. E. B. Stuart and his 1st Virginia Cavalry troopers arrived at Fairfax Court House around 9:30 a.m. on July 23. Only 12 miles from Washington, the Confederates found no shortage of reminders of the recent Federal retreat. John S. Mosby, destined for fame as a partisan fighter, wrote, "The county looked very much like Egypt after a flood of the Nile—it was strewn with the debris of [the] army."[1]

Stuart's men were flush from their victory at Manassas. Stuart himself gathered acclaim from both Gen. Joseph Johnston, commanding the Army of the Shenandoah, and Brig. Gen. Thomas Jackson, soon-to-be-known as "Stonewall," who wrote that Stuart and his men "deserve great praise for the promptness with which they moved to my left and secured the flank by timely charging the enemy and driving him back."[2]

At Fairfax Court House, Stuart screened the advance of the Confederate army. His men fanned out from Fairfax, closing in on small towns like Falls Church and Annandale. They would be there for the months to come.

The troopers captured a trio of hills just outside of Alexandria, known as Upton's, Munson's, and Mason's hills. By controlling them, the Confederates restricted access to turnpikes leaving Washington, D.C., and gained vantage points from which the occupiers could stare directly into the city. As July became August, Confederates worked at building entrenchments and signal towers atop the trio

---

1 John S. Mosby, *The Memoirs of John S. Mosby*, ed. *Charles W. Russell* (Boston, 1917), 50.

2 *OR* 2, 477, 481.

of hills. The officer in charge of signal operations, Maj. Edward Porter Alexander, found Mason's Hill especially useful and added that with a "fine astronomical glass," he "could easily count the panes . . . in the windows in Washington City."[3]

P. G. T. Beauregard worried that the Federals would strike out from Washington and push back the thin screen of cavalry pickets outside of Alexandria. Stuart's troopers were reinforced by infantry under the command of Brig. Gen. James Longstreet, and soon after Beauregard sent seven more infantry brigades to supplement the Confederate presence. Longstreet personally set up his headquarters at Fairfax Court House, not far from Stuart's. The two worked together closely in the weeks to come.[4] In tours of duty lasting as many as five days, Longstreet's infantry rotated in and out to Mason's Hill.[5]

With infantry support coming up behind him, Stuart pushed his cavalry pickets even closer to the Federal outposts. Though still a colonel, he found his responsibilities growing. On August 10, Johnston wrote to President Jefferson Davis. He asked for more cavalry, and the appointment of Stuart to command them. Making his case, Johnston described Stuart as "Calm, firm, acute, active, and enterprising, I know no one more competent than he to estimate the occurrences before him at their true value." From that point on, all cavalry near the front answered to Stuart.[6]

The cavalry was under strict regulations on the front line. An officer in the 1st Virginia explained how the pickets—known as videttes—established their posts under Stuart's orders:

> A company went down to relieve the guard every morning. Company headquarters were in the village and the outposts half a mile beyond. Each outpost consisted of from four to six men under command of a non-commissioned officer, and each of them kept a vidette, always mounted, one or two hundred yards in advance; the men on the post could dismount, but kept their reins in their hands. These posts were relieved every four hours from company headquarters in the village. At the

---

3 Edward P. Alexander, *Fighting for the Confederacy: The Personal Recollections of General Edward Porter Alexander*, ed. Gary W. Gallagher (Chapel Hill, 1989), 66. Mason's Hill was named for Capt. Murray Mason of the U.S. Navy, who remained a Unionist when war broke out. His more-famous brother was James Mason, who became one of the two famed Confederate delegates arrested in the tumultuous *Trent Affair* in Nov. 1861; Bradley E. Gernand, *A Virginia Village Goes to War: Falls Church During the Civil War* (Virginia Beach, 2002), 53.

4 *OR* 5, 778-779; James Longstreet, *From Manassas to Appomattox: Memoirs of the Civil War in America* (Philadelphia, 1896), 59.

5 Robert G. H. Kean, *Inside the Confederate Government: The Diary of Robert Garlick Hill Kean*, ed. Edward Younger (Oxford, 1957), 3; Holland, *Recollections of a Private*, 6; Morgan, *Personal Reminiscences*, 87.

6 *OR* 5, 777.

reserve in the village a sentinel was kept on duty to listen for firing on the line of outposts. In case the enemy appeared, the vidette fired, the men on his post galloped to his rescue and began skirmishing, the sentinel at headquarters gave the alarm and the reserve then mounted their horses ready for action.[7]

Stuart's men had daily encounters with their Union counterparts. These little skirmishes never amounted to much; a few shots here and there before the two sides separated, but it kept the videttes on high alert.

Munson's Hill, where Stuart put his field headquarters, became a magnet for such skirmishes. From Munson's, Confederates stared down at an intersection known as Bailey's Crossroads, where Federals built outposts and entrenchments of their own. The Union soldiers also put up a few observation balloons filled with hydrogen gas from where observers eyed the Confederate lines. Confederate soldiers made a sport of firing at the balloons, including with a rifled cannon.[8] Their positions atop Munson's Hill placed the Confederates about half a mile from the Union soldiers.[9]

The days went on, with light skirmishing being the general rule of the day. It made a lot of noise, but did not do much else. It wasn't until August 28 that Stuart had his first real challenge near Munson's Hill.[10] From Bailey's Crossroads, approximately 250 Federal soldiers deployed into a skirmish line and began to advance towards Munson's Hill. From atop the hill Stuart's men opened fire, and a rifled artillery piece added to the din.[11]

The fighting on August 28 continued throughout the day and into the evening before darkness stopped the firing. It did not lead to many casualties—Stuart reported one man killed and six wounded—but it earned the Confederate cavalier attention and respect.[12] James Longstreet, who had been appointed to command the "Advance Forces" outside of Alexandria, especially took note of Stuart's performance. Three days later, on August 31, Stuart pushed back another Federal force from Bailey's Crossroads.[13]

---

7 W. W. Blackford, *War Years with Jeb Stuart* (1945; repr. Baton Rouge, 1993), 52.

8 Joseph C. Scott, "The Infernal Balloon: Union Aeronautics During the American Civil War," in *Army History*, No. 93 (Fall 2014): 10-12; Morgan, *Personal Reminiscences*, 87.

9 *The Daily Exchange*, Sep. 5, 1861.

10 Thomas Goree, *Longstreet's Aide: The Civil War Letters of Major Thomas Goree*, ed. Thomas W. Cutrer (Charlottesville, 1995), 35.

11 *OR* 5, 120-121; *OR* 51, pt. 1, 38.

12 *OR* 51, pt. 1, 38. Federal casualties were not listed, but could not have been very high either.

13 Jeffry Wert, *General James Longstreet: The Confederacy's Most Controversial Soldier* (New York, 1994), 85; *OR* 5, 121-122.

As the daily skirmishes continued, the Federal army mustered its strength for when it would send more than 250 men at the rebel positions.

*   *   *

On July 22, Maj. Gen. George B. McClellan received a foreboding telegram from Winfield Scott that started, "Circumstances make your presence here necessary." McClellan, whom Gov. Curtin had desperately wanted to command the Pennsylvania Reserves, had spent the spring and early summer campaigning in western Virginia against Robert E. Lee. That campaign made McClellan a hero in Washington and left some in Richmond questioning Lee's abilities. In the aftermath of the Union defeat at Manassas, Scott ordered "Come hither without delay."[14]

Upon his arrival in Washington, McClellan set out to reorganize the army and determine his next move. It would take time, but McClellan approached the tasks with an engineer's efficiency. His slow approach was not always up to Lincoln and Scott's liking, but McClellan was wary of moving out of Washington's defenses because he consistently believed Confederate forces outnumbered him. McClellan wrote to his wife, "the enemy have 3 to 4 times my force—the Presdt is an idiot, the old General in his dotage, they cannot or will not see the true state of affairs."[15] In another letter, McClellan spelled out his hesitations: "Beauregard probably has 150,000 men—I cannot count more than 55,000!"[16]

The Confederates, though, only had around 45,000 men. They were spread out from outside Washington, down to Manassas, and to the west towards Leesburg. Johnston wrote to President Davis in late August that almost 10,000 soldiers were sick in camp, negating any kind of offensive capability. That caused friction between Johnston and Beauregard, who continued to advocate pushing troops closer and closer to Washington. Johnston, on the other hand, who outranked Beauregard, disagreed, and began to think about pulling his men back towards Manassas.[17]

As the days passed without a Confederate attack, McClellan grew more confident. He began taking daily rides into Virginia, scoping out the terrain. McClellan again wrote to his wife, "I feel sure that the dangerous moment has

---

14 *OR* 2, 753; Thomas L. Boeche, "Victory in Western Virginia: McClellan's First Campaign," in *America's Civil War* 10, No. 6, Jan. 1998.

15 McClellan, *Civil War Papers*, 85-86.

16 Ibid., 87.

17 Joseph T. Glatthaar, "Confederate Soldiers in Virginia, 1861," in *Virginia at War*, 1861, eds. William C. Davis and James I. Robertson, Jr (Lexington, KY, 2005), 51; Williams, *Napoleon in Gray*, 99-100; Alfred Roman, *The Military Operations of General Beauregard in the War Between the States, 1861 to 1865*, Vol. 1 (New York, 1884), 136.

Major General George B. McClellan

LOC

passed."[18]   Englishman   William Russell noted "From an observation [McClellan] made, I imagined that the General would make an effort to recover his lost ground."[19]

The skirmishing at Munson's Hill on August 28 and 31 gave McClellan hope for pushing out of the Washington defenses. He wrote that he was "much pleased" with the action and began making efforts to follow them up.[20]

McClellan made his move just a few days later. On September 3, he directed brigades of infantry to cross the Potomac River using the Chain Bridge, located about six miles northwest of Washington's center. Soldiers were ordered to have "their knapsacks packed + at least one day's cooked rations in their haversacks." McClellan also instructed a team of topographical engineers to escort the troops across the river and lay out works for their arrival. To lead the vanguard, McClellan looked to one of his closest friends in the army.[21]

Colleagues at West Point called him Baldy. It was a straightforward nickname for William Farrar Smith, who explained as a young man "his hair was rather fine, like a child's." Graduating fourth in the Class of 1845, Smith served as a topographical engineer and as a professor of mathematics at West Point. When conflict came in 1861, Baldy Smith jumped to action, serving as a mustering officer in New York before making his way to the front lines.[22]

It did not hurt Smith's prospects to be a close friend of McClellan's. The latter had been one class behind Smith, and their friendship continued in the late 1850s

18 McClellan, *Civil War Papers*, 90-91.

19 Russell, *My Diary*: Vol. 1, 522.

20 *OR* 5, 121.

21 George Brinton McClellan Papers: Correspondence I, 1783-1888, 1861, Sep. 3-15, 21.

22 William B. Styple, ed., *Generals in Bronze: Interviewing the Commanders of the Civil War* (Kearny, NJ, 2005), 219; Cullum, Volume 2, 210.

Major General William F. "Baldy" Smith
LOC

when McClellan, vice president of the Illinois Central Railroad, worked alongside Smith in Chicago. Smith frequently referred to McClellan as "Mac" and kept in touch as the war began.[23]

Smith received a colonelcy in the 3rd Vermont Infantry and arrived at his regiment's camp in late July near the Chain Bridge. There the Vermonters peered into Fairfax County. One of the men in the 3rd Vermont was not impressed, writing, "The country about here is very rough and uneven and appears to be all run out. The inhabitants in this quarter are the poorest kind and I don't see what they live on."[24]

Smith jumped from a captain in the engineers to a colonel in the infantry, but soon after his arrival, he received more responsibilities. Likely because of his friendship with McClellan, Smith received a dispatch from headquarters on August 1. The dispatch from McClellan put Smith "in command of all the troops in the vicinity of the Chain Bridge." The order instructed Smith to report directly to McClellan. Two weeks later came a promotion for Smith to the rank of brigadier general. The turnaround happened so quickly that a soldier in the 3rd Vermont wrote home, "Our Officers are getting promoted quite fast."[25]

---

23 George Brinton McClellan Papers: Correspondence I, 1783-1888, 1857, Jan. 1-1861, May 6, 198-199. Russel Beatie says Smith was among McClellan's "best friends from the old army;" Russel H. Beatie, *Army of the Potomac, Vol. II: McClellan Takes Command, September 1861-February 1862* (Cambridge, 2004), 171.

24 Carlos Reed, Aug. 30, 1861, Letter, Quoted on "Vermont Civil War," accessed May 22, 2019. https://vermontcivilwar.org/get.php?input=27052.

25 Special Orders No. 4, Aug. 1, 1861, copy found in William F. Smith's CSR, NARA; Cullum, Volume 2, 210; Smith would not be confirmed by Congress until Dec. 1861, but the date of his commission was backdated as Aug. 13, 1861. *Journal of the Executive Proceedings of the Senate of the United States of America 12* (Washington, 1887), 5; Emerson A. Boynton, Aug. 17, 1861, Letter, quoted in "Vermont Civil War," accessed May 22, 2019. https://vermontcivilwar.org/get.php?input=643.

Smith had about two weeks to get acclimated to his new brigade before he received orders to push his men across the Chain Bridge. The soldiers gathered their equipment and mobilized on September 3. They crossed the bridge and "advanced into Virginia three miles," one Vermonter wrote home.[26] Listening to the stomping feet and the rumbling of artillery wheels, William Russell called it "a considerable movement of troops."[27] Just as the Federals began their advance, the skies opened. The soldiers bedded down in the rain and "slept on our arms until morning, the rain pouring down in torrents."[28]

As his men bivouacked, Smith realized just how close the rebels were. He quickly jotted a note to Washington reporting that the enemy was "within three fourths of a mile" of his picket line. The engineers that McClellan ordered up had to work quickly to set out defensive works if Smith was expected to maintain his foothold.[29]

Come morning, Smith's waterlogged soldiers began to construct defenses. A Vermonter wrote, "We worked pretty hard there for a week." That work paid off, and the breastworks started to take shape in what the Federals christened Camp Advance.[30] Meanwhile, the rain continued to fall, all but halting any advance. With nothing else to do, the soldiers at Camp Advance kept working, with engineer Lt. Orlando Poe laying out Fort Ethan Allen, named for Vermont's Revolutionary War hero.[31]

The force at Camp Advance and Fort Ethan Allen grew. McClellan ordered another brigade, under the command of Brig. Gen. Rufus King, to support Smith's mission. King brought three regiments with him, hardy westerners from Wisconsin and Indiana, who set to the same daily fatigue duties. Those soldiers in turn were reinforced by regiments including the 79th New York, so that a week after Smith led the way across Chain Bridge, his brigade-sized command had grown to a small division.[32]

---

26 Leo Hyde, Sep. 20, 1861, Letter, quoted in "Vermont Civil War," accessed May 22, 2019. https://vermontcivilwar.org/get.php?input=3253

27 Russell, *My Diary*: Vol. 1, 523.

28 *Lamoille Newsdealer*, Sept. 27, 1861.

29 George Brinton McClellan Papers: Correspondence I, 1783-1888, 1861; Sep. 3-15, 36.

30 Benedict, Volume 1, 92; Paul G. Zeller, *The Second Vermont Volunteer Infantry Regiment, 1861-1865* (Jefferson, NC, 2002), 43.

31 Paul Taylor and Phil Shiman, *Orlando M. Poe: Civil War General and Great Lakes Engineer* (Kent, OH, 2005), 47.

32 Charles King, "Rufus King: Soldier, Editor, and Statesman," in *The Wisconsin Magazine of History* 4, No. 4 (Jun. 1921): 377-378; Alan D. Gaff, *On Many a Bloody Field: Four Years in the Iron Brigade* (Indianapolis, 1999), 51; Hazard Stevens, *The Life of Isaac Ingalls Stevens*, Vol. 2 (Boston, 1900), 327-328.

Everyday Smith's pickets clashed with Confederate forces, both sides exchanging pot shots and some desultory artillery fire. On September 6, McClellan wrote to Smith, warning him that, "It is said the enemy at Manassas struck their tents and marched this morning." The next day, McClellan followed his message with a general directive to all subordinate commanders, instructing them to "Hold your command in constant readiness to move at the shortest notice with two days cooked rations." On September 10, McClellan, joined by President Lincoln and Secretary Cameron, visited Smith's lines, and eyed the enemy in the distance.[33]

On the same day that McClellan visited Smith at Camp Advance, other Federals had already come directly into contact with J. E. B. Stuart's men. Just six miles south of Chain Bridge lay the tiny town of Lewinsville. The town was dismissively described by a newspaper correspondent as "a miserable, broken-down village, very Virginian in aspect."[34] Another soldier wrote the town "would hardly be dignified with the name of village in Wisconsin. It consists of a church, a one-horse store, four dwelling houses and a sign-post."[35]

However, the location of Lewinsville mattered; five roads converged at the center of the town. Some of those roads were little more than farmers' paths cut into the countryside, but others offered access to much larger avenues like the Leesburg & Georgetown Pike or the Leesburg & Alexandria Pike. Taking Lewinsville and its intersections was a vital step in helping the Federals gain a stronger foothold in Virginia. Lewinsville was just twelve miles from Dranesville.[36]

Baldy Smith ordered a detachment of infantry to head toward Lewinsville around 1:30 a.m. on September 10. The soldiers came from two columns. The first, totaling about 160 men, was detached from the 79th New York and led by Capt. David Ireland, while the second column consisted of three companies from the 5th Wisconsin led by Capt. Elisha Hibbard. Ireland's job was to ambush any Confederates trying to reinforce Lewinsville; Hibbard was to head straight for Lewinsville and "capture or break up a body of the enemy known to be there."[37]

Ireland's men moved through the darkness and closed in on a meandering stream called Pimmit Run. Misidentified in his orders as "Pirnett Run," the stream

33 George Brinton McClellan Papers: Correspondence I, 1783-1888, 1861; Sep. 3-15, 101, 116; William Todd, *The Seventy-Ninth Highlanders New York Volunteers in the War of Rebellion* (Albany, 1886), 73.

34 *Harper's Weekly*, Dec. 14, 1861.

35 Edwin B. Quiner "Scrapbooks: Correspondence of the Wisconsin Volunteers, 1861-1865, Volume 1," *Wisconsin Historical Society*, 221, 226.

36 See "Map of N. Eastern Virginia and Vicinity of Washington," Library of Congress, accessed Mar. 1, 2017. https://www.loc.gov/resource/g3881s.cw0468000/ for the road network.

37 *OR* 5, 165-166.

The town of Lewinsville, as seen in a print of the December 14, 1861, edition of *Harper's Weekly*.

LOC

offered a chokepoint where Capt. Ireland's men could set up an ambush. The Federals took up positions on either side of the road crossing Pimmit Run and waited. Ireland's location along Pimmit Run blocked the road to Falls Church, just south of his position. Any rebels who rode north from Falls Church would run into Ireland's contingent.[38]

While Ireland set up his ambush, Hibbard's men advanced closer to Lewinsville. The Wisconsinites found the going tough, because, as one soldier wrote home, "The country is very hilly, and scouting is exceedingly difficult." The Federals moved forward with the aid of Unionist locals who guided them through the countryside. Rumors circulated that there were as many as 150 rebel cavalrymen encamped at Lewinsville, so the men of the three Wisconsin companies held tense fingers near their triggers.[39]

Hibbard's soldiers surrounded Lewinsville near daylight on September 10. Rather than the 150 cavalrymen, the 5th Wisconsin found just a small squad of "ten or a dozen." One of the Confederates spotted the infantry column and raised the alarm. The squad of cavalrymen bolted, outnumbered by the roughly 200 bluecoats. Hibbard's men leveled their muskets and opened fire, engaging in "a most desperate *running* fight for a few minutes." In those brief moments the Wisconsinites captured one and killed or wounded three others. The other Confederates escaped through the countryside and out of reach.[40]

38 *OR* 5, 166; Todd, *The Seventy-Ninth Highlanders*, 74.

39 Quiner, "Scrapbooks," 220.

40 Ibid., 220-21. Emphasis in original.

Hibbard's musketry alerted Capt. Ireland's men that the raid had started, but also alarmed the Confederate forces around Falls Church. Mounting up, Company K of the 1st Virginia Cavalry galloped towards the firing. Its troopers rode straight into Ireland's ambush.[41]

According to one New Yorker, the Virginians were alerted to their presence by a barking dog. The Confederates slowed down at the noise, and some began to turn around. The New Yorkers on Ireland's left saw their chance slipping away and "without any word of command, our muskets were discharged at the enemy, who galloped off." On the right flank, the New Yorkers "blazed away" at a wagon amongst the Confederate column, killing the two mules at the front. One New Yorker was killed in the exchange of gunfire.[42]

The Virginians got out of the killing zone without suffering heavily. In his report, Ireland stated he believed his men had killed four, wounded two, and captured one. However, records from the 1st Virginia Cavalry indicate that just two men were captured.[43]

Once they were back at Camp Advance, the Federals reported on their busy day. The action around Lewinsville gave Baldy Smith an idea. Hibbard's men had expected Confederates in Lewinsville but had found next to nothing. If the rebels would not use the town, Smith would. He directed Col. Isaac Stevens, commander of the 79th New York, to go to Lewinsville the next day, September 11, "to determine all the facts that would be required for its permanent occupation and defense."[44]

When Col. Stevens left Camp Advance around 7:30 a.m. on September 11, he brought his own 79th New York, a battalion each from the 65th New York, 19th Indiana, and 3rd Vermont, two companies from the 2nd Vermont, about 100 cavalry troopers, and a battery of artillery. All told, Stevens's expedition to Lewinsville totaled about 1,800 men, and was accompanied by a contingent of engineers under Lt. Poe.[45] Before his departure, Smith received a message from McClellan: "Caution your reconnoitering party to look out and not fall into a conflict with an overpowering force." Smith repeated those orders to Stevens, who

---

41 Robert J. Driver, *1st Virginia Cavalry* (Lynchburg, VA, 1991), 18.

42 Todd, *The Seventy-Ninth Highlanders*, 75; *OR* 5, 166.

43 *OR* 5, 166.

44 Ibid., 169.

45 Ibid. 169; Stevens did not mention the presence of two companies from the 2nd Vermont, but a report of Lt. Col. George Stannard mentions he was in command of Companies A and F during the day and supported the Federal artillery in the ensuing fight. See Ibid., 176-177.

departed "with the strictest injunction not to bring on a general engagement under any circumstance."[46]

Stevens's column got to Lewinsville around 10:00 a.m. As it neared the tiny village, Company G of the 3rd Pennsylvania Cavalry advanced to clear it out. The Pennsylvanians returned and reported that, while in their estimation some "100 to 200 of the enemy's cavalry" had been there the night before, it was now empty. Stevens put one cannon from Capt. Charles Griffin's Battery D, 5th U.S. Artillery, on each of the three major roads leading out of town. The colonel put Griffin's fourth cannon in reserve and used infantry to guard the last two roads. Focusing his attention on the road to Falls Church— the same road Capt. Ireland had ambushed the day before—Stevens deployed almost 500 infantrymen in a wide skirmisher's net to block approaching rebel forces. Stevens left the rest of his infantry about a third of a mile out of Lewinsville and ready to deploy quickly in any direction. His dispositions completed, Stevens gave the go-ahead for Lt. Poe's engineers to get to work.[47]

Poe's men moved quickly. In about four hours, the engineers, "noted houses, places of business, names of owners, water supply sources . . . public and long farm roads, areas of woodland . . . and meadow and cultivated land." In the distance the Federals could see Confederate pickets eyeing them but thought little of it.[48]

By 2:00 p.m., Poe's work was finished. The engineer alerted Stevens, who ordered the skirmishers to fall back towards Lewinsville and reform into their marching columns. It took nearly forty minutes for the Federals to form up, much to Stevens's annoyance, but just as the pocket watches read 3:00 p.m., the soldiers were ready to march back to Camp Advance.

Then all hell broke loose.[49]

*   *   *

Company K of the 1st Virginia Cavalry had recovered from its near disastrous ambush the day before. When the Federals bedded down on the night of September 10, the Virginians returned to their picket posts outside Lewinsville. The next day, as the Federal column closed in on Lewinsville the Confederates sped quickly south, linking up with another company from the 1st Virginia. These were the men

---

46 George Brinton McClellan Papers: Correspondence I, 1783-1888, 1861, Sep. 3-15, 173; Stevens, *Life of Isaac I. Stevens*: Vol. 2, 329.

47 *OR* 5, 169-170.

48 Edgar R. Hon, "A Civil War Action at Lewinsville, Virginia, 11 September 1861," in *The Historical Society of Fairfax County, Virginia Yearbook* 29, (2003-2004), eds. Edith Moore Sprouse and Paulsa Elsey, 46.

49 Stevens, *Life of Isaac I. Stevens*: Vol. 2, 330.

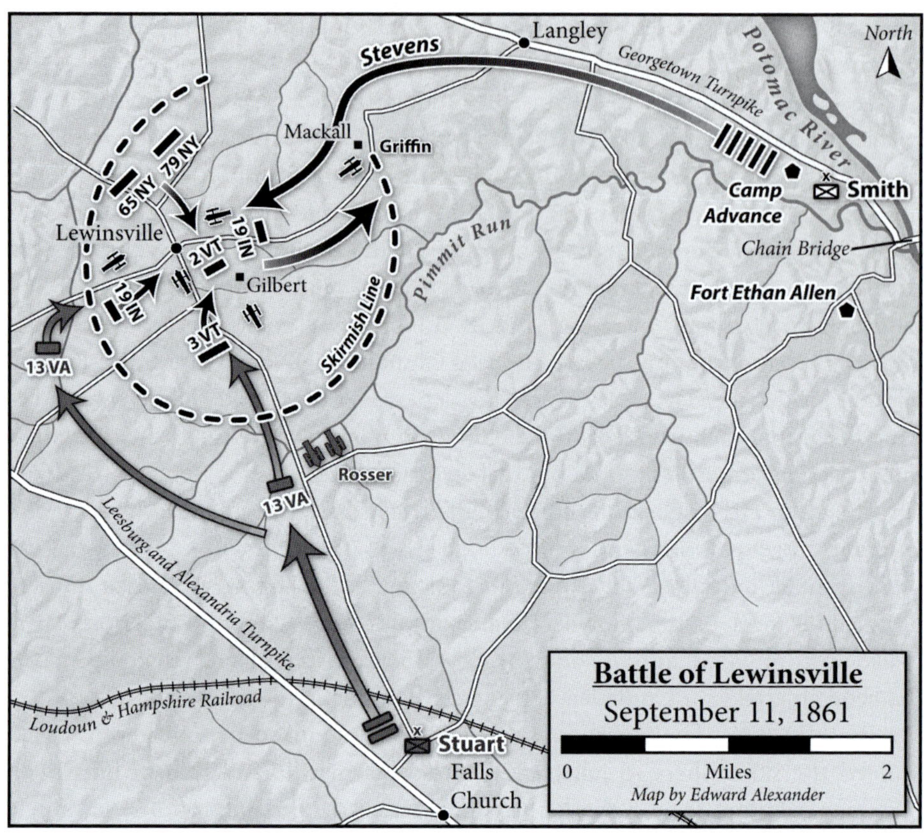

the Federals spotted as they reconnoitered. While the Union soldiers dismissed the small force of mounted Confederates, they did not know that riders were making their way to J. E. B. Stuart's headquarters at Munson's Hill.[50]

As soon as he learned of the Federals' incursion, Stuart made plans to stop them. He gathered a few companies from the 1st Virginia Cavalry, a battalion 305 strong from the 13th Virginia Infantry, and a section of two guns from the Washington Light Artillery under the command of Capt. Thomas Rosser. All told, Stuart's force numbered around 500 men. The Confederates set out from Falls Church around noontime.[51]

They neared Lewinsville, but Stuart did not attack immediately, opting instead to watch the enemy's movement. He deployed the 13th Virginia, commanded by Maj. James Terrill, through the heavy woods outside of Lewinsville.

50 Driver, *1st Virginia Cavalry*, 19.

51 *OR* 5, 183.

As Terrill's men advanced into position, they ran into a small squad of soldiers from the 19th Indiana. The Indianans saw the Confederates and dashed forward for a chance to fire their muskets. But the inexperienced soldiers, facing combat for the first time, "forgot their office of sending back information of the approach of the enemy." The Indianans were still dressed in gray uniforms, giving the 13th Virginia a momentary pause of confusion. Terrill's soldiers soon recovered and captured three Hoosiers. Because the Indianans never notified their commanding officer what they saw, Col. Stevens remained unaware of Stuart's presence.[52]

As the 13th Virginia moved into position, Capt. Thomas Rosser maneuvered his two cannon, one rifled gun and one smoothbore, to within 600 yards of the Federals who were forming up for their return to Camp Advance. As Rosser's men finished unlimbering their guns, a sudden scattering of musketry announced the beginning of the battle, such as it was, of Lewinsville.[53]

The musketry started on the 19th Indiana's front. As the squad of soldiers were scooped up by the 13th Virginia, one Hoosier, Pvt. Hiram Antibus, escaped capture by fleeing back to Federal lines as quick as his legs would carry him. He ran so fast his shoes fell off. The Virginians fired at him as he went, but Antibus escaped capture. The Confederates rushed forward, "yelling like so many devils, firing as they ran."[54]

As the crackle of musketry continued, Rosser's gunners pulled the lanyards of their cannon. The sharp boom of artillery sent shells arcing through the air and landing amongst the column of Union infantry. Shells exploded in fireballs of flying iron, and half a dozen soldiers in the 3rd Vermont went down, one killed outright and one dying soon after. Another shell struck the 79th New York, wounding three. A soldier in the 19th Indiana wrote "the bombs came aflying over our heads thick and fast."[55]

Captain Charles Griffin responded quickly. An 1847 graduate of West Point, Griffin would become one of the Army of the Potomac's best generals by the end of the Civil War. According to one historian, his soldiers called him "King of the War Dogs," and as Rosser's shells continued inflicting casualties amongst the infantry, Griffin jumped to his guns. He deployed two of them and opened fire, suppressing the Confederates.[56]

---

52 Ibid., 170; Gaff, *On Many a Bloody Field*, 55.

53 *OR* 51, pt. 1, 43.

54 *OR* 5, 173; Charles Preston Poland, Jr., *The Glories of War* (Privately Published, 2006), 99.

55 Benedict, Volume 2, 134; Todd, *The Seventy-Ninth Highlanders*, 77; Gaff, *On Many a Bloody Field*, 56.

56 Francis A. O'Reilly, *The Fredericksburg Campaign: Winter War on the Rappahannock* (Baton Rouge, 2003), 364; *OR* 5, 171.

Under Griffin's covering fire, the Federal infantry fell back to Camp Advance. The opposing gunners made a show of blasting away at each other. Griffin's section of two guns expended 40 shells within a matter of minutes, while Rosser reported that "the road here was plowed by my projectiles and thick with fragments of shell." Rosser's two cannon fired a total of 107 shells. A cavalryman in the 1st Virginia wrote, "The shot and shell whistled over my head making pretty but *nervous* music."[57]

While his soldiers pressed forward, Stuart engaged in a little joking around. At West Point, he had been two years ahead of Orlando Poe, the Federal engineer. Learning it was Stuart after them, Poe left a small note to the cavalier. Addressing Stuart with his Academy nickname, Poe wrote, "My Dear Beauty, I am sorry that circumstances are such that I can't have the pleasure of seeing you although so near you. Griffin says he would like to have you dine with him at Willard's at 3 o'clock on Saturday next. Keep your 'Black Horse' off me if you please." Stuart left a reply behind: "I have the honor to report that 'circumstances were such' that they could have seen me if they had stopped to look behind, and I answered both at the cannons' mouth. Judging from his speed Griffin surely left for Washington to hurry up the dinner."[58]

The shooting at Lewinsville lasted about an hour before Stevens's column moved out of range of Rosser's artillery. Union soldiers encountered a worried Baldy Smith, who, hearing the firing, gathered a battery of New York artillery and rode to the sound of the shooting. That New York battery included a 32-Pounder Parrott Rifle, which unlimbered on a nearby hill and opened fire. The shuddering boom of the large cannon convinced the Confederates to end their pursuit.[59]

Though the Union soldiers were already leaving Lewinsville, Stuart's apparent victory there raised morale among his troops and earned him high praise from his superiors. The hour-long shooting match killed three Federals, wounded roughly a dozen more, and Stuart's men captured the three overanxious Hoosiers. In exchange for that, Stuart reported "not a scratch to man or horse." He gloated, too, "The prisoners reported . . . that the occupancy of Lewinsville was to be permanent. Alas for human expectations!"[60]

With a numerically inferior force Stuart was able to intercede and force a Federal column to retire—even if they were already retiring. Stuart's victory also

---

57 *OR* 5, 179; *OR* 51, pt. 1, 42-43; Driver, *1st Virginia Cavalry*, 19.

58 Orlando Poe to J. E. B. Stuart, Sep. 11, 1861, J. E. B. Stuart Papers Section 3, Virginia Museum of History & Culture (Hereafter VMHC).

59 *OR* 5, 178.

60 Ibid., 173-175, 184.

Captain Charles Griffin commanded a battery of artillery at Lewinsville and was the namesake of a Federal camp created there. *LOC*

further impressed his superiors. One of Longstreet's staffers, Thomas Goree wrote, "We had a little fight yesterday which I hoped might bring on a large one, but it has not." Stuart, in Goree's opinion, "would storm Washington with his regiment alone if ordered to do so."[61]

When Longstreet forwarded Stuart's report about Lewinsville, he summarized the cavalier's actions over the past two months. "He has been most untiring in the discharge of his duties. . . . Where he has lost a man, he has brought in at least two of the enemy, dead or alive." Longstreet finished by writing, "Colonel Stuart has, I think, fairly won his claim to brigadier, and I hope the commanding generals will unite with me in recommending him for that promotion." Joseph Johnston endorsed the recommendation.[62]

Stuart received his promotion on September 24. With it came a new command to oversee the Confederates' brigade of cavalry. He had foreseen the promotion, writing to his wife Flora, "You need not be surprised to see your hubbie a Brigadier. . . . [I] feel sure that I can command better than many I saw."[63]

61 Goree, *Longstreet's Aide*, 43.

62 *OR* 5, 181, 182.

63 Thomas, *Bold Dragoon*, 87; Jeffry Wert, *Cavalryman of the Lost Cause: A Biography of J. E. B. Stuart* (New York, 2008), 65.

High command in the Confederate army had some reservations, however. The main concern regarded Stuart's usage of artillery. While Rosser's section had dueled with the Federals ably, the generals worried about Stuart's "free use" of the cannon and worried that future usage of artillery so close to the enemy would result in its loss. Longstreet wrote to Stuart, reassuring him, "I took it upon myself to deny the report of imprudence, attributed to you." Stuart would have to learn to be more careful with his artillery.[64]

Ironically, Federal authorities also saw their mission to Lewinsville as a success. Stevens's force had completed its objective: it went to Lewinsville, scouted the area, and returned. George McClellan shared the favorable view of Lewinsville, proudly proclaiming, "Our men came back in perfect order & excellent spirits. They behaved most admirably under fire. We shall have no more Bull Run affairs."[65]

McClellan thought the expedition successful enough that he ordered Smith to repeat it two weeks later. On September 25, Smith left Camp Advance, this time at the head of 5,100 infantry, 16 cannon, and 150 cavalry troopers—a force that dwarfed Col. Stevens's expedition. This time, though, instead of scouting the area for engineer drawings, Smith's men loaded up 90 wagons worth of forage. A soldier in the 5th Wisconsin wrote that they gathered "hay, straw . . . and about a hundred cattle and several horses."[66]

Confederates from Falls Church mobilized again and moved to intercept the Federals. Smith was ready this time, and except for some long-range artillery fire—once more between Thomas Rosser and Charles Griffin—nothing came of it. Pleased with his haul of forage, Smith returned to Camp Advance the same night.[67]

The numerous Federal expeditions in and around Lewinsville, as well as near Bailey's Crossroads, brought an end to the Confederate line of works along Upton's, Munson's, and Mason's Hills. Johnston had always been uneasy about those works, and as the Federal army became more mobile and stretched out from Washington, the position of the Confederate army, as Johnston wrote, "became

---

64 Johnston's and Beauregard's concerns, and Longstreet's letter to Stuart both in Wert, *Cavalryman of the Lost Cause*, 64.

65 *OR* 5, 168.

66 *OR* 5, 215-17; Quiner, "Scrapbooks," 223.

67 *OR* 5, 217; Gernand, *A Virginia Village*, 95. Gernand writes of the skirmish on Sep. 25, "Yet again an inferior (in number) force of Confederates had bested a superior (in number, not in leadership clearly) Union force"; 95. This is a baffling summary of the actions on Sep. 25. Smith's men were not "bested"—they in fact wanted the Confederates to attack. It was Confederate leadership that balked at fighting the heavy presence near Lewinsville. Simply because Smith returned to Camp Advance does not mean he retreated. He went to Lewinsville, successfully gathered almost 100 wagons full of forage, and then safely and without loss of life went back to his starting point. It was not Smith's objective to establish a permanent encampment at Lewinsville, so of course he would return to Camp Advance at the end of the day.

more hazardous." In late September, Johnston began to pull the army's forces back to Centreville.[68]

Before withdrawing, Stuart had one final fight atop Mason's Hill. When the Confederates pulled back, they accidentally left some supplies and materials behind. To regather those supplies, the Confederates' 1st Kentucky Infantry was sent forward.

The Kentuckians were a long way from home, a divided one at that. Kentucky's governor had refused to fill Lincoln's quota of volunteers, and instead naively tried to pass a "Declaration of Neutrality." Nevertheless, volunteers from the Bluegrass State poured North and South to fight for their cause.[69] Around Louisville Thomas Taylor, a lawyer, was "among the most active in recruiting companies." He headed east, and by August 1861, his companies were consolidated with other lonesome Kentuckians to form the 1st Regiment of Infantry.[70] When the Kentuckians first arrived in Virginia, they attracted attention, with the Richmond *Daily Dispatch* declaring, "They are all dressed in the blue Kentucky hunting shirt, and a finer body of men the world has never produced."[71] In Richmond, the Kentuckians received training at the hands of cadets from the Virginia Military Institute and were soon ready for war.[72]

On September 28, the Kentuckians moved towards Mason's Hill for their first experience with the enemy. Taylor's men passed by a contingent of Confederate cavalry, who warned them "the enemy was in possession" of Mason's Hill. The Kentuckians deployed their battle line on both sides of the Columbia Turnpike "and at the word of command marched steadily to the base of the hill, where, being ordered, they charged bayonets to its summit."[73]

At the top, the Kentuckians found Mason's Hill abandoned but for a small holding force, probably from the 32nd New York. Captain James Harvey's Company A pushed the Union soldiers back towards Bailey's Crossroads. It was

---

68 Joseph E. Johnston, *A Memoir of the Life and Public Service of Joseph E. Johnston*, ed. Bradley T. Johnson (Baltimore, 1891), 77.

69 On KY's neutrality see James M. McPherson, *Battle Cry of Freedom: The Civil War Era* (Oxford, 2003), 293-294.

70 Clement Evans, ed., *Confederate Military History*, Vol. 9 (Atlanta, 1899), 34.

71 *Richmond Daily Dispatch*, May 4, 1861; Bruce S. Allardice and Lawrence Lee Hewitt, *Kentuckians in Gray: Confederate Generals and Field Officers of the Bluegrass State* (Lexington, KY, 2015), 259.

72 *Richmond Dispatch*, Mar. 13, 1902.

73 *OR Supplement* 23, pt. 2, 174.

one final victory for the Confederate outposts and, once the Kentuckians secured the supplies, they marched back the way they had come half an hour earlier.[74]

The last few minutes of fighting atop Mason's Hill on September 28 ended two months of almost daily skirmishing between the armies. With McClellan's forces occupying all three hills that same day, he wrote to his wife, "They can no longer say that they are flaunting their dirty little flag in my face, & I hope they have taken their last look at Washn."[75]

McClellan continued to push his men further out, creating a buffer in front of Washington. On October 10, he ordered Smith to advance back to Lewinsville. This time, there would be no skirmishing or artillery fire. And this time, the Federals stayed put. They constructed Camp Griffin, named for Charles Griffin, whose guns had done so much firing there in September. Those soldiers were still there a month later when word arrived of murder and mayhem along the Potomac River, just north of Dranesville.[76]

74 Ibid.; Documents of the Assembly of the State of New York, Vol. 10 (Albany, 1867), 285.

75 McClellan, *Civil War Papers*, 104.

76 Benedict, Volume 1, 96.

Chapter Six

"Putting Five Bullets Into Him, Killing Him on the Spot"

The Ambush at Lowe's Island

Herkimer County, New York, is about 400 miles from Dranesville. The county sits nestled roughly equidistant between Syracuse and Albany. Because of the events of 1861, soldiers from Herkimer were soon to run into Home Guardsmen from Dranesville. It was a clash of cultures that sent bloody shock waves through both communities.

The people of Herkimer County poured forth to answer Lincoln's call in the spring of 1861. Men eagerly enlisted in numerous volunteer companies. "Sermons bristling with a fiery and bayonet patriotism, from nearly all northern pulpits" pushed them to arms, one man remembered.[1] One of those soldiers, Oliver P. Darling, enlisted on May 1. Darling, 26-years-old, lived with his wife Amanda— whom he had married the year before—and his parents, scratching out a simple farmer's life.[2] The new soldier soon found himself in Company B of the 34th New York Infantry. He answered to Capt. Wells Sponable, who was described as "a capable and ambitious young man."[3]

With each passing day, the 34th grew until the regiment had enough men to warrant moving toward Virginia at the end of May. Exuberance marked the day. A

---

1 Louis N. Chapin, *A Brief History of the Thirty-Fourth Regiment, N. Y. S. V.* (Privately Published, 1903), 9.

2 Oliver P. Darling 1860 Census, Herkimer County, New York; Amanda W. Darling Widow's Pension, NARA.

3 Chapin, *A Brief History of the Thirty-Fourth Regiment*, 9.

soldier in the 34th wrote home that when they passed through Penn Yan, "As long as it remained light enough to see we had fun enough giving and answering cheers."[4]

The New Yorkers continued their move south, passing through Baltimore where they saw African Americans "waving their pocket-handkerchiefs and cheering us as we marched [with] fixed bayonets through the streets." By early July, the 34th arrived in Washington and soon set up camp at Kalorama Heights on the northwest edge of the city.[5]

The New Yorkers explored Washington, even visiting the White House where they "rested on the sofa and chairs."[6] When not playing tourist, they escaped the hot July weather by jumping into a "very big creek where we go swimming every day," Pvt. Arthur O'Keeffe wrote home.[7]

O'Keeffe soon became a tent mate of Oliver Darling's, alongside three others. The five men squeezed into one tent and spent their nights sleeping on straw. Together the five soldiers decided to name their tent "Camp Independence."[8]

Aside from their recreational activities, the New Yorkers also learned how to be soldiers. Shortly after they arrived in camp the men exchanged their old worn-down muskets for newer Enfield rifles. "Every day we go out for target practice in the woods that surrounds us," O'Keeffe wrote. Soon the soldiers were "spoiling for a fight they go out scouting every day to see if they can't find a secessionist or any other 20 men that they can lick and they feel greatly disappointed when they cannot."[9]

Though the men of the 34th missed the battle at Manassas, they soon had their own orders. They moved about 20 miles outside of Washington and then split into two detachments, with three companies at Great Falls, and the others continuing further up the Potomac to Seneca Mills. Their objective was to guard the crossings of the river and prevent rebel excursions against the locks and dams of the Chesapeake & Ohio (C&O) Canal. A correspondent to the *New York Herald* explained that between the two wings of the 34th were "six good fords in the river

---

4 Henry Lyon, *Desolating This Fair Country: The Civil War Diary and Letters of Lt. Henry C. Lyon, 34th New York*, ed. Emily N. Radigan (Jefferson, NC, 1999), 22.

5 Arthur O'Keeffe to family, Jul. 6, 1861, O'Keeffe Family Papers, New York State Library, Albany, NY.

6 Lyon, *Desolating This Fair Country*, 27.

7 O'Keeffe to his family Jul. 10, 1861, O'Keeffe Family Papers.

8 O'Keeffe to his family, Jul. 13, 1861, O'Keeffe Family Papers.

9 Ibid.

. . . where the enemy can cross, the depth being, at the ordinary stages of the river, from two to three feet."[10]

Securing the fords proved easy for the 34th and other Federal regiments in the area. More difficult, however, were the miles of the canal intervening. Constructed between 1828 and 1850, the canal stretched 184 miles from the outskirts of Washington, D.C. to Cumberland, Maryland. It cost more than 11 million to construct, but by 1861, "the fortunes of the canal seemed to be approaching their lowest point."[11] Before the war, miners used the canal to send hundreds of thousands of tons of coal and other goods east, but the waterways closed with Virginia's secession.[12] As Federal forces occupied larger portions of the Potomac River, workers set about repairing the damage done by Confederates and shoring up weaker parts of the canal damaged by incessant rain in the summer of 1861.[13]

The 34th's Company B, with two others, was stationed in early August along the Maryland side of Great Falls. There the Potomac River's rapids crashed into the rocks, splashing white foam in every direction. Along the Falls, the companies deployed their sentinels. "We guard the river about a mile on each side," one of O'Keeffe and Darling's tent mates wrote. At first the soldiers' biggest concern was the mosquitoes, "so large that several of them would weigh a pound."[14]

The mosquitoes were soon replaced by a different enemy. Across the river, Confederates began to open fire. "Almost every day one of our men get shot," Arthur O'Keeffe wrote home.[15] The Federals returned the shots, blazing away, but their foe remained elusive. When a soldier in Company B was shot in the calf, his comrades went "every way in search of the rebel but nothing was to be found."[16] Frustration built among the soldiers as they remained unable to come to grips with their enemy.

By the middle of August, the three companies at Great Falls received orders to slide down the river and link up with the rest of the regiment at Seneca Mills. The area got its name from the Seneca Creek that lazily meandered towards the

10 Ibid.; *New York Herald*, Sep. 16, 1861.

11 Harlan D. Unrau, *Historic Resource Study: Chesapeake & Ohio Canal* (Hagerstown, MD, 2007), 226; Walter S. Sanderlin, "A History of the Chesapeake & Ohio Canal," PhD dissertation (University of Maryland, 1945), 246.

12 *Wisconsin State Journal*, Apr. 25, 1861.

13 Unrau writes, "Heavy rains at the beginning of July caused additional damage to the canal," 713. It rained for 18 of August's 31 days in 1861; Robert K. Krick, *Civil War Weather in Virginia* (Tuscaloosa, AL, 2007), 34.

14 J. Michael O'Brien to O'Keeffe family, Aug. 7, 1861, O'Keeffe Family Papers.

15 Arthur O'Keeffe to his brother, Aug. 8, 1861, O'Keeffe Family Papers.

16 J. Michael O'Brien O'Keeffe family, Aug. 7, 1861, O'Keeffe Family Papers.

Potomac River. Spanning the Potomac in the immediate area was a dam and Locks No. 23 and 24 of the C&O. The river, nearly a mile wide at this point, could easily be crossed via the dam, which made "an excellent ford," necessitating the presence of the 34th New York. The New Yorkers built their camp "on a hill-side, in full view of the Virginia shore, and a half-mile back from the river."[17] From their new location along the river, the 34th was just five miles north of Dranesville.

The soldiers' attention was soon drawn to the fugitive enslaved people coming to their camps. They arrived by the dozens, seeking sanctuary among the blue-clad soldiers. Many of the soldiers gladly took them in, hiring them to serve as camp cooks or laundresses. Even Capt. Wells Sponable hired one while the regiment was still in Washington.[18] A private in the 34th New York wrote that these moments "were the first working of the Hellish system that I have seen."[19]

The enslaved people were creating conundrums for the Federal command, however. In early August, Congress passed the First Confiscation Act, a law declaring that if rebel enslavers used their slaves to help the Confederate war effort, the enslaved would be deemed "lawful subject of prize and capture wherever found."[20] However, that law did not apply to the border states that had not seceded: Kentucky, Missouri, Delaware, and Maryland. Congressmen in Washington feared that if they tried to legislate against slavery in any of the border states, it could potentially push those states into joining the Confederacy. While the law made sense to the politicians in the Capitol, that did not mean much to the soldiers on the front lines, dealing with the refugees firsthand.[21]

It fell to the commanders to make decisions on the spot. The New Yorkers reported to Brig. Gen. Charles P. Stone. Under Stone's orders, enslaved people claimed by their loyal enslavers were quickly returned to bondage. Stone's position was supported by George McClellan, who similarly ordered the return of enslaved people.[22] A soldier wrote of one person being sent back: "It was the bitterest pill I

---

17 *New York Times*, Oct. 11, 1861; Wilmer H. Helmer his brother, Aug. 19, 1861, Lewis Leigh Collection, United States Army Heritage and Education Center, Carlisle, PA (hereafter USAHEC).

18 Chapin, *A Brief History of the Thirty-Fourth Regiment*, 22.

19 Lyon, *Desolating This Fair Country*, 35.

20 *Statutes at Large, Treaties, and Proclamations of the United States of America*, Vol. 12 (Boston, 1863), 319.

21 James Oakes, *Freedom National: The Destruction of Slavery in the United States, 1861-1865* (New York, 2013), 145-146.

22 Beatie, *McClellan Takes Command*, 120; Stone later testified to Congress that he returned the enslaved people because he believed it was his duty to uphold the law as written. The Fugitive Slave Act of 1850 was still technically the law of the land, and Stone said, "Until you gentlemen change the laws, I am bound to let any civil magistrate order a search of my premises, under the laws of the State in which I am serving." *Report of the Joint Committee on the Conduct of the War, Volume 1, Part 2:*

ever swallowed to stand by and see the old Dark going off to bondage but could not help him."[23]

Frustration built among the New Yorkers, causing more problems. They were constantly on edge, with daily shelling that caused little damage, but kept the soldiers on their toes. The soldiers began to eye the Virginia shore. It was "a region of special interest and inquiry among both officers and men." The "temptation to steal over" proved too much to resist, and the New Yorkers began to cross the Potomac, either using small boats or via the dam. Once on the opposite shore, the soldiers foraged liberally, and then returned to Seneca Mills. None of those crossings led to any confrontations with Confederate forces.[24] That changed on September 16. Herkimer County, New York, was about to collide with Dranesville, Virginia.

Captain Sponable was ordered to cross the river and gain as much information as possible about rumored Confederates near Dranesville. As Sponable readied to go, Pvt. Oliver Darling from Company B and Corporal Robert Gracey, Company H, volunteered to go with him. The three men set out and were soon joined by another ten or so soldiers, "who were on their way to obtain some of the rebels' green corn on the island."[25] Sponable said his little expedition "crossed the river around sundown," putting it a little past 6:00 p.m.[26]

By the time the New Yorkers reached Virginia, they were already being watched.

*   *   *

The strip of land that Sponable's men headed towards was called Lowe's Island. Formed by an offshoot of a creek known as Sugarland Run, a part of the C&O known to the locals as "the old channel," and the Potomac River, Lowe's Island sat on the far fringes of Loudoun County.[27]

McCarty Lowe and his wife Ann lived on the island in 1861. Throughout the summer, Lowe fumed as the Federals came across the Potomac and carried off food from his property. The Lowes had been unable to stop them from taking "six of Mrs. Low[e]'s horses." On another occasion, "a party came over to Mrs. Low[e]'s

---

Bull Run—Ball's Bluff (Washington, D.C., 1863), 280 (hereafter *JCCW*). For further examination of McClellan and his involvement in returning the enslaved, see Ethan S. Rafuse, *McClellan's War: The Failure of Moderation in the Struggle for the Union* (Bloomington, IN, 2005), 121-122.

23 Lyon, *Desolating This Fair Country*, 35.

24 Chapin, *A Brief History of the Thirty-Fourth Regiment*, 23.

25 Ibid.

26 Ibid.; Krick, *Civil War Weather in Virginia*, 36.

27 James W. Head, *History and Comprehensive Description of Loudoun County, Virginia* (Washington, D.C., 1908), 17.

and broke open her kitchen." Reaching his limit and his frustration boiling, Lowe made his way south to Dranesville.[28]

He found three Confederate officers and told his story. These three officers, identified only as Captains Gardner, Harvey, and Miller, were on the prowl for Union soldiers on the southern side of the Potomac River. Listening to Lowe, the officers began to plan a way to intercept the Federal incursions. September 16 would be their first chance.[29]

The first thing the captains needed was men to fight the Federals. They found them aplenty amongst the Dranesville Home Guard. John T. Day later told authorities, "These captains came to me the morning before the affray at the landing and insisted upon my going down with them to attack the pickets that night."[30] The doctor claimed he declined, but plenty of others did not. By the evening of the sixteenth, there were over a dozen volunteers joining the captains. They gathered and set off from town, heading north towards Lowe's Island.[31]

Arriving at Lowe's Island, the party made themselves comfortable, and waited. Though nightfall had come and gone, the moon was nearly full on September 16, with clear skies over northern Virginia that night.[32] Under the stars, the Confederates checked their firearms—including rifles, pistols, and shotguns—and soon spotted Capt. Sponable's small patrol.

After disembarking, Sponable's men made their way forward. He took the lead, with Oliver Darling and Robert Gracey behind him. Further back came the others, including Cpls. Christian Zaugg and Cyrus Kellogg, who took up the rear.[33] Sponable said later his patrol crossed over a small marsh and skirted around a cornfield. Behind him, the other soldiers were still crossing through the marsh when he "heard a slight noise in the cornfield on my left, probably not over three rods distant from me."[34] And then the entire world seemed to explode.

---

28 John T. Day Case File, 35.

29 William B. Day Case File, 13. The captains' first names, and their units, have proven elusive thus far in research.

30 John T. Day Case File, 35.

31 William B. Day Case File, 13-14.

32 Krick, *Civil War Weather in Virginia*, 36; Moon Phases, Sep. 16, 1861, accessed June 1, 2019. https://bit.ly/3GZnKiG.

33 Chapin, *A Brief History of the Thirty-Fourth Regiment*, 23-24. Zaugg's name is spelled "Zugg" in Chapin, "Zaug" on his service record, and "Zaugg" in the 34th NY Roster; Roster of the 34th NY Infantry, retrieved from the NY State Military Museum and Veterans Research Center, accessed May 1, 2017. https://dmna.ny.gov/historic/reghist/civil/rosters/Infantry/34th_Infantry_CW_Roster.pdf.

34 Chapin, *A Brief History of the Thirty-Fourth Regiment*, 23. A rod is 16.5 feet.

"Instantly thereafter," Sponable said, "I heard the command to fire given, which was followed by a volley of rifles; how many there were I cannot say." The captain "dropped on his face and hands so that the volley passed over him without touching him," Arthur O'Keeffe wrote home. O'Keeffe was not part of the expedition, so Sponable must have told the tale when he arrived back in camp. Sponable's hat was "knocked off my head by a rebel bullet," and he quickly noticed "both of my companions fall." The captain returned fire, blazing away with his revolver.[35]

Once Sponable had emptied his pistol, he made a quick judgment call—it appeared to him both Darling and Gracey had been felled by the first volley, and there "was nothing left for him to do but to run or get shot or taken prisoner."[36] The captain made a beeline for the Potomac, and "in much less time than it now takes to tell it, I turned to the right, passed through the woods, and came out about half a mile further up the river than I had crossed earlier in the evening," he recalled. With no boat to carry him to safety, Sponable plunged into the river and began to swim, as quickly as he could, with the Confederates "firing about twenty shots at me."[37] He arrived on the Maryland side of the river and was discovered by the 34th's Company C. The entire 34th "was alarmed by the firing of guns and [hollering] down the river," a soldier wrote.[38] Sponable "lost one boot, leggings, and revolver in swimming the river," Company C's captain wrote. "I was overjoyed to see him, but could not help laughing at his ridiculous appearance."[39]

It was anything but a laughing matter back at Lowe's Island. Sponable had seen his companions Darling and Gracey fall, but neither of the privates was dead. The volley of projectiles had sliced through the Federal patrol, wounding at least Gracey and Zaugg. In the confusion of the night, Zaugg, though hit in the cheek, made a quick retreat. Reaching the same conclusion as Sponable that his safety rested within the Potomac, "he threw in his gun and plunged in himself, lying on his back and resting his head upon a stone, with his mouth and nostrils above the water." Zaugg spent close to three hours in the river before being discovered by other Federals who brought him back to the safety of camp.[40]

35 Ibid.; Arthur O'Keeffe his brother, Sep. 17, 1861, O'Keeffe Family Papers.

36 Arthur O'Keeffe his brother, Sep. 17, 1861, O'Keeffe Family Papers.

37 Chapin, *A Brief History of the Thirty-Fourth Regiment*, 23-24.

38 Charles Willoughby, "Extracts from Journal of Charles H. Willoughby, Private Company C., Thirty-Fourth New York Volunteers," *Documents of the Assembly of the State of New York, Ninety-First Session*, Volume 40 (Albany, 1868), 477.

39 Chapin, *A Brief History of the Thirty-Fourth Regiment*, 24.

40 *New York Times*, Sep. 22, 1861.

Sponable and Zaugg escaped, as did the eight other Federal soldiers who were further behind, near the marsh. That left Kellogg, Gracey, and Darling alone on Lowe's Island to face off against the fifteen or so men shooting at them. Gracey was hit in the left shoulder by a bullet that ricocheted, broke a rib, and finally burst out his back; he dropped in a heap. [41] The remaining two New Yorkers put up a brief stand.

Oliver Darling soon found himself face to face with Capt. Miller. Darling raised his rifle, but the gun "would not go off." The two combatants closed on one another, and Darling reached out and grabbed the Confederate "by the throat." Miller tried to grab Darling's Enfield. As the two struggled, Philip Carper, a member of the Dranesville Home Guard, ran up with a pistol, put the "pistol muzzle to [Darling's] heart" and then, as Robert Gracey watched helplessly, "fired his revolver at Darling, putting five bullets into him, killing him on the spot."[42]

The fight was over. Darling was dead; Christian Zaugg was wounded and hiding in the river; Robert Gracey was wounded and soon surrounded by his foe; and Cyrus Kellogg, unwounded, was taken prisoner. The Dranesville Home Guard suffered no casualties.[43]

Although the fighting ended, McCarty Lowe was not finished. He walked up to Gracey, wounded on the ground, pointed his pistol, and fired twice. The first ball "penetrated Gracey's back in a slanting direction and came out on his left side." Lowe's second ball "entering the back, lodged in his left lung." One of the three captains stopped Lowe from firing a third time.[44]

The Dranesville Home Guard picked Gracey up and carried him into town. Cyrus Kellogg was herded along as a prisoner. According to an enslaved woman, the entourage arrived back in town around 3:00 a.m., still exuberant over their victory. The Confederates bragged about their night and "laughed when they talked about it," Unionist Minor Crippen said.[45]

Gracey, suffering from three gunshot wounds, was put inside Charles Coleman's house. He remained there for the next two weeks, during which time

---

41 "The Dead Alive, And The Lost Found," in Unknown Newspaper Publication, 34th Regiment NY Volunteers Civil War Newspaper Clippings, New York State Military Museum and Veterans Research Center, accessed May 1, 2017. https://dmna.ny.gov/historic/reghist/civil/infantry/34thInf/34thInfCWN.htm.

42 David Johnson Testimony, in George Coleman Case File, 44; Caroline Jackson Testimony, in William B. Day Case File, 16; Arthur O'Keeffe to his family Oct. 16, 1861, O'Keeffe Family Papers.

43 Arthur O'Keeffe to his brother, Sep. 17, 1861, O'Keeffe Family Papers.

44 *New York Times*, Oct. 18, 1861.

45 Ibid.; Caroline Jackson Testimony, William B. Day Case File, 14; Minor Crippen Testimony, Charles W. Coleman Case File, 54.

the town's two doctors, William and John Day, "saw him, but gave him no advice." There were some in town, especially a man named Walker, who advocated that they just lynch Gracey and be done with it.[46] Cyrus Kellogg was sent to Richmond as a prisoner of war.

For the Dranesville Home Guard, the celebrations continued in the days to come. Not only did the men continue to brag over their success, but they also went back to Lowe's Island. William Day, who by all accounts did not go to the island on September 16, did make the trek on September 17. They found Darling's body where they left it, and Day stripped the corpse of his clothes. He brought the garments back to town and gave them to some of his slaves.[47] Thomas Coleman found some of Darling's letters and delighted in reading them aloud.[48]

The wounded Gracey took efforts to make sure Darling was buried. He paid two dollars to a local, identified only as Jimmy, to bury the dead man. Gracey also thought Capt. Sponable had been killed, and he instructed Jimmy to bury him as well. Because Jimmy was paid to bury *two* bodies, word spread through the area, including into the ears of the local enslaved population, that two Union soldiers had been killed.[49] That discrepancy would cause a great amount of confusion later. With his two dollars in tow, Jimmy went to Lowe's Island and did a quick job of the interment; Darling's decomposing body persuaded Jimmy not to take too much time. His hasty work, a thin covering of soil, was soon discovered by hogs, who uprooted the body and devoured it.[50]

Gracey's stay at Dranesville lasted for two weeks. In early October, it ended abruptly when he was sent to Fairfax Court House. He was placed in a hospital, where attendants gave him daily dosages of opium. Gracey, a large man, claimed the Confederates said they wanted to help him recover so they could "exhibit him, *a la Barnum,* as a fine specimen of the living Yankee, who couldn't be killed."[51] As he regained his strength, Gracey plotted his escape.

That escape plan involved his regular doses of opium. Bearing his pain, Gracey squirreled the opium away until he was finally ready to make his move. Around October 11, he mixed the opium into the drinks of his unsuspecting guards, putting them to sleep. Moving with the darkness and the shadows, Gracey spent the next three days moving north towards the Potomac River. On October 14,

---

46 "The Dead Alive, And The Lost Found."

47 Joseph Ordwick Testimony, William B. Day Case File, 19.

48 Caroline Jackson Testimony, William B. Day Case File, 15.

49 Chapin, *A Brief History of the Thirty-Fourth Regiment,* 23.

50 Ibid., 17.

51 *New York Times,* Oct. 18, 1861.

nearly a month since he left camp, Gracey walked right back into the bivouac of the 34th New York.[52]

"You may imagine with what acclamation he was greeted when he made his appearance in camp," one of the 34th's soldiers wrote. "Gracey is telling big stories of what the rebels say," another noted. Among those stories, Gracey told of his lack of treatment at the hands of the Day doctors. A New York newspaper printed forebodingly of the Days, "let these names be remembered." Arthur O'Keeffe angrily scribbled, "We have sent to headquarters for permission to cross over and get the body." He was prepared to "give the fellows on the other side Hell if they interfere with us."[53]

But there was to be no recovery. Other events along the Potomac were occupying Federal commanders' attention more than this small skirmish. Yet the ambush at Lowe's Island changed everything for the people of Dranesville. The Home Guard had spent nearly five months acting as the strong arm of secession in the area. Their late-night visits to households like Kitty Hanna's now paled in comparison to what happened at Lowe's Island. The consequences of that ambush were far-reaching—more people were going to die because of it. While the 34th New York was forced to move on from the trauma of Lowe's Island, the people of Dranesville did not know that they would soon be hosting close to 10,000 Union soldiers. The Pennsylvania Reserve Corps was about to become intimately familiar with the area.

52 Ibid.; Willoughby, "Extracts from Journal of Charles H. Willoughby," 480.

53 Lyon, *Desolating This Fair Country*, 14; Willoughby, "Extracts from Journal of Charles H. Willoughby," 480; "The Dead Alive, And The Lost Found"; Arthur O'Keeffe to his family Oct. 16, 1861, O'Keeffe Family Papers.

Chapter Seven

"Shake the Enemy Out of Leesburg"

The Pennsylvania Reserves' Reconnaissance to Dranesville

After two months of waiting, the time had come. On October 9, Brig. Gen. George McCall led his three brigades of Pennsylvanians over the Potomac River and into Virginia. They had arrived in late July, answering the distress call of a worried capital. Through the late summer, the soldiers drilled and built earthworks to protect the capital.[1] And now, after champing at the bit for so long, the Pennsylvanians were heading further south.

The division was organized into three brigades of infantry, four batteries of artillery, and a cavalry regiment. Later in the war, a division like that might number, at best, about 3,500 men. But in October, McCall led nearly 11,000 soldiers over the Chain Bridge and into Virginia.[2] McCall commanded, in that window of time, just a fraction less than what George Washington led in the Continental Army at Yorktown in 1781.[3] The Reserves were an army unto themselves.

For almost two and a half months McCall's men had been bivouacked at Tenallytown, near Washington's northwestern edge, about four miles from Georgetown.[4] From Tenallytown it was little more than a quick jaunt to the impressive Chain Bridge and into Virginia.

---

1 Uzal Ent, *The Pennsylvania Reserves in the Civil War: A Comprehensive History* (Jefferson, NC, 2014), 18-19.

2 Sypher, *Pennsylvania Reserve Corps*, 111-113.

3 Jerome Greene, *The Guns of Independence: The Siege of Yorktown, 1781* (New York, 2005), 79. The American strength at Yorktown, counting both Continental units and militias, totaled about 13,000.

4 M. D. Hardin, *History of the Twelfth Regiment Pennsylvania Reserve Corps* (New York, 1890), 6. Tenallytown is now known as Tenleytown.

George McClellan ordered McCall to "move your entire command to a position on the right of Genl. Smith." Baldy Smith then dispatched an aide to "point out the ground" that McCall was to take up.[5]

McCall's men soon "broke camp and marched across [C]hain [B]ridge into Virginia as soldiers to battle," the Pennsylvanians' historian wrote later. "The cheerful spirit and the delight with the change was universal; the bands of music played 'Dixie's Land,' and the men rent the air with patriotic cheers." On the ninth, the vanguard of the Reserves crossed the river, with the remaining coming across the next day.[6]

The Pennsylvanians made their camp about two miles from the river and ten miles or so from Washington. It was near the small village of Langley, "a few plank-houses, clustering around a tavern and a church," as one correspondent described it.[7] While McCall's men bedded for the night around Langley, Baldy Smith's division returned to Lewinsville a couple of miles away and began to set up Camp Griffin.[8] Once the march was finished, Smith, writing for both himself and McCall, reported back to McClellan, "All is quiet."[9]

When the Pennsylvanians' "baggage, stores, and camp equipments" arrived at the rear of the column, they made camp, staking down tents and posting pickets around their new home: Camp Pierpont, named for the Unionist Francis Pierpont, who led Virginia's loyal Restored Government.[10]

Camp Pierpont soon became a bustling community of white tents. The men spent the following days continuing their training, which, according to some of their commanders, they desperately needed. "I almost despair," scoffed the First Brigade's commander Brig. Gen. John F. Reynolds, "from what I have seen of them since I have been here."[11] Brigadier Gen. George Meade, commanding the Second Brigade, echoed the sentiments. In a letter to his wife, Meade admitted his men

---

5 George Brinton McClellan Papers: Correspondence I, 1783-1888; 1861, Sep. 16-Oct. 11, 213-214.

6 Sypher, *Pennsylvania Reserve Corps*, 123; Rauch and Thomson, *"Bucktails"*, 68; Hardin, *History of the Twelfth Regiment Pennsylvania*, 7.

7 George Alfred Townsend, *Campaigns of a Non-Combatant* (New York, 1866), 14. Today, Langley is most known as the location for the headquarters of the Central Intelligence Agency.

8 See Chapter Five.

9 George Brinton McClellan Papers: Correspondence I, 1783-1888; 1861, Sep. 16-Oct. 11, 218.

10 John Bard, *John Bard's History of the Old Bucktails* (West Conshohocken, PA, 2013), 15.

11 Edward J. Nichols, *Toward Gettysburg: A Biography of General John F. Reynolds* (Gaithersburg, MD, 1986), 79.

were certainly brave enough, but "Soldiers they are not in any sense of the word."[12] For the time being Col. John S. McCalmont commanded the Third Brigade.

The soldiers went about their business. Vernon Henderson, a soldier in the Third Brigade's 6th Reserves, wrote, "Cornfields are destroyed, fences are going as fast as possible." Henderson continued, "Men are detailed every day to chop and the timber is falling fast."[13] General Reynolds, a commander firmly of the opinion that civilians' private property should not be trifled with, complained, "They proceeded at once to plunder and destroy everything in the houses left by the people."[14]

On October 10, McCall set up his headquarters in a local tavern known as the Langley Ordinary.[15] General McClellan rode across to oversee the crossing and met with both McCall and Smith at Lewinsville.

McClellan feared a Confederate attack against the two divisions and expected one at any time.[16] On October 6, three days before McCall crossed, McClellan had received a message from a spy near Leesburg, thirty miles west of Langley. That message warned that "the forces at Leesburg have been kept up to nearly 27,000."[17] The threat of almost 30,000 Confederates within marching distance of Washington unnerved McClellan. He moved both McCall and Smith to shore up his right flank, but in his opinion, it was still dangerously weak.

Except the spy, a man named Francis Buxton, was wrong. Exponentially wrong. There were not 27,000 Confederates at Leesburg; there were in fact only about 2,800.[18] Buxton over-inflated the rebel strength an astounding nine times its actual size. Men died because of that faulty intelligence in another embarrassing Federal defeat: the battle of Ball's Bluff.

The farce started with a Confederate withdrawal. Following the Federals' capture of the trio of hills just outside Washington, Gen. Joseph Johnston ordered his army to pull back from its positions, as outlined in Chapter 5. Those movements

---

12 George G. Meade, *The Life and Letters of George Gordon Meade*: Vol. 1, ed. George G. Meade (New York, 1913), 223.

13 Vernon Henderson Diary, Oct. 13, 1861, *Civil War Times Illustrated Collection*, USAHEC.

14 Nichols, *Toward Gettysburg*, 79.

15 Carole L. Herrick, *Images of America: McLean* (Charleston, SC, 2011), 30; Elizabeth David, "National Register of Historic Places—Nomination Form: Langley Fork Historic District" (Fairfax County Office of Comprehensive Planning, May 1980), 3; Rafuse, *Army of the Potomac*, 138.

16 Rafuse, *Army of the Potomac*, 138; McClellan, *Civil War Papers*, 106; McClellan, *Civil War Papers*, 108.

17 *OR* 5, 613.

18 James A. Morgan III, *A Little Short of Boats: The Battles of Ball's Bluff & Edwards Ferry, October 21-22, 1861* (El Dorado Hills, CA, 2011), 3.

were ongoing in the middle of October, and while most of the Confederate army was taking up new positions around Centreville, a lone outpost remained near Leesburg. Those forces, a brigade of infantry alongside some cavalry and artillery, were under the command of Col. Nathan Evans, ordered to watch the Potomac River and its fords. However, Evans, like McClellan, feared a massive attack on his lines. Unlike McClellan, however, who worried about legions of Confederate soldiers who simply did not exist, Evans faced a very real threat of tens of thousands of Union soldiers—not only far to his right at Langley and Lewinsville, but also thousands of soldiers directly across the Potomac. With Johnston and Beauregard moving their forces closer to Centreville, Evans was alone with his tiny brigade—a pebble in a sea of Union soldiers.

Evans feared what would happen if the Federals in Maryland and down by Langley attacked simultaneously. His little force would be useless to stop them. Reacting to this threat, Evans moved his soldiers back on October 16. Evans's new position at Carter's Mill lay almost seven miles to the southwest of Leesburg, and he figured that from there he could avoid being swallowed whole by attackers coming across the river.[19]

Evans's move horrified his superior, Gen. Beauregard. On October 17, as soon as he heard about Evans abandoning the Leesburg line, Beauregard sent a tersely worded message to the independent-thinking brigade commander. He explained that preventing a conjunction of the Federals across the river from Leesburg and McClellan's main force "is of the utmost military importance, and you will be expected to make a desperate stand, falling back only in the face of an overwhelming enemy." If Evans insisted on staying at Carter's Mill, Beauregard went on, he was ordered to keep at least one regiment constantly at Leesburg.[20] Evans decided if he had to send part of his brigade, it made the most sense for everyone to go back. Orders were soon cut that sent regiments backtracking to Leesburg.[21]

In their brief absence, however, the situation along the river had changed. When McClellan got word that the Confederate force in Leesburg was pulling out, he figured this was his chance to capture the town and secure lodging for more Federal camps. That involved sending the Pennsylvania Reserves halfway to Leesburg, where the Pennsylvanians were to assess the feasibility of closing on Leesburg from the Turnpike. The town that lay halfway between Camp Pierpont and Leesburg was, of course, Dranesville.

---

19 Jess. N. McLean Sr., ed., *The Official Records of the 13th Mississippi Infantry Regiment . . . as told by those who were there* (Privately Published, 2015), 50.

20 *OR* 5, 347.

21 McLean, *The Official Records of the 13th Mississippi*, 51.

McCall got his orders in the evening of October 18, which stipulated he was to "move his command . . . to Dranesville, and to thoroughly reconnoiter the country, and map the roads and topography as accurately as possible."[22] McClellan had grander plans in mind, as well. Across the river from Leesburg were troops under Brig. Gen. Stone. If McCall's mission to Dranesville was successful, McClellan figured he could order Stone across and hopefully "shake the enemy out of Leesburg."[23]

The Reserves left Camp Pierpont on Saturday morning, October 19 to begin the eleven-mile march to Dranesville.[24] At the front rode the 1st Pennsylvania Cavalry, screening the division's movements. The Pennsylvanians, still anticipating close to 30,000 rebels in front of them, "thought we were going into battle," a trooper wrote home. "I resigned my fate into the hands of my God and advanced without the slightest fear whatever."[25]

McCall's three brigades marched in a long column down the Leesburg & Alexandria Turnpike. As the division came to Difficult Run, about four miles from Dranesville, McCall ordered Col. John McCalmont's brigade to halt and hold steady along the Run. The rest of the division kept marching, and McCall next stopped George Meade's brigade a couple of miles closer to town.[26] At the same time, Baldy Smith took his division from Lewinsville and advanced west; this movement protected McCall's left.[27]

With Meade's and McCalmont's brigades stopped, that left just Reynolds's First Brigade and the three artillery batteries to continue down the road and into Dranesville. The soldiers reached the town and McCall set up his headquarters in the Thornton House, a large brick structure on the eastern edge of town. In two months, some of McCall's soldiers would be using the same home as an impromptu fort during the battle of Dranesville.[28]

Once settled in, McCall wrote to McClellan that "All is quiet [,] no enemy seen." Remembering his mission to reconnoiter the area, McCall gave his quick impressions. "Country for one mile beyond Difficult Creek, broken + woody

22 Sypher, *Pennsylvania Reserve Corps*, 124.

23 *JCCW*, 508.

24 Sypher, *Pennsylvania Reserve Corps*, 124.

25 Thomas Lucas, *I Seat Myself to Write You a Few Lines: Civil War and Homestead Letters from Thomas Lucas and Family*, eds. Dona B. Sauerburger and Thomas L. Bayard (Privately Published, 2002), 29.

26 *JCCW*, 257.

27 E. M. Woodward, *Our Campaigns; Or, The Marches, Bivouacs, Battles, Incidents of Camp Life and History of Our Regiment During Its Three Years Term of Service* (Philadelphia, 1865), 67-78.

28 *The Alleghanian*, Oct. 31, 1861; *OR* 5, 481.

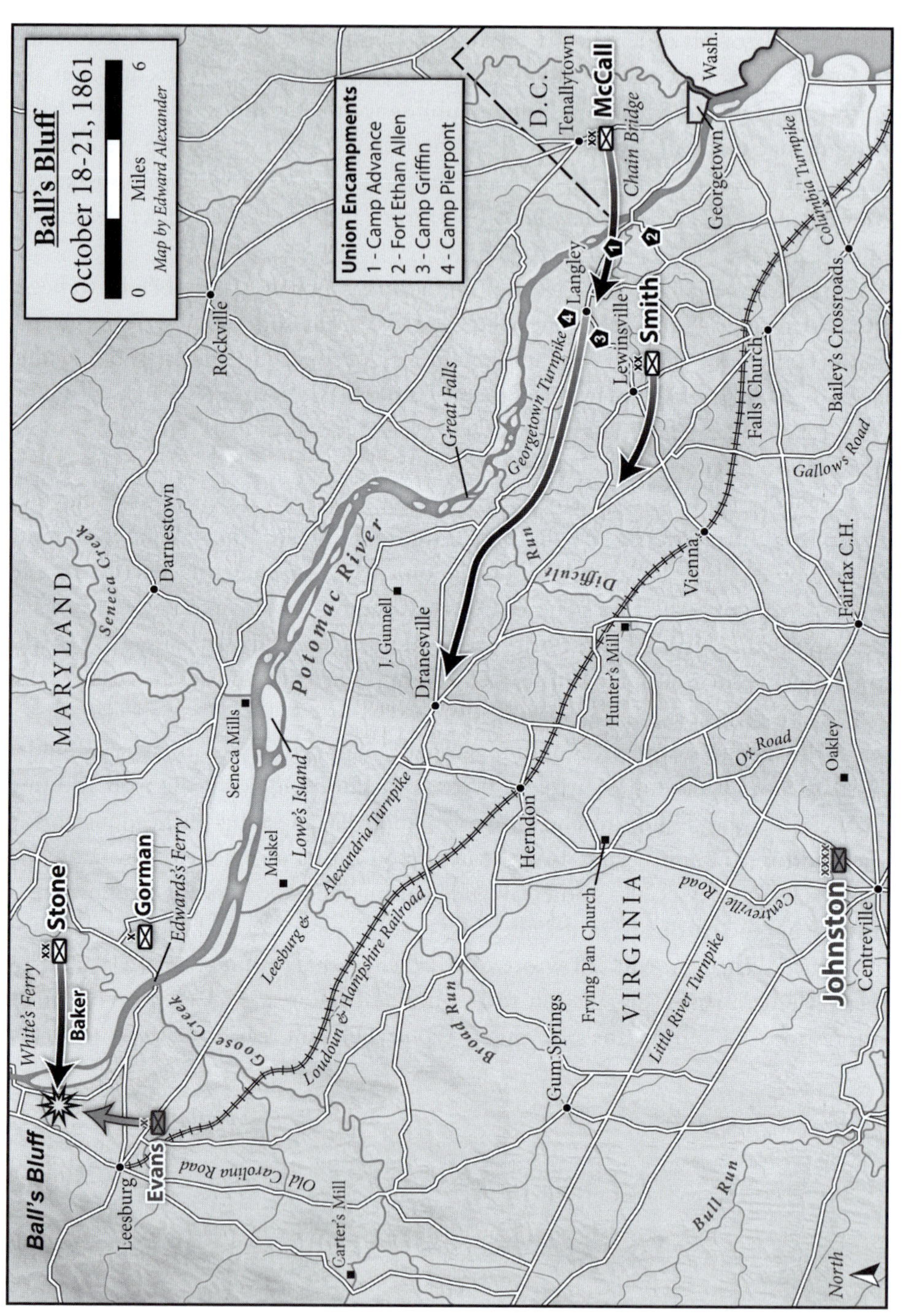
Ball's Bluff
October 18-21, 1861
Map by Edward Alexander
Miles
0
6
Union Encampments
1 - Camp Advance
2 - Fort Ethan Allen
3 - Camp Griffin
4 - Camp Pierpont
McCall
Wash.
D.C.
Tenallytown
Chain Bridge
Georgetown
Columbia Turnpike
Langley
Smith
Lewinsville
Falls Church
Bailey's Crossroads
Georgetown Turnpike
Gallows Road
Great Falls
Difficult Run
Rockville
Potomac River
Vienna
Fairfax C.H.
Darnestown
Seneca Creek
J. Gunnell
Dranesville
Hunter's Mill
MARYLAND
Ox Road
Oakley
Seneca Mills
Lowe's Island
Alexandria Turnpike
Herndon
VIRGINIA
Frying Pan Church
Centreville Road
Johnston
Miskel
Stone
White's Ferry
Gorman
Edwards's Ferry
Leesburg & Hampshire Railroad
Broad Run
Gum Springs
Little River Turnpike
Centreville
Baker
Goose Creek
Leesburg
Evans
Old Carolina Road
Carter's Mill
Ball's Bluff
Bull Run
North

[,] bad country to manoevre." In his opinion, "Nothing but skirmishing could be done by infantry, artillery could not leave the Road." Two months before the battle occurred, George McCall was foretelling the problems both sides would face fighting over this same ground.[29]

As Reynolds's brigade entered Dranesville, his soldiers only saw a couple of Confederate pickets, who quickly raced out of town. The Dranesville Home Guard was nowhere to be found. Content to harass local Unionists and shoot at soldiers in the middle of the night, the Home Guard fled to the countryside when word arrived that the Federals were coming in force. Charles Coleman later claimed that he was one of only "four men in the village" who remained, and he happily fed paying soldiers hot food in his public house. Coleman also sold McCall "100 bushels of oats" during the general's stay.[30]

Other residents of the town were not as hospitable. Members of the 1st Reserves found a bucket of water with "An aged lady and two young girls" standing guard over it. The women told the Pennsylvanians, "Only for the soldiers, none for officers." But when Reynolds rode up and asked for water, a sergeant handed the cup to his general. As Reynolds rode off and the sergeant tried to refill his cup, one of the girls snapped, "You gave your cup of water to that officer, and you cannot have any more." Continuing the verbal sparring, the sergeant replied, "I'll give my Brigade commander a cup of water every time, even if it deprives me of a drink, at the hands of a she rebel." At that, the girl spat twice on the sergeant, who, composing himself, walked away from the confrontation, but not before scooping up the bucket and taking it with him.[31]

Besides the few anecdotal meetings between soldiers and civilians, not much happened in Dranesville. Evan Woodward, 2nd Reserves, wrote, "We found a number of houses abandoned by their occupants who had fled on our approach under the impression we were Mamelukes and Bedouins coming to murder and destroy all we found." The soldiers also saw the evidence of the Home Guard's work, such as "Houses that had been abandoned for some time, their inhabitants having been driven away by their neighbors on account of their Union sentiments."[32]

The Pennsylvania Reserves bedded down for the night. Come morning, October 20, the soldiers woke up and went to work, "cutting down the chestnut trees in the woods to get the nuts, and the squealing of pigs was heard in various

---

29 George Brinton McClellan Papers: Correspondence I, 1783-1888, 1861, Oct. 12-21, 156.

30 *OR* 2, Series 2, 1287-1288.

31 H. N. Minnigh, "A Rebel Girl 'Spit in His Face,'" in *History of Company K., 1st (Inft,) Penn'a Reserves* (Duncansville, PA, 1891), 29-30.

32 Woodward, *Our Campaigns*, 68.

directions."[33] While some soldiers had little to do, the same could not be said for the 1st Pennsylvania Rifles.

The eccentric Lt. Col. Thomas Kane received an order from McCall that morning putting him in command of a detachment protecting engineers sent to map the area. Kane, with his riflemen in tow, ensured the safety of the engineers as they took notes and made geographic plans.[34]

As patrols spread out in every direction, Kane personally accompanied Maj. Amiel Whipple, the commander of the engineers. Together they rode south, going as far as Hunter's Mill, about five miles from Dranesville. The patrols occasionally ran into Confederate pickets, who shied away once the Pennsylvanians opened fire. Whipple wrote that Kane "afford[ed] every facility for the reconnaissance in his power, and kindly gave me the odometer distances taken under his direction."[35]

While the riflemen went out on patrol, back in Dranesville, George McCall received a visitor. Riding up with his entourage, the Army of the Potomac's commanding general arrived on the scene sometime in the afternoon. McClellan and McCall discussed the movements of the day, and the commanding general directed the division commander to pull back elements of Reynolds's brigade. McClellan further directed McCall to return to Camp Pierpont once the engineers were finished with their duty, and then returned to his headquarters in Washington. McCall, however, realized he would not have enough time to both finish the reconnaissance and return to Langley the same day. He wrote to McClellan, explaining the situation; McClellan replied, "If you finish in the morning, return." That gave the Pennsylvanians more time to become familiar with the area—a fact that surely helped them two months hence.[36]

McCall staying at Dranesville complicated matters, though. While most of his patrols had no trouble during the day, one of McCall's couriers was captured, and the dispatches brought to Nathan Evans in Leesburg. Evans now knew what force, and in what strength, McCall had at Dranesville, and he prepared by bringing more of his soldiers onto line at Goose Creek.[37]

Furthermore, McCall's positioning at Dranesville encouraged McClellan to write to Charles Stone across the river. McClellan told Stone, "General McCall occupied Dranesville yesterday and is still there. . . . The general desires that you will keep a good lookout upon Leesburg, to see if this movement has the effect to drive

33 Ibid.

34 Thomas Kane Papers, Box 23, Folder 4, Item 15, BYU; *OR* 5, 288.

35 *OR* 5, 288.

36 Beatie, *Army of the Potomac*, 46; *JCCW*, 258-259.

37 *OR* 5, 349.

them away." And if McCall did shake Evans at Leesburg, McClellan continued, "Perhaps a slight demonstration on your part would have the effect to move them." In the words of historian James Morgan, "This suggestion, almost an afterthought, led to the unintended battle that occurred the next day at Ball's Bluff."[38]

While McCall's men returned to their bivouacs around Dranesville for the second night, Stone planned his "slight demonstration." But in a list of errors that continued to grow, he got a dispatch from McClellan's headquarters on the night of October 20, asking "if there was a road from 'Darnesville' to Edwards's Ferry." It was a straight-forward question, except for the fact that there was no such place as "Darnesville." As Stone explained it later, "I took it for granted that the operator had made a mistake, and had meant Drainesville, instead of 'Darnestown,' which was the name of a place in Maryland." Thinking McClellan intended to find a good road that McCall could use to travel to Leesburg as Stone crossed the river, the latter figured he would have the Pennsylvanians on hand in case anything went awry.[39] With that fact to comfort him, Stone issued orders for his command to prepare a reconnaissance across the river.[40]

Everything quickly spun out of control. On Monday, October 21, Federals began to cross the Potomac, landing on the opposite bank and winding their way up Ball's Bluff before sunrise.[41] Stone ordered some of his soldiers to scout west of Leesburg along the Leesburg & Alexandria Turnpike, keeping an eye out for the arrival of McCall's vanguard, which Stone still figured was on its way.[42]

But McCall was not coming—in fact, quite the opposite. Around 8:00 a.m. he received orders from McClellan to bring his division back to Camp Pierpont. "We fell in in a hurry supposing we were to advance," Vernon Henderson, a soldier in the 6th Reserves wrote. But when the regiments turned away from Leesburg, and instead towards Langley, "all felt disappointed."[43]

Some historians have criticized McCall for marching back to Camp Pierpont. Russell Beatie, in his history of the Army of the Potomac, wrote, "McCall followed his orders to the letter. . . . By not exercising his discretion and marching to the

---

38 Ibid., 32; Morgan, *A Little Short of Boats*, 18.

39 *JCCW*, 489.

40 Jim Morgan, "Unintended Consequences: Ball's Bluff and the Rise of the Joint Committee on the Conduct of the War," in *Turning Points of the Civil War*, eds. Chris Mackowski and Kristopher D. White (Carbondale, IL, 2018), 25.

41 Ibid., 34.

42 *OR* 5, 294.

43 Vernon Henderson, Diary Oct. 21, 1861, USAHEC.

sound of the guns, he lost a critical opportunity for himself and McClellan."[44] But it is worth asking: what guns? Around the time that McCall set off for Camp Pierpont, roughly 10:00 a.m., the battle of Ball's Bluff was little more than some desultory skirmishing between the sides. And even if McCall heard that type of shooting from Dranesville, it would have been nothing out of the ordinary; there was picket firing across the river almost daily. How was McCall to differentiate those potshots from a budding battle?[45]

The three brigades of Pennsylvanians arrived back at Camp Pierpont around 1:00 p.m. A dispatch from McClellan was waiting for McCall; stay at Dranesville, it read, if the Pennsylvanians had not already left. Stone had telegraphed McClellan a little past 11:00 a.m., describing an action that was steadily growing in size. But with McCall's three brigades back at Camp Pierpont, it was too little, too late. The Federals atop Ball's Bluff were on their own.[46]

Stone dispatched Col. Edward Baker, a sitting U.S. Senator, and a close friend of President Lincoln's, across the river to assume command of the front. Fighting began in earnest around 3:00 p.m., and within two hours Baker was dead. The surviving Federal forces scrambled into the Potomac River. Ball's Bluff, the grand culmination of a comedy of errors and poor intelligence, was an embarrassing and unnecessary event that left close to 1,000 Union soldiers killed, wounded, or captured.[47]

Finger-pointing and scapegoating followed. In his official report about the battle, Stone wrote that he made the decisions he had because of his false impression that McCall would be on the scene to assist him. Worried that the report "put me in a false position entirely," McCall went to McClellan's headquarters, trying to clear the confusion. For his part, McClellan put the blame on Col. Baker, who could not defend himself from the grave.[48]

The soldiers in the Pennsylvania Reserve, though, were not part of those discussions. Many of them were disappointed that they had not been able to fight at Leesburg, and many believed that the battle would have gone differently had they been there. But the march to Dranesville and the two days spent in the immediate area had not been a waste of time. The knowledge the Pennsylvanians

---

44 Beatie, *Army of the Potomac*, 72.

45 Ted Ballard, *Battle of Ball's Bluff: Staff Ride Guide* (Washington, D.C., 2001), 44-45.

46 Sypher, *Pennsylvania Reserve Corps*, 125; *OR* 5, 33.

47 For a full description of the battle of Ball's Bluff, see Morgan, *A Little Short of Boats* and Morgan, "Unintended Consequences," 36; *OR* 5, 308.

48 *JCCW*, 261; Morgan "Unintended Consequences," 38.

This depiction of the battle of Ball's Bluff done by Currier & Ives
shows the death of Col. Edward Baker. *LOC*

gained would pay dividends when it came time to fight on December 20. In the
meantime, they went about their daily responsibilities at Camp Pierpont.

*   *   *

In mid-November, Charles Veil, a soldier in the 9th Pennsylvania Reserves,
received orders to report and serve as the brigade commander's orderly. "When
I arrived at the headquarters I saw an ordinary-looking kind of elderly man, in a
common soldier's uniform with an overcoat and a very greasy cap, overseeing some
work being done about the tents," Veil wrote. The orderly-to-be "inquired of him
as to where the general's tent was." When Veil knocked and found no one inside,
he returned to the man, saying, "The general ain't here." Looking up from his work,
the man "In a very short and 'snappy' way . . . indicated the one I was inquiring
for." Finding an "officer at a desk in full uniform," Veil figured he had located
the general to whom he was to report. But the officer instead walked him back
outside to the man in the greasy cap and saluted. Veil, realizing the man he "had
so unceremoniously accosted" was to be his commander, "felt like sinking into the
ground."[49] Charles Veil's first meeting with Brig. Gen. Edward Otho Cresap Ord,
the new commander of McCall's Third Brigade, had not gone according to plan.

"General Ord seems to be a very precise and particular man," James Chadwick,
10th Reserves, wrote home. "Last Sunday he inspected the regiments of the Third
Brigade and 'came down' very hard on captains of companies whose men had the

49 Veil, *The Memoirs of Charles Henry Veil*, 12.

Brigadier General Edward O. C. Ord

NARA

least bit of dust or tarnish on their muskets." Ord clearly intended his regiments to shape up and prepare for action. He joined Reynolds and Meade in their stringent drilling.[50]

Ord certainly made impressions on those he came across. A staff officer later in the war described him as "a tall man, with bushy eyebrows and a nervous manner, who looked like an excentric Irishman who was about to tell a funny story." Another soldier said Ord "looks just like a Russian Marshal with his fierce Mustachios and beard."[51] Ord had a soft spot, too. During his first night with the brigade, one of Ord's staff officers, A. B. Sharpe, went to bed with just one blanket. "The night was cold, and I felt it," Sharpe wrote years later. But "In the night [Ord] got up quietly, got a pair of blankets and covered me with them and tucked them around me as carefully as if I had been his child."[52]

Family lore said Ord's grandfather was George, Prince of Wales (later King George IV). While the connection was likely no more than family lore, Ord's immediate ancestry was nonetheless English. His father James, born in London in 1786, was adopted by a seagoing uncle. That uncle arrived in the new United States, bringing James with him.[53]

50 James Chadwick his father, Nov. 28, 1861, Allegheny College.

51 David W. Lowe, ed., *Meade's Army: The Private Notebooks of Lt. Col. Theodore Lyman* (Kent, OH, 2007), 230; Quoted in Timothy B. Smith, *Corinth 1862: Siege, Battle, Occupation* (Lawrence, KS, 2016), 109.

52 *Carlisle Herald*, Jan. 1, 1886.

53 Bernard Cresap, *Appomattox Commander: The Story of General E. O. C. Ord* (London, 1981), 2-3. As it pertains to the rumors of Ord's royal ancestry, Cresap and George IV biographer Shane Leslie both believe them to be unfounded. But Saul David, another biographer of George IV, is not so convinced, saying James Ord was "the most likely candidate" of a child born to the then-Prince of Wales during a short-lived marriage to a woman named Maria Fitzherbert; Shane Leslie, *George The Fourth* (London, 1926), 198-201; Saul David, *Prince of Pleasure: The Prince of Wales and the Making of the Regency* (New York, 1998), 76.

James Ord went to Georgetown as a young man with intentions of becoming a Jesuit priest, but when his uncle died, he suffered a crisis of faith. He joined the navy, but soon after discovering he had not inherited his uncle's sea legs, became a commissioned officer in the army instead. Stationed in Cumberland, Maryland, James married Rebecca Cresap in 1814. Four years later they welcomed their third child, a son named Edward.[54]

At the age of 16 Edward followed his father's footsteps into the army, gaining admission to West Point in 1835. Over the next four years Ord maintained an average academic standing. For three consecutive years, he ranked 21st in his class-standing, and came perilously close to the maximum of 200 demerits a cadet could receive in a year without fear of expulsion. Prior to the start of the 1836 school year, Ord met William T. Sherman, and the two became life-long friends. Still running in the middle of the pack, Ord graduated 17th out of a class of 32 in 1839. With his commission in hand, Ord joined the 3rd United States Artillery on service in Florida against the Seminoles.[55]

A mundane career followed. While other classmates were making names for themselves in the Mexican War, Ord arrived in California after the fighting had ended. He served there with Sherman, the two men doing not much more than twiddling their thumbs The war ended with nothing to show on Ord's resume, though in 1849 he did help survey the Los Angeles valley.[56]

In 1854 Ord married Mary Thompson, the daughter of a well-to-do lawyer in San Francisco. The marriage resulted in 13 children and lasted until Edward's death in 1888.[57]

More years of garrison duty followed, with a couple of campaigns chasing American Indians thrown in. The actions were fleeting, though, and to pass the time Ord read anything he could get his hands on pertaining to the study of military history.[58] In 1858, Ord was put in charge of the Artillery School of Practice at Fort Monroe. Teaching the next generation of gunners kept Ord's skills sharp, and he studied to stay one step ahead of his pupils, "so as not to be 'stumpt' by my section," he wrote later.[59]

---

54 Cresap, *Appomattox Commander*, 7.

55 *Official Register of the Officers and Cadets of the U.S. Military Academy, 1818-1872*, Class Ranking of 1839; Cresap, *Appomattox Commander*, 14; Cullum, *Volume 2*, 6.

56 J. Gregg Layne, "Edward Otho Cresap Ord: Soldier and Surveyor," *Quarterly Publication* (Historical Society of Southern California) 17, No. 4 (Dec. 1935).

57 Cresap, *Appomattox Commander*, 34-35.

58 Ibid., 52.

59 Ord to William T. Sherman, Apr. 12, 1888, William T. Sherman Papers, LOC.

John Brown put a hold on Ord's tutelage. In October 1859, orders came for Ord to bring a company of soldiers to help suppress the attack at Harpers Ferry. By the time Ord and his men got to Baltimore, however, another telegram arrived alerting him that Brown had been captured and ordering Ord to return to Fort Monroe. A pattern appeared to be forming that anytime there was action, Ord missed it.

As the sectional crisis worsened, Ord believed radical abolitionists were the ones pushing the country to the brink. He firmly believed in the law, and if the law said slavery was legal, then so be it. As he admitted to Sherman, "I was in [18]49 and until [18]54 a pro-slaveryman." In the words of his biographer, the passage of the Kansas-Nebraska Act "cooled his ardor" regarding the issue of slavery, but even in 1859-60 Ord still adhered to the belief that the institution was something best left alone. He supported Southern Democrat John Breckinridge for president in 1860.[60]

His belief in the law also kept Ord firmly convinced that the Union had to be preserved. As the secession crisis began, Ord used his connections and wrote to Congressman John Sherman of Ohio, William T.'s younger brother, detailing what should be done about forts like Sumter and the Norfolk Naval Base. But Ord, still a captain even 21 years after graduating West Point, was just another voice lost in the cacophony.[61]

The start of the war found him back on the west coast, serving at Fort Vancouver in the Washington Territory. Urgently wishing to be back east, Ord tried to pull every string he had. He wrote to senators, congressmen, friends, and friends of friends, hoping for something, *anything*, to do. As the armies back in Virginia mobilized and began to fight, Ord was still at Fort Vancouver.

His saving grace proved to be Major Julius Garesché, Assistant Adjutant General of the United States Army. The two men had served together in the early 1850s and Garesché wrote that "Ord nursed me during my sickness" when he was laid low with a bout of camp fever.[62] In 1861, when Ord found himself locked in place at Fort Vancouver, Garesché was in Washington. With his position alongside Adjutant General Lorenzo Thomas, Garesché proved to be "the means of procuring

---

60 Ord to Sherman, Aug. 14, 1863, William T. Sherman Papers, LOC; Cresap, *Appomattox Commander*, 58-59.

61 Cresap, *Appomattox Commander*, 59.

62 Louis Garesché, *Biography of Lieut. Col. Julius P. Garesché, Assistant Adjutant-General, U. S. Army* (Philadelphia, 1887), 162.

commissions for many worthy subjects." Among the names for whom Garesché advocated that spring was Edward Ord.[63]

A promotion came, dated September 14, 1861. Ord jumped from captain, a rank he had held for 11 years, to brigadier general. He packed his bags as quickly as he could and made his way east. Ord never forgot what Garesché did for him, and after the latter was killed at the battle of Stones River in 1862, Ord wrote to the man's widow, "It is one of the happinesses of my life to have known your husband, and to think he was my friend."[64]

Ord arrived in Washington, D.C., on November 6, and joined the Pennsylvania Reserve Corps just under two weeks later.[65] It seems odd for Ord to have been given command of the division's Third Brigade. Unlike every other field commander in the division, Ord was not from Pennsylvania. But Garesché's pull went far, and Ord took the helm of the four regiments. Colonel John McCalmont, commanding the brigade before, arrived back from a leave of absence to find Ord moved into the brigade commander's tents. What could have easily been an awkward, if not caustic relationship, instead proved respectful and easy-going. "My relations with General Ord were of the most agreeable kind," McCalmont remembered. "He was a frank, communicative, considerate, and very gallant officer." While Ord settled into the brigade command, Col. McCalmont returned to his regiment, the 10th Reserves.[66]

As he continued his reviews and drill observations, Ord wrote contentedly to his wife, "I have been a short time with my Brigade, am much pleased with it." He hoped to continue training the brigade so "that I can trust to put them in a tight place." Ord would not have long to wait until he found out whether he could or not; one month remained before the battle of Dranesville.[67]

63 Ibid., 358.

64 Ibid., 498. Ord went further to commemorate his friend, naming a son born in 1866 Jules Garesché Ord. The young Ord was killed at San Juan Hill in 1898.

65 Cresap, *Appomattox Commander*, 67; Ent, *The Pennsylvania Reserves in the Civil War*, 30.

66 J. H. Stine, *A History of the Army of the Potomac* (Philadelphia, 1892), 37.

67 Edward Ord to his wife, Nov. 26, 1861, Edward Ord Papers, Box 1, Folder 3, Item 10, Stanford University.

Chapter Eight

"Some of Them Spattered With Blood"

George Bayard's Dranesville Raid

On the road about halfway between Fairfax Court House and Centreville sat a home owned by the Millan Family, which they called Oakley. The Millans fled Oakley right before the battle of Manassas, leaving an empty structure through the summer and fall of 1861. In late October, newly minted Brig. Gen. J. E. B. Stuart decided to make Oakley his headquarters for the winter.[1]

He named his quarters Camp *Qui Vive* ("Who Goes There"), and he and his entourage quickly moved into the structure. With all the Millans' furniture gone, "the house was bare and bleak," a staffer wrote. But Stuart's men made the most of it. "General Stuart's headquarters was always a pleasant place to visit," another officer wrote, "and I spent a many good evenings there."[2]

Stuart still commanded the advance posts of the Confederate Army of the Potomac, though the area had quieted down. Most of the army was camped around Centreville and the Federal army still licked its wounds after Ball's Bluff; the daily skirmishing of the summer was all but gone. Stuart occasionally took the field and led reconnaissances near enemy lines, although their most interesting prisoner was a wild raccoon. Back at Camp *Qui Vive*, the Confederates looped a leash around the raccoon and tied it to a cannon. The racoon provided no small amount of amusement. It was "black, wary, with snarling teeth, and eyes full of 'fight'!"[3]

---

1 Photo Record of Oakley Farm, American Civil War Museum, Richmond, Virginia.

2 John E. Cooke, *Wearing of the Gray: Being Personal Portraits, Scenes and Adventures of the War* (New York, 1867), 195; Blackford, *War Years with Jeb Stuart*, 54.

3 Trout, *With Pen and Saber*, 50; Cooke, *Wearing of the Gray*, 196.

J. E. B. Stuart's winter headquarters, Camp *Qui Vive*, at the Millan family home, Oakley. The home is seen here near the turn of the century. In a state of disrepair, it was torn down in the 1960s and the site is now the Fairfax County Fire and Rescue Academy. *Courtesy of the Fairfax County Public Library Photographic Archive*

But Stuart wanted more than just a raccoon. He wrote to his wife on November 20, "We are still anxiously hoping for the enemy to advance," and then, four days later, *"Why don't he come?"*[4] He itched for more action, but it seemed like the front was settling down for the winter. Frank English, from the camps of the 6th South Carolina, wrote, "It is generally thought that the Campaign on the Potomac is finished for this year."[5]

The weather certainly portended winter. Starting around the same time that Stuart set up Camp *Qui Vive*, weather reports noted the presence of frost settling in. Snow began to fall, driving both armies to construct winter quarters.[6] Soldiers who would soon find themselves under Stuart's command at Dranesville began to replace their tents with wooden huts. The soldiers were proud of their constructions,

4 J. E. B. Stuart, *Letters of General J. E. B. Stuart to his Wife, 1861*, ed. *Bingham Duncan* (Atlanta, 1943), 17, 19.

5 Franklin English to his mother, Dec 3, 1861, Frank English Letters.

6 Krick, *Civil War Weather in Virginia*, 40.

one private in the 10th Alabama noting, "Our cabins were comfortable warm as we kept a good fire nearly all the time."[7]

As the soldiers settled in for what they presumed to be a long winter's rest, they found other recreational activities. They "passed time with games of different sorts, such as foot-ball, bandy, and other kinds, including cards," wrote a soldier in the 11th Virginia.[8]

But the Confederates continued to keep their eyes open for their Federal counterparts. It all boiled down to what Stuart had complained about on November 24: "*Why don't he come?*" Little did Stuart know that the soldiers in blue would soon have reason to move out of their works.

* * *

It began when three people walked into Camp Griffin on November 26 and said they had a story to tell. Their names were Caroline Jackson, Joseph Ordwick, and Isaac Madison, and up until a week before, they were enslaved by the Coleman family in Dranesville.

More specifically, the three had been enslaved by Eliza Coleman—Charles and Thomas's mother. In Isaac Madison's case, he had been "born the slave of the Coleman family," and had spent his whole life in Dranesville.[9]

The three were cousins and on November 19, they fled from the town. It took them a week to traverse the roughly eleven miles to Camp Griffin at Lewinsville, evading patrols by day and moving by night. They were brought into the camp that, over the past few weeks, Baldy Smith's division had built into a large tent city. Once in the camp, the three were sent to meet with one of Smith's brigadiers, Winfield S. Hancock.[10]

They described what they had witnessed, including what the Dranesville Home Guard had done since the spring, especially the ambush at Lowe's Island. Caroline, in her testimony, remembered the two Federal soldiers brought back to town—Robert Gracey and Cyrus Kellogg—and described Thomas Coleman reading the dead Oliver Darling's letters.[11] Isaac Madison spoke of William Day coming back with Darling's uniform; he told the Federals "that the names of the slaves who

---

7 McClelen, *I Saw the Elephant*, 18.

8 Dorothy Sue Simmons Kessler, ed., *The Fincastle Rifles* (Fincastle, VA, 1979), 4.

9 Isaac Madison Statement, William B. Day Case File, 18.

10 William B. Day Case File, 12.

11 Caroline Jackson Statement, William B. Day Case File, 13-14.

wore the clothes thus stripped from the Union soldiers were Jack Murgeon, slave of Stephen Farr . . . and John Lee, slave of Dr. Wm. B. Day about 15 years old."[12]

The pivotal moment of the Dranesville saga hung in the balance. Hancock could simply have kicked the three people out of the camp, like Charles Stone had done to others. Or he could have chosen not to believe them, and nothing else likely would have happened. But he did listen, and he took careful notes.

Joining Hancock that day was John Hawxhurst, a local Unionist, and a member of the Restored Government of Virginia. Hawxhurst had lived just east of Lewinsville, and a historian described Hawxhurst as "one of the most radical Republicans in the Restored government during the war."[13] When Hawxhurst was not attending to political matters, he aided the Federal army in identifying both Unionists and suspected rebels in Fairfax County.[14] Together, Hancock and Hawxhurst proved eager listeners as the three recounted their story.

Caroline Jackson gave the most pertinent information. After describing the attack at Lowe's Island, she proceeded to name the 14 men who took part in the ambush. Except for the three captains (Gardner, Harvey, and Miller), all the men were citizens of Dranesville. Quickly copying the names down, Hawxhurst sealed the list and forwarded it to officials in Washington. Hancock sent Caroline, Isaac, and Joseph into the city as well, away from Dranesville and their enslavers.[15]

This information set off a chain reaction that made the rest of November 26 a whirlwind. With the names of the accused Dranesville residents in hand, now it was just a matter of apprehending them. It proved an easy choice as to what unit would go get them.

Which soldiers had just been to Dranesville a month ago? Which soldiers had spent the intervening period on near-daily patrols and reconnaissances, and thus knew the roads? At Camp Pierpont, George McCall received the directive that same hectic day. He passed the order to the commander of his cavalry regiment, Colonel George D. Bayard, to go and round up the accused men.

The 25-year-old Bayard was a no-nonsense officer who had instituted a rigorous drill system when he took command of the mounted Pennsylvanians in September 1861. Before that, after graduating from West Point in 1856, Bayard served in the 1st U.S. Cavalry, fighting under

12 Isaac Madison Statement, William B. Day Case File, 19.

13 Richard Lowe, *Republicans and Reconstruction in Virginia, 1856-70* (Charlottesville, VA, 1991), 37.

14 Joseph Cockrell Southern Claims File, Fairfax County, Virginia, 57. Hawxhurst is identified in Federal papers as "Hawkshurst," but his deposition in the Southern Claims and his gravestone are both spelled Hawxhurst.

15 Caroline Jackson Statement, William B. Day Case File, 13; *OR 2*, Series 2, 1286.

Colonel George Bayard
1st Pennsylvania Cavalry
LOC

J. E. B. Stuart against the Kiowa people.[16] In a July 1860 fight, Bayard was shot through the cheek with an arrowhead, which remained in his face for five weeks before it could be removed in St. Louis.[17] The war's outbreak found him teaching cavalry instruction at West Point, but by the middle of September he was commissioned by Gov. Curtin as colonel of the 1st Pennsylvania Reserve Cavalry.[18]

Bayard told his troopers to be mounted and ready to go by 8:00 p.m. An hour later the 600-man regiment set out from Camp Pierpont. It was a miserable night; the sun had set four hours prior, and temperatures hovered near freezing. The moon did not offer much light as the troopers made their way towards Dranesville. They stuck to byroads at first, moving "all night at a break-neck gait," as one trooper wrote. Another described the countryside around him as, "one of the darkest and most dismal pine thickets I ever saw."[19]

Bayard later reported the journey as "a very tedious and toilsome march."[20] Within a few miles of Dranesville, Bayard split the regiment: two companies veered onto the Leesburg & Georgetown Turnpike, while the remaining eight stayed on the Leesburg & Alexandria Pike. Perhaps Bayard expected more resistance leading into town, but there was none. It was close to 5:00 a.m. on November 27 as the

---

16 Cullum, *Volume 1*, 647.

17 Samuel Bayard, *The Life of George Dashiell Bayard* (New York, 1874), 172, 175-177.

18 Cullum, *Volume 1*, 647; Sypher, *Pennsylvania Reserve Corps*, 104; Bayard, *The Life of George Dashiell Bayard*, 196.

19 Bayard, *The Life of George Dashiell Bayard*, 196; OR 5, 448; Krick, *Civil War Weather in Virginia*, 40; Lucas, *I Seat Myself to Write You*, 40.

20 OR 5, 488.

troopers closed in on their objective; their ride had taken close to eight hours in near complete darkness.[21] Sunrise was still two hours away.[22]

Opposing Bayard's men was a small picket from the 2nd Virginia Cavalry.[23] The picket consisted of two soldiers, Privates Alex Whitten and Frederick Hildebrand. Neither, however, were proving very good at their job. A comrade of theirs wrote, "They were, I understand, tight, and when ordered to leave by their sergeant, refused." In other words, both Whitten and Hildebrand were drunk.[24]

The inebriated Confederates were captured without a fight by Capt. Jacob Stadelman's Company B. With the picket captured, the road lay open to Dranesville. The Leesburg & Georgetown and the Leesburg & Alexandria turnpikes converged at Dranesville. Major S. D. Barrows, at the head of the two companies Bayard had detached, closed on the town from the north while Bayard headed straight into town from the east. Not a single shot was needed for the Pennsylvanians to take control of the town.[25]

The Union soldiers set about their mission, kicking in the doors of houses throughout the town and dragging their targets back outside. John B. Farr's daughter remembered the Pennsylvanians "seized my father who was then in his bed."[26] On the eastern side of town the soldiers went into Robert Coleman's home. He pledged his loyalty and said "he was working for them." The Pennsylvanians left Robert and his family alone, but from their home the Colemans "could hear the women and children screaming."[27]

Bayard's soldiers arrested six men: William and John Day, Charles Coleman, Richard Gunnell, John DeBell, and John Farr. One of the Pennsylvanians wrote that the men "were guilty of deeds almost too horrible to relate." Many of the soldiers "were all eager to tear them to pieces, and would have done so, if the colonel had not interfered." Bayard insisted the civilians be treated as prisoners of war. As the captives were loaded into wagons for the ride back to Langley,

21 Ibid.

22 Krick, *Civil War Weather in Virginia*, 40.

23 *OR Supplement*, pt. 2, vol. 69, 694; Rufus H. Peck, *Reminiscences of a Confederate Soldier of Co. C, 2nd Va. Cavalry* (Fincastle, VA, 1913), 12.

24 Robert W. Parker, *Lee's Last Casualty: The Life and Letters of Sgt Robert W. Parker, Second Virginia Cavalry*, ed. Catherine M. Wright (Knoxville, 2008) 50.

25 *OR* 5, 448.

26 *OR* 2, Series 2, 1288.

27 Ann Coleman Southern Claims Commission, NARA.

the soldiers ignored "the women and children, who were running around in their night clothes, pleading for us to spare their fathers, brothers, sons, husbands etc."[28]

The Pennsylvanians had not succeeded in finding everyone. Philip Carper and Thomas Coleman, two men Caroline Jackson had mentioned for their roles in the ambush at Lowe's Island, were nowhere to be found. The 1st Pennsylvania Cavalry reformed and began the ride back to Camp Pierpont.

They would not get back without a fight.

*   *   *

William Downs Farley hailed from South Carolina. As a young man he attended the University of Virginia, and before he graduated, he embarked on a tour of northern Virginia. Eight years later, the knowledge gained on that tour helped the 25-year-old Farley as a scout in the Confederate army.[29]

Farley joined the Confederate war effort as a private in the 1st South Carolina Infantry, a unit in which he fought at the battle of Manassas. He became a scout after the battle, and his friend John Cooke wrote "if any daring deed was undertaken . . . Farley was sure to be there."[30] In his capacity as a scout, Farley excelled. Through the summer and fall of 1861, he routinely went out "either alone or with small groups of handpicked men," and gathered intelligence about the Federals nearby. Those scouting missions frequently ended in small skirmishes, and a South Carolina newspaper wrote happily of Farley, "He has made several Yankee scouts bite the dust."[31]

On November 26, Farley heard that the Federal cavalry "were going to make an expedition towards Dranesville," as he told Cooke later. He wanted to "waylay the party, whatever its strength, and attack it from the woods on the side of the road; then, during the confusion, to make our escape in the thicket, if necessary."[32] In his endeavor to ambush the enemy, Farley was joined by another officer, and, from Dranesville, Philip Carper and Thomas Coleman.[33] Carper and Coleman's presence with Farley had prevented their arrest earlier that morning.

---

28 *OR* 5, 448; Bayard, *The Life of George Dashiell Bayard*, 197.

29 Robert J. Trout, *They Followed the Plume: The Story of J. E. B. Stuart and His Staff* (Mechanicsburg, PA, 1993), 107.

30 John E. Cooke, "Captain William D. Farley, The Partisan," in *The Confederate Reader: How the South Saw the War*, ed. Richard B. Harwell (New York, 1989), 93.

31 J. Tracy Power, "The Confederate as Gallant Knight: The Life and Death of William Downs Farley," in *Civil War History* 37, No. 3, (Sep. 1991): 249; *Yorkville Inquirer*, Sep. 5, 1861.

32 Cooke, *Wearing of the Gray*, 425.

33 Ibid.; D. M. Kelsey, *Deeds of Daring by the American Soldier North and South* (Chicago, 1897), 96. It remains unclear who the other officer with Farley was. In his official report, Bayard identified

Captain William D. Farley ambushed Bayard's men. *Courtesy of Virginia Museum of History & Culture*

Farley's original intention was to hit the Federal cavalry as they came out of Camp Pierpont. He and his compatriots closed to within "a mile or so" of Langley and "took post in the woods." There they waited until darkness. Realizing his ambush would not pay off, Farley led his small party to the nearby house of a Confederate sympathizer. They had a "a good supper" that night, and the next morning "a hot cup of coffee at daylight" before returning to the road.[34]

As the Confederates started back, they saw Bayard's cavalry coming toward them in the distance. Farley had a decision to make. He could still try to ambush the 1st Pennsylvania—though with the entirety of Bayard's men on hand the odds were about 150:1, or he could scramble off into the woods and fight another day. The young South Carolinian made up his mind: they would hit the Pennsylvanians. He explained later that he figured the Federal troopers would "think we are a heavy force sent to ambush them," and he thought once the shooting started, he and his comrades could escape into the woods.[35] The four men took up a place just off the road amid some pines and readied their pistols, carbines, and shotguns.[36]

Meanwhile, Col. Bayard's column kept coming. According to one of the troopers, they had put their prisoners at the "front of the column under a strong

---

the man as "F. De Caradene, lieutenant 7th South Carolina." However, that name does not appear on the remaining roster rolls of the 7th South Carolina. In a fanciful retelling of the story, in both Cooke and Kelsey, the name Decaradeux is used— but in those same retellings Farley is intentionally changed to "Darrell." Thus, those sources cannot be used either in attempting to identify the mystery officer. *OR* 5, 449; Cooke, *Wearing of the Gray*, 427; Kelsey, *Deeds of Daring*, 96.

34 Cooke, *Wearing of the Gray*, 425-26.

35 Ibid.

36 The soldiers' armament comes from a list of captured weapons compiled by Colonel Bayard. He wrote of "5 shot-guns, 1 Hall's rifle, and 2 pistols"; *OR* 5, 449.

guard," unknowingly putting the civilians directly in the line of Farley's fire. Colonel Bayard rode at the head of his regiment, alongside his lieutenant colonel, major, and regimental staff, including both the surgeon and assistant surgeon.[37]

When the Pennsylvanians were within twenty yards, Farley cried out, "Now, boys!"[38] The four men opened a small but rapid scattering of gunfire. Bayard was nicked twice, and his horse was killed. The regimental surgeon, David Stanton, "had three balls through his clothes."[39] Private John Lewis, from Company G, was shot in the leg.[40] The worst of the wounded were Assistant Surgeon Samuel Alexander and Company D's Pvt. Joel Houghtaling. Alexander was hit three times, "one striking him in the abdomen, one in the thigh, and one just above the knee."[41] Private Houghtaling died later that same day; Assistant Surgeon Alexander lasted two days before succumbing to his wounds.[42]

At the first firing, the Pennsylvanians reeled away in surprise. One of the soldiers wrote he was "right in the midst of the muss, and for a short time enjoyed quite as much of the music of whistling bullets as was pleasant."[43]

Bayard recovered from his horse's death and the sudden onset of the shooting. His instincts kicked in, and he began shouting commands to his troopers. "We pitched into them," Pennsylvanian Thomas Lucas wrote home.[44] To combat the rebels, "One company dismounted and pushed into the woods on foot and the other Companies surrounded the woods mounted," Sergeant Thompson Snyder from Company D recalled.[45]

At this point in the war, there were roughly only ten Sharps carbines per company in the 1st Pennsylvania. Those who had them now plunged into the pine thickets after their foe.[46]

---

37 *Centre Democrat*, Dec. 12, 1861.

38 Cooke, *Wearing of the Gray*, 427.

39 Bayard, *The Life of George Dashiell Bayard*, 191.

40 *The Cecil Whig*, Nov. 30, 1861.

41 *Centre Democrat*, Dec. 12, 1861.

42 *The Press*, Nov. 29, 1861; *Lewistown Gazette*, Dec. 12, 1861. Alexander's remains were brought back home where he was buried in Wilmington, DE. A Pennsylvanian wrote, "His wife arrived in camp about two hours after he died, expecting to find him slightly wounded. She was almost frantic on hearing of his death"; *Lewistown Gazette*, Dec. 4, 1861.

43 *Centre Democrat*, Dec. 12, 1861.

44 Lucas, *I Seat Myself to Write You*, 40.

45 Snyder, "Recollections of Four Years with the Union Cavalry," unpublished manuscript in Bound Volume 42, Fredericksburg & Spotsylvania National Military Park (hereafter FRSP).

46 Report of J. R. Taylor, 5, in Bound Volume 42, FRSP Archives.

Meanwhile Farley and the others kept firing. Farley later claimed to be the one who killed Bayard's horse and Surgeon Alexander. He heard Bayard cry out "Steady! steady, men!" Another shouted, "*Here's* the First Pennsylvania! Bully for us, boys!"[47]

In a matter of moments, the Confederates were outmatched. Farley had "fired all [his] loads, and stopped under a sapling to reload." The other officer with him was shot in the hand and soon out of the action. Farley began to make his way out of the pines when Pvt. A. B. Selheimer rode up to him and swung his carbine down, smashing Farley with the barrel of the gun. The blow knocked Farley unconscious, and he was further wounded when Selheimer's horse's hoof came down on him, leaving him "all bruised and bloody."[48]

The fight inside the pines quickly descended into an every-man-for-himself brawl. While Farley made his getaway attempt, the two Dranesville men also made their stand. Philip Carper was captured without much difficulty; he was the only Confederate of the four with no reported injuries. Thomas Coleman, on the other hand, was a different matter entirely.

Since April, the 21-year-old Coleman had been a central figure in the Dranesville Home Guard. He had gone alongside the other Guards as they rode to Unionist households and intimidated those inside. He had actively taken part in the ambush at Lowe's Island, and according to Caroline Jackson had even taken a pistol from the dead Oliver Darling.[49] Maybe now, in the pines just a few miles from home, Coleman used that same pistol to shoot at the Pennsylvanians. Maybe he used the pistol John Day, now sitting as a prisoner not far from him, had sold him because he "was going to fight the Yankees with it."[50]

Whichever gun Coleman used, his defense did not last long. Closing in on him came Cpl. Christian Romich. At close range Romich fired, striking Thomas Coleman "through the head, the ball entering at one temple and coming out his opposite ear."[51]

The fight in the pines had lasted only a few minutes. Bayard's loss tallied two dead horses, one enlisted man wounded, and two mortally wounded. Captain Farley's entire party was captured. Farley himself slowly came to, awaking to

---

47 Cooke, *Wearing of the Gray*, 427.

48 Selheimer's identity is revealed in a letter to the editor of the *Lewistown Gazette*, Dec. 4, 1861, and corroborated in another letter to the *Lewistown Gazette*, published Dec. 11, 1861; Cooke, *Wearing of the Gray*, 428.

49 Caroline Jackson Testimony, William B. Day Case File, 14.

50 Timothy Johnson Testimony, John T. Day Case File, 29. See Chapter Four.

51 Romich's identity is given in *Lewistown Gazette*, Dec. 4, 1861. The quote comes from a letter written by James Chadwick, Nov. 28, 1861, Allegheny College.

Corporal Christian Romich, 1st Pennsylvania Cavalry, shot and mortally wounded Thomas Coleman. Romich was killed at the Battle of Brandy Station in 1863. *Courtesy of John Deppen*

mocking voices.[52] Bayard put the barely alive Thomas Coleman and his own wounded soldiers "in an ambulance together," and continued his return to Camp Pierpont.[53]

The shooting had not gone unnoticed back at Langley. When couriers arrived from Bayard describing the fight, McCall ordered Reynolds's First Brigade to arms, and alongside Capt. Mark Kerns's Battery G, 1st Pennsylvania Artillery, set out to relieve Bayard.[54]

A little after 1:00 p.m. on November 27, Bayard's cavalry returned to Camp Pierpont. A trooper summed up the whole affair: "We arrived in camp pretty well worn out, both horse and man, having been in our saddles sixteen hours, and traveled forty miles without taking time to water our horses."[55] The infantrymen in McCall's division watched the riders pass by in amazement. James Chadwick, 10th Reserves, wrote that the troopers were "Not a pleasant sight, some of them spattered with blood and horses without riders."[56]

Thomas Coleman died that night. Chadwick wrote, "The poor fellow was sensible till the moment of his death." The next morning, the Pennsylvanians buried both Coleman and Joseph Houghtaling, who "died about the same time." They "were buried in the honors of war, and it was a very impressive scene," recalled Pvt. Lucas.[57] The war's brutal reality had come to Dranesville.

While Thomas Coleman lay dying at Camp Pierpont, the other prisoners were readied for transport to Washington. Captain H. J. Biddle, the assistant adjutant-general for McCall's division, prepared the papers. He wrote to Brig. Gen. Andrew

---

52 Cooke, *Wearing of the Gray*, 428.

53 Lewis Prall unknown recipient, Dec. 1, 1861. Author's Collection.

54 *OR* 5, 448.

55 Bayard, *The Life of George Dashiell Bayard*, 198.

56 James Chadwick to his father, Nov. 28, 1861, Allegheny College.

57 Ibid.; Lucas, *I Seat Myself to Write You*, 41.

Porter, the provost marshal in the city, and explained the civilians were "secessionists of known activity in furnishing supplies to rebel forces or taken in arms."[58] On the night of November 27, the civilians and captured soldiers were "put in a wagon, and carried to Washington," said Farley.[59]

Their destination turned out to be "a depressing jumble of structures strewn along" a short way east of the United States Capitol.[60] The complex was located at the intersection of First and A Streets, and at "its heart was a three-story pile of dingy brick . . . an old rookery that had degenerated into a tenement."[61] The whole place was known simply as the Old Capitol Prison.

It had gotten its name in the wake of the British burning of Washington in 1814. Needing a place to convene, Congress moved just a block or so away from the debris of the Capitol Building and began to hold its sessions in the brick structure. In 1817, James Monroe's presidential inauguration took place within its walls. By 1819, with the replacement Capitol Building on the Hill far enough along, members of Congress stopped using their temporary quarters. Though Congress vacated after only four years of using the building, the name stuck: The Old Capitol.[62]

The building served as a boarding house from the 1820s through the start of the Civil War. One advertisement proclaimed that the building "containing 50 rooms, enables the subscriber to offer every accommodation to members of Congress and travelers."[63] Its most famous tenant, John C. Calhoun, died there in 1850.[64]

Starting in 1861, though, most inhabitants of the building were not there voluntarily. The boarding house closed before the war, and the Federal government bought the complex.[65] Locks were added to the doors, and "A high wall was built

58 *OR* 2, Series 2, 1286.

59 Cooke, *Wearing of the Gray*, 430.

60 Curtis Carroll Davis, "The 'Old Capitol' and Its Keeper: How William P. Wood Ran a Civil War Prison," in *Records of the Columbia Historical Society, Washington, D.C.*, Vol. 52, (1989), 207.

61 Ibid.

62 Harold H. Burton and Thomas E. Waggaman, "The Story of the Place: Where First and A Streets Formerly Met at What Is Now the Site of the Supreme Court Building," in *Records of the Columbia Historical Society, Washington, D.C.*, Vol. 51/52, (1951/1952), 142-143.

63 Hopper Striker Mott, ed., *The New York Genealogical and Biographical Record*: Vol. 44 (New York, 1913), 114.

64 Burton and Waggaman, "The Story of the Place," 144-145; John Niven, *John C. Calhoun and the Price of Union: A Biography* (Baton Rouge, 1988), 1.

65 N. T. Colby, "The 'Old Capitol' Prison," in *The Annals of the War Written by Leading Participants North and South* (Philadelphia, 1879), 503.

The Old Capitol Prison in Washington, D.C.
NARA

around the prison yard on the east."[66] In July, William P. Wood from Alexandria, Virginia, was appointed the prison's superintendent.[67]

By August the prison contained "sixty-five military prisoners and five 'contrabands,'" reported a Washington newspaper. The latter were escaped enslaved people sent to Washington and were kept in a different building from the prisoners.[68]

The prisoners scooped up by Col. Bayard arrived on November 28. Farley, Carper, and the other officer from South Carolina were imprisoned on the third floor.[69] It is not noted in any records which floor or room the civilians from Dranesville were kept, though one source familiar with the jail wrote, "Rooms No. 14, 15, and 18 were usually filled with citizens of Virginia." These rooms

66 Burton and Waggaman, "The Story of the Place," 145.

67 Davis, "The 'Old Capitol' and Its Keeper," 206.

68 *Washington Evening Star*, Aug. 12, 1861; Davis, "The 'Old Capitol' and Its Keeper," 211-212.

69 Cooke, *Wearing of the Gray*, 430.

were on the second floor and made up what used to be chambers for the House of Representatives.[70]

On the first floor the prisoners were led into a large room where they were searched and questioned. From there, guards brought the prisoners to the rooms where they would be confined. One such room was described by another prisoner, later in the war as:

> large, and divided from the room in front by folding-doors, which were locked, and barred on the other side. Two windows without blinds opened on a large yard. . . . The room was one mass of dirt; spider-webs hung in festoons from the ceiling, and vermin of all kinds ran over the floor. The walls had been papered, but dampness had caused most of it to fall off, which all over that which was left were great spots of grease. . . . The furniture consisted of an iron bedstead, pillows, and a mattress of straw, a pair of sheets, and a brown blanket.[71]

The six citizens of Dranesville arrived at the jail when it was still relatively empty. By the end of the war, Superintendent Wood estimated 30,000 prisoners, mostly civilians, came through the doors of the Old Capitol Jail. In November 1861, the prison's population numbered less than 100.[72]

The Dranesville men were thoroughly confused, and up to that point, did not know why they had even been arrested. All they were aware of was the fact that they had gone to bed on November 26 and woke the next morning with guns in their faces. After five days in prison, Charles Coleman wrote a letter to Provost Marshal Andrew Porter. Coleman said he was arrested, but "for what charge I do not know unless it was for feeding Confederate pickets." Coleman insisted, "I have never been in arms against the United States at any time." He tugged at Porter's heartstrings, writing, "I have a wife and three little children at home, with no person to do anything for them."[73] At least for now, no answer came. Coleman and the other men with him had no choice but to continue sitting in their rooms wondering what lay ahead of them.

*　　*　　*

70 John A. Marshal, *American Bastille: A History of the Illegal Arrests and Imprisonment of American Citizens During the Late Civil War* (Philadelphia, 1881), 323.

71 Maria Miller, *The Old Capitol and Its Inmates* (New York, 1867), 66-67.

72 Wood quoted in Davis, "The 'Old Capitol' and Its Keeper," 208; *OR 2*, Series 2, 237 has a chart entitled "List of persons received at the Old Capitol Prison other than prisoners of war since the 1st of March, 1861." For the Dranesville citizens' date of arrest, Nov. 27, there are only roughly 50 names.

73 *OR 2*, Series 2, 1286.

While this whirlwind of events around Dranesville occurred, J. E. B. Stuart remained at Camp *Qui Vive*. Stuart and his staff filled their days with frivolity, and he wrote to his wife about some of the more humorous aspects. In one letter he said, "My beard flourishes like the gourd of Jonah." In another letter, Stuart thanked his brother, William, for the "splendid cheese which I received + demolished long ago."[74]

But even the good times at headquarters did not keep Stuart fully away from the matter at hand. "We still expect [McClellan] daily," he wrote to Flora. "That he will advance, there can be little doubt, but when & where—aye there's the *rub*."[75]

He would get his answer soon enough. The Pennsylvania Reserves were not finished with Dranesville. Sixteen days remained until the battle.

74 Stuart, *Letters of General J. E. B. Stuart*, 21, 23; J. E. B. Stuart to William Alexander Stuart, Jan. 6, 1862, in William A. Stuart Papers, Virginia Historical Society.

75 Stuart, *Letters of General J. E. B. Stuart*, 23.

Chapter Nine

"Move in Command of Your Brigade at 6 a.m. To-Morrow"

Planning for Battle

As November became December, temperatures continued to drop. Both armies kept working on the construction of their winter quarters, which proved beneficial when the weather turned "quite snowlike."[1]

The souring weather increasingly vexed both armies, as they sought for food and supplies not just for their men, but for their horses, mules, and oxen, too. According to the United States Army's Regulations, each horse in service was allotted "fourteen pounds of hay and twelve pounds of oats, corn, or barley" every single day. Mules were given daily rations of "fourteen pounds of hay and nine pounds of oats, corn, or barley."[2] The daily total needed for the army's sustenance reached a staggering 400 tons.[3] In the Confederate lines, commanders fretted over their inability to get enough forage, and Beauregard ordered winter structures be built to house the army's animals.[4]

It fell to the respective quartermaster generals of both armies to oversee the acquisition and distribution of these mountains of provisions. In Washington, D.C., Quartermaster General Montgomery Meigs administered his department well and became an unsung hero in the Federal war effort. Forage remained a "continuous difficulty" for Meigs and his officers. Not only did Meigs have to

---

1 Krick, *Civil War Weather in Virginia*, 42.

2 United States Army, *Revised United States Army Regulations of 1861* (Washington, D.C., 1863), 166.

3 *OR* 11, pt. 1, 157.

4 Joseph T. Glatthaar, *General Lee's Army: From Victory to Collapse* (New York, 2008), 210.

gather the supplies, but then he had to ensure there was adequate transportation to bring it to the field. His problems included soldiers discarding tens of thousands of dollars' worth of equipment during long marches, and agents and contractors continuously trying to undercut each other, resulting in fraud and poor quality of materials and food.[5]

The problem was amplified for Meigs's counterpart in Richmond, quartermaster general of the Confederate army Abraham C. Myers. A graduate of West Point, Myers found himself appointed quartermaster in the spring of 1861. Myers faced the same problems as Meigs in Washington, but Meigs at least had an infrastructure with which to work; Myers was starting from scratch. If the logistics alone were not hard enough, Myers's personality did not help. Many people saw him as "a dandy," and he "affected a lifestyle of opulence that inspired criticism." He reported directly to the Secretary of War LeRoy Walker, but their relationship soon soured, and John Jones, a clerk in Richmond, noted in his diary that the men "really hated" each other.[6]

The proximity of the armies to each other left northern Virginia stripped of food. Because it was getting more difficult gathering supplies, Federal and Confederate officers began looking beyond their lines. With Confederate forces still at Leesburg and Federals around Langley, Dranesville was square in the middle. Up until now, the fields around the town had been relatively untouched.

That changed in early December. On the third of the month, George McCall sent the brigades of John Reynolds and George Meade out of Camp Pierpont and towards Dranesville. The heavy force made its way into the countryside, the recent ambush against Bayard's cavalry still fresh in the men's minds. There were also rumors—false as it turned out—that the Confederates "have reappeared at Dranesville, where it is believed, they are entrenching themselves."[7] A soldier wrote, "We returned home in the evening, without seeing or doing anything of interest."[8]

Three days later McCall ordered a repeat excursion. Meade's brigade, accompanied by artillery and cavalry, left Camp Pierpont and headed for Dranesville. Meade had specific orders this time to head for the home of John Gunnell, where there was reportedly plenty of forage for the taking. Furthermore, two of Gunnell's nephews, John and George Coleman, were supposedly there. The

---

5 Sherrod E. East, "Montgomery C. Meigs and the Quartermaster Department," in *Military Affairs* 25, No. 4 (Winter, 1961-1962): 187, 192; Robert O'Harrow Jr., *The Quartermaster: Montgomery C. Meigs, Lincoln's General, Master Builder of the Union Army* (New York, 2016), 125, 136.

6 Harold S. Wilson, *Confederate Industry: Manufacturers and Quartermasters in the Civil War* (Jackson, 2002), 4-11; Jones, *A Rebel War Clerk's Diary: Vol. 1*, 61.

7 *The Press*, Dec. 4, 1861.

8 *The Globe*, Dec. 12, 1861.

Coleman men were rumored to have taken part in the ambush at Lowe's Island but had thus far proved elusive to Federal patrols. The Federals did not expect much resistance, but rumors continued that the Confederate army was also making plans to gather fodder from Gunnell's rich fields, creating urgency for Meade's men.[9] They arrived at the house around noon.[10]

The Pennsylvanians' intelligence had been correct: they found both John and George Coleman, and soon packed them off to Washington. Both Colemans joined the other Dranesville men sitting in the Old Capitol Prison. The newcomers were charged with "Aiding and comforting the Insurgents, + oppressing Union men," in George's case and "Procuring recruits for [the] Insurgent army," in John's.[11] At this point, the Coleman family's genealogy thoroughly confused Federal officials; in correspondence gathered later, John is noted as having the alias "Richard." Except they had made a mistake—there were in fact two locals named Richard Coleman. One was John's younger brother, the other was a cousin who had recently moved to Virginia from Missouri. Federal forces also arrested the Missouri-transplant Richard, but sheepishly let him go once it became obvious there had been an embarrassing mix-up.[12]

With the arrest of the Colemans accomplished, the Pennsylvanians turned to the other matter at hand. One soldier wrote to his local newspaper, "We took, I suppose, about five hundred bushels of corn, one hundred bushels of potatoes, twenty-five or thirty hogs, quite an amount of wheat, an ox-team and a number of horses." The soldiers went beyond just filling the army's wagons. They took for themselves "several private appropriations of turkeys, chickens, ducks, and other necessaries of camp life."[13] Five of the eight horses taken were pressed into service by Lt. Charles Campbell from the Pennsylvania Light Artillery, and the artillerists even found a "spring wagon" that they took as well.[14] At the end of the expedition, an artillerist wrote, "We got everything that we wanted, except a fight, and we're in hopes of getting that the next time."[15]

9 *OR* 5, 455; Meade, *Life and Letters of George Gordon Meade*: Vol. 1, 234.

10 Krick, *Civil War Weather in Virginia*, 42; Meade, *Life and Letters of George Gordon Meade*: Vol. 1 234.

11 *OR* 2, Series 2, 1287; *Proceedings of the Commission Relating to State Prisoners*, Vol. 1, RG 59, NARA.

12 See Fairfax 1860 County Census for brothers John and Richard Coleman. See *Proceedings of the Commission Relating to State Prisoners*, Vol. 1, RG 59, Richard Coleman Case File, 50, for the Missourian's brief trial (hereafter Richard Coleman Case File).

13 *The Alleghanian*, Dec. 19, 1861.

14 *The Globe*, Dec. 12, 1861.

15 Ibid.

Just a couple of miles from John Gunnell lived his brother, James. Both men were off in the Confederate army, and the Pennsylvanians found James's home ripe for the picking. The soldiers loaded another "forty-three wagons with provisions" but were prevented from taking anything else by James's wife, Catherine, who stood "barring the way to the cellar of the house when the Yankees tried to take her last ham." The Pennsylvanians let her be and finished their foraging elsewhere on the property.[16] Meade's men returned to Camp Pierpont, bringing with them not only the brimming wagons but also two of John Gunnell's enslaved men, who used the Reserves' presence to secure their freedom.[17]

Back in camp, Meade contemplated the march to Gunnell's and wrote to his wife, shamefully reflecting on the soldiers' actions. "I never had a more disagreeable duty in my life to perform," the general wrote. "The great difficulty was to prevent the wanton and useless destruction of property which could not be made available for military purposes." Meade went on, "The men and officers got into their heads that the object of the expedition was the punishment of a rebel, and hence the more injury they inflicted, the more successful was the expedition, and it was with considerable trouble they could be prevented from burning everything." He continued, "it made me sad to do such injury, and I really was ashamed of our cause, which thus required war to be made on individuals."[18]

An officer with 26 years of experience, and a member of the army's conservative core, Meade's sentiments are not that surprising. He fell into line politically with men like George McClellan and Charles Stone. The reigning thought among them was to wage war against the enemy's army, not the enemy's people.[19] However, there were surely no tears shed by the area's Unionists, who had spent the year fearing for their lives because of John Gunnell and his colleagues' actions. The Pennsylvania Reserves had been to Dranesville in force at least four times.

Once during its October reconnaissance, a second time led by George Bayard, and now the two foraging expeditions on December 3rd and 6th. Added to that were near-daily smaller patrols, both by cavalry and infantry. The next time the Pennsylvanians returned to Dranesville in substantial size would be December 20, and then they would find themselves engaged in battle.

<hr>

16 Tanya Edwards Beauchamp and Karen Washburn, "National Register of Historical Places—Nomination Form: William Gunnell House," (2002), 14.

17 Joseph Gibbs, *Three Years in the Bloody Eleventh: The Campaigns of a Pennsylvania Reserve Regiment* (University Park, PA, 2002), 65.

18 Meade, *Life and Letters of George Gordon Meade.* Vol. 1, 234.

19 For more on the evolving Federal approach to the war and civilians, see Mark Grimsley, *The Hard Hand of War: Union Military Policy Toward Southern Civilians, 1861-1865* (Cambridge, 1997).

Brigadier General D. H. Hill
LOC

---

*   *   *

The Federal excursions into the countryside proved vexing for the Confederate commander in Leesburg. After his victory at Ball's Bluff, Col. Nathan Evans received a promotion and transfer. His replacement, Brig. Gen. D. H. Hill, arrived on December 4, and now had the task of finding a way to stop the Union soldiers' raids.[20]

Hill had just one brigade of infantry at Leesburg, limiting his options. He pushed pickets down the Leesburg & Alexandria Turnpike to keep eyes on the blue-clad soldiers, but those pickets were in no position to start a fight. "Successful foraging parties of the enemy constantly depredate around Dranesville," Hill wrote to Beauregard on December 16.[21]

Hill did not get much help from his superiors in Centreville. Joseph Johnston responded, "We are too far to be able to give him assistance after an attack is begun and too weak to send him re-enforcements whilst there is an uncertainty as to the point of attack." Beauregard "concur[red] fully with these views."[22]

Receiving less-than-helpful instructions from his commanding officers, Hill still sought ways to prevent the Federals from getting the forage in Dranesville, or, even better, to recover it himself. Part of the problem, Confederate officials figured, were the Unionists in the area helping the Federal cause.

In late November, just three days after Bayard's raid, Confederate authorities arrested several Unionist civilians and sent them to Richmond. One of these locals was a man named Edward Johnson, "residing near Dranesville." Now, a month later, Hill planned a similar roundup.[23]

---

20 Hal Bridges, *Lee's Maverick General: Daniel Harvey Hill* (Lincoln, NE, 1961), 30; *OR* 5, Series 2, 981.

21 *OR* 5, 999.

22 Ibid., 1000.

23 *Richmond Daily Dispatch*, Nov. 30, 1861.

Or at least that is what came out of the rumor mill. Back in Dranesville, it would have been a fair assessment to say nearly all the men were gone. Between Unionists fleeing, Confederate-sympathizers enlisting, and the remainder getting arrested by Union or Confederate forces, the town was fully in the hands of its women. And they, just like everyone else, wanted to get involved.

One of these women, Jane Crippen, had married Minor Crippen in 1852. By 1860, they lived just north of the town with their two young children.[24] After Virginia's secession, Minor's Unionist opinions became known, and he soon fled to Washington with his neighbors Nelson Voorhees and Henry Bishop.[25] Jane remained at home while, in Washington, Minor and Voorhees became guides for the Federal forces. Routinely Crippen and Voorhees snuck back towards Dranesville, gathering intelligence to bring back to Washington. If Jane heard anything around town that she wanted to pass along, "she would come to the window and raise it a little and talk to us so that nobody could hear if there was anybody hiding outside," Voorhees testified after the war.[26] And in the middle of December, Jane had plenty to say.

She told them that the Confederates "were coming at such a time to get all the forage in our neighborhood and were going to turn all the Union people out of doors." According to Voorhees, the trio had their secret window meeting on Tuesday, December 17. The two men raced back east, heading straight for Camp Pierpont.[27]

George McCall, not one to believe idle gossip, sent Voorhees back to Dranesville "two or three times to ascertain if it was the fact" over the following days.[28] Each time Voorhees returned to Langley and affirmed the news: Confederates were planning any day to come to Dranesville to try and collect forage. All that remained to be known was *when.*

While McCall waited for more information, his counterpart, D. H. Hill, was still deliberating how to get a force to Dranesville to retrieve the forage. If Johnston and Beauregard could not send reinforcements, and Hill could not abandon Leesburg per his orders, then he would have to find someone else to go. J. E. B. Stuart, commander of the Advance Outposts, seemed to fit the bill.

*   *   *

---

24 Sprouse, Volume 1, 415.

25 See Chapter Four.

26 Voorhees Testimony, Minor Crippen Southern Claims, 8-9.

27 Ibid.

28 Ibid.

As the commanders studied their maps and made plans, their soldiers continued with their day-to-day lives in camps from Washington to Centreville. They played, they wrote home, they drilled, and for one individual, they challenged others to duels.

Thomas Kane, 1st Pennsylvania Rifles, lay in bed at Willard's Hotel in Washington with a high fever. Kane thought the fever so bad it would soon kill him, writing to his brother in Philadelphia, "Come on at once. The game is up."[29] But the fever did not preclude Kane from writing a challenge to his former commanding officer, Charles Biddle.

As discussed in Chapter 3, Biddle and Kane were on opposite political spectrums—Biddle a Peace Democrat, and Kane a pro-war Republican. Biddle's actions, or, in Kane's opinion, lack thereof, drove the lieutenant colonel crazy at Cumberland. Finally, it seemed that Biddle would be out of Kane's hair; elected to Congress, Biddle resigned his commission in the Pennsylvania Rifle. Then, in a letter that Biddle wrote to Democratic friends on December 6, he wrote that Republicans "had so persistently abused that part of the American people that lived across a geographical line that they had come, at last, to underrate and despise them, and Republican oratory summoned its hearers . . . only to pay and pillage."[30]

Other officers steamed at Biddle's words. George Bayard wrote that Biddle "made an ass of himself." Captain Charles F. Taylor, a company commander in the Bucktails, wrote, "I was greatly astonished to read his letter."[31]

Kane went further. On December 17, he wrote to Biddle from his sick bed: "My time has come. The acceptance of your resignation places you out of the protection of the Articles of War. If you can shoot me, I will not have you sent to Fort Lafayette. If you do not, I shall denounce you as a traitor and intriguer as well as an ingrate and a liar." Kane gave the letter to Bayard, who agreed to act as Kane's second in the coming duel.[32]

Biddle did not answer. Kane, growing angrier, wrote a day later, "The least dishonorary inference I can draw is that you fear to suffer me to be the challenged party. You shall have every advantage. Name your own arms and terms, with time and place of meeting." And still Biddle ignored the feverish Kane. Events soon to transpire took Kane's attention away from his challenge.[33]

---

29 Thomas Kane Papers, Box 20, Folder 4, Item 6, BYU.

30 *Northumberland County Democrat*, Dec. 6, 1861.

31 Charles F. Hobson, et al., "Colonel of the Bucktails: Civil War Letters of Charles Frederick Taylor," in *The Pennsylvania Magazine of History and Biography* 97, No. 3 (Jul. 1973): 343.

32 Thomas Kane Papers, Box 20, Folder 4, Item 9, BYU.

33 Ibid.

Across the lines, soldiers did not have nearly so eventful a couple days as Kane. Some, in fact, did not even want to be soldiers anymore. Frank English enlisted in the 6th South Carolina even before Fort Sumter was fired on. It seems, though, that English was growing tired of it all. When the prospect of war had been fresh and exciting, thousands like himself had rushed to the service. Now, after months of picket duty and sicknesses, that adrenaline wore off. In early November, English wrote home, requesting his father to ask politicians in Columbia, "concerning my discharge." In another letter, written on November 22, he again asked that his father request a discharge, wanting to resume his school studies. In a subsequent letter, English specified all that needed to be done was for his father to write to James Chesnut, who could then write to the 6th South Carolina's commanding officer. "I would like to be home about Christmas," English pleaded. On December 17, English wrote his last letter before the battle of Dranesville. He did not ask again about a furlough, but simply spoke about camp matters: "The troops here are [now] principally engrossed in bedding Winter Quarters & throwing up entrenchments." He finished the letter by passing along well wishes from his uncles, company commanders in the 6th, "in love to you all."[34]

While Frank English hoped for a discharge, 2nd Lt. Benjamin Ashenfelter, Company G, 6th Pennsylvania Reserves, went into Washington, D.C., on December 19. With some money in his pocket, he set off in search of a sword. He soon found one, and wrote home, "I paid $15 for it at the government store." In just twenty-four hours he would draw it in battle.[35]

At Camp Pierpont, the Pennsylvanians were restless. Their cavalry went out on patrols, but the three brigades of infantry did not have much to do. Officers tried to find ways to keep their men busy. During the afternoon of December 19, the 2nd Reserves, Reynolds's brigade, "practiced with blank cartridges," and the 12th Reserves, Ord's brigade, received orders to "parade for Battalion drill this day at 1.30 P.M."[36]

Not all the soldiers had to drill, though. Private A. F. Hill, 8th Reserves, wrote that on December 19, with nothing else to do, a comrade said, "Come boys, let's have a little game of foot-ball." According to Hill, "About two hundred followed," and "The centre was soon agreed upon; also the goals, which were the extreme ends of the field." With the field laid out "Soon the ball was going—kick, bat,

---

34 Frank English Letters, Nov. 12, 1861, Nov. 22, 1861, Dec. 3, 1861, Dec. 17, 1861, USC.

35 Benjamin Ashenfelter to his mother, Jan. 3, 1862, Harrisburg Civil War Round Table Collection, USAHEC.

36 Woodward, *Our Campaigns*, 74; Regimental Letter and Order Book, Vol. 2, Entry for Dec. 19, 12th PA Reserves, NARA.

spang, and away it would go—now back, now forth—now to, now fro—hither and thither." Hill played until he accidentally kicked a root sticking up from the ground and sheepishly admitted, "I didn't play any more foot-ball *that* day."[37] The soldiers, many not much older than mere boys, were having their fun. Perhaps in the frenzy of the ball game they did not see the courier ride into camp.

Throughout the day, Company F of the 1st Pennsylvania Reserve Cavalry was posted out of town. Through the grapevine those soldiers heard about an impending Confederate raid into Dranesville, and one of the troopers raced back to Camp Pierpont to tell McCall.[38]

Two days earlier, Nelson Voorhees and Minor Crippen had reported to McCall about the rumored enemy presence around Dranesville, and now he had confirmation from his own division. The general immediately started to make plans for the next day.

McCall wrote to Gen. McClellan that he figured the Confederates "had advanced to within 4 or 5 miles of our lines and carried off two good Union men and plundered and threatened others." McCall's intentions, as he told McClellan, were "to surround and capture this party, and at the same time to collect a supply of forage from the farms of some of the rank secessionists in that vicinity." In other words, he planned to return to John Gunnell's home.[39]

Perhaps because Reynolds and Meade had already been to Dranesville on previous occasions, and possibly because he wanted Ord to have the same experience, McCall decided to send his Third Brigade on the expedition. Ord received his instructions that evening. McCall's intentions were laid out in extreme detail and are worth copying in their entirety:

> GENERAL: You will please move in command of your brigade at 6 a.m. to-morrow, on the Leesburg Pike, in the direction of Dranesville. The First Rifles, Pennsylvania Reserves, Lieutenant-Colonel Kane, have been ordered to form right in front on the pike near Commodore Jones' house and await your arrival, when the commanding officer will report to you for further orders. Captain Easton's battery has been directed to form on the left of the Rifles. The captain will report to you for orders. Two squadrons of cavalry will also be placed under your command. The senior officer will report to you this evening for orders. Sherman, the guide, will likewise report to you for duty. The object of this

---

37 A. F. Hill, *Our Boys: The Personal Experience of a Soldier in the Army of the Potomac* (Philadelphia, 1865), 169-170.

38 Lucas, *I Seat Myself to Write You*, 46.

39 *OR* 5, 474.

expedition is twofold: In the first place, to drive back the enemy's pickets, which have recently advanced within 4 or 5 miles of our lines (leaving a force of about 70 cavalry at Henderson's), and carried off two good Union men, and threatened others; and, secondly, to procure a supply of forage. It has to-day been reported to me that there is a force of about 100 cavalry lying between Dranesville and the river. This force might be captured or routed by sending a regiment of infantry up the pike beyond their position, to strike their rear by a flank movement to the right, while your disposable cavalry, after picketing the cross-roads near Dickey's, might move near the river, and attack them in front or on the left. Should you not arrive at Dickey's in time to make this movement and leave the ground on you[r] return before nightfall, it must not be undertaken, as I do not wish any part of your command to remain out over night. The forage will be procured at Gunnell's or at some other rank secessionists in the neighborhood of Dickey's. Direct your quartermaster to confine the selection of forage to corn and hay. Captain Hall will have charge of the wagon train. The regiment intended to move forward from Dickey's (if you think proper, Jackson's) might ride in the wagons as far as Dickey's, and then be fresh for the forward movement. I am, very respectfully, your obedient servant, Geo. A. McCall.[40]

Orders in hand, Ord passed fresh instructions down to his regimental commanders. His brigade—the 6th, 9th, 10th, and 12th Reserves—all received similar instructions. "This Brigade will march tomorrow morning at 6 O'clock a.m. armed and equipped with forty (40) rounds of ammunition and one days rations, cooked, canteens filled with coffee or tea, toward Drainesville," Ord commanded. "The Capts. will form their companies before 6 A.M. The Doctors will accompany the Regiments with ambulances and attendants. . . . Regiments will march without music except the drummers and each to sound calls."[41]

While the men of Ord's brigade prepared their packs, McCall ordered Reynolds to take his brigade as far as Difficult Run, east of town, "to be ready to support Ord in the event of his meeting a force stronger than his own."[42]

It seemed all was set for the morning. Anxious soldiers lay down in their tents to try to get some sleep. For some, it was their last sunset.

*   *   *

40 Ibid., 480-481.

41 Records of the Adjutant General's Office Book Records of Volunteer Union Organizations 6th PA Reserve Infantry Regimental Letter, Order Book, Volume 2, 12th PA Reserve Infantry, Dec. 19, 1861.

42 *OR* 5, 474.

Other soldiers were getting ready that night, too. These men wore gray and butternut uniforms, and their camps were scattered about Centreville. As the day wore on, four regiments of infantry received orders to prepare for a march in the morning.

Unlike George McCall and Edward Ord, there is not much of a paper trail when it comes to J. E. B. Stuart's preparations for his movement to Dranesville. In his after-action report, Stuart wrote, "I was placed in command of four regiments of infantry, 150 cavalry troopers, and a battery of four pieces of artillery," but he did not specify *who* put him in command of those forces. Stuart wrote later that he went for the "purpose of covering an expedition of all the wagons of our army that could be spared (after hay) to the left of Dranesville."[43]

Because Stuart never explicitly laid out who gave him the command of the various regiments, it is left to historians to speculate, though there is strong evidence that D. H. Hill at least suggested the expedition. It was Hill who knew of the plentiful forage in the area, and it was Hill who knew that if someone did not go get it, the Federals would fill their wagons first. After the battle, Stuart's first dispatch was not addressed to Beauregard or Johnston, but to Hill. If Hill had not coordinated with Stuart, why would the latter have even written to him at all?[44]

Aside from his regular brigade of cavalry troopers, Stuart's command fluctuated constantly, as regiments rotated on and off picket duty. The infantry that accompanied Stuart on his march were regiments whose turn had come up on the picket line. They were the 1st Kentucky, 6th South Carolina, 10th Alabama, and 11th Virginia. Only the Kentuckians, who had attacked Mason's Hill in late September, and the Virginians, who had fought at Blackburn's Ford on July 18, were veterans of any fighting. The 6th South Carolina, though in service the longest, had still not seen any action beyond some potshots on the picket line, and the 10th Alabama likewise lacked experience. Within 24 hours, all four regiments could, with confidence, say they had seen the elephant.[45]

Alongside the infantry, Stuart planned to bring a cavalry contingent with him. He grabbed 100 men from the 1st North Carolina Cavalry and 50 more from the 2nd Virginia—both units of Stuart's cavalry brigade. The Virginians were

---

43 Ibid., 490.

44 Ibid. A scouring of Stuart's personal papers at the Virginia Historical Society reveals nothing in his writings to either confirm or deny the theory. Pending the discovery of a long-lost piece of paper from Stuart going more in depth about his preparations prior to Dranesville, only guesswork remains.

45 "Seeing the elephant"—the experience of combat—was a common expression used by both sides; Glatthaar, *General Lee's Army*, 318; McPherson, *Battle Cry of Freedom*, 409.

commanded by Capt. Andrew Pitzer and the North Carolinians by Maj. James B. Gordon. As the senior officer, Gordon would command both detachments.[46]

To complete his expedition, Stuart needed artillery. For that, he rode towards the Stone Bridge on the Manassas battlefield where Battery A, 11th Georgia—the Sumter Flying Artillery—had its headquarters. He arrived in camp "in full uniform and riding a magnificent charger," Pvt. Felix Callaway of the Georgian battery remembered.[47]

Stuart met with the battery's commander, Capt. Allen S. Cutts, an experienced veteran of the Mexican War who became captain of the Sumter Flying Artillery upon its organization at the outbreak of war. In Virginia the battery had been outfitted with captured Federal cannon from Manassas. Cutts's men had not yet seen combat, but his leadership experience was probably what brought Stuart into their camp on the evening of December 19.[48]

Stuart explained the situation. Felix Callaway, eavesdropping, wrote later that Stuart said, "he had found out where was stored away a fine lot of forage," and interestingly added, "that he had permission from Gen. Beauregard to go and get it." Stuart told Cutts that Beauregard's instructions were "to take with him what artillery he would need." To give the go-ahead for Cutts to leave, Stuart wanted a courier from the battery to ride to Joe Johnston's headquarters and get permission from the army commander.[49]

There is nothing, at least nothing yet found, from Beauregard to Stuart concerning the march to Dranesville. One reporter, researching the battle for an article after the war, wrote angrily that "Johnston says nothing about the Battles of Dranesville . . . nor does Beauregard." Thus, the only account of Beauregard's blessing comes from Callaway.[50]

---

46 *OR* 5, 490; James B. Gordon to his mother, Dec. 23, 1861, Gordon Papers, North Carolina State Archives.

47 Felix Callaway, *The Bloody Links* (Shreveport, LA, 1907), 29. One may wonder why Stuart did not have John Pelham with him at Dranesville. Pelham would make himself a hero of the Confederacy because of his exploits in 1862 and early 1863, but in the winter of 1861, he was still a lieutenant struggling for a command. The Horse Artillery battery that Pelham would lead with excellence had been approved by the Confederate War Department, but he was still recruiting for it and bringing it up to strength. Pelham had even gone back to his home state of AL, "in late December 1861 or early January 1862," and thus may not have been in camp when the battle of Dranesville took place; see Robert J. Trout, *Galloping Thunder: The Stuart Horse Artillery Battalion* (Mechanicsburg, PA, 2002), 25.

48 Speicher, *The Sumter Flying Artillery*, 30-31; *OR Supplement*, Pt. 2, Vol. 5, 698.

49 Callaway, *The Bloody Links*, 30.

50 Henry T. Owen Letters, Folder 10, Library of Virginia.

Cutts agreed to send a rider to Johnston though he "would not send his courier as he was a mere boy," Callaway wrote later. Cutts instead picked Callaway "as I was older and could stand more." Borrowing a horse from the battery's orderly, Callaway set off. "It was then dark and cold, almost beyond endurance," he remembered.[51]

While Callaway rode off into the night, some soldiers remained unaware of what was in their future. Nearby, in the camp of the 6th South Carolina, Pvt. R. Wade Brice wrote a letter to a friend. Brice, hoping to get the letter sent off, quickly jotted, "Wishing you a Merry Christmas," and signed it. But then, below his signature, is a P.S.: "I got in too late for the mail to day. We have just got orders to be ready to march tomorrow morning at 5 o'clock with one day's rations. I suppose as we report to Genl. Stewart, the commander of the outposts, we are going out on a scout & may have a brush with the Yankees."[52]

Meanwhile, Felix Callaway continued to ride. It was only a few miles from the Sumter Flying Artillery's camp to Centreville, but it took Callaway most of the night. "I came near freezing," he wrote later. But eventually, well into the night, Callaway found Johnston. Due to the lateness of the hour, Callaway probably found his way to Johnston's headquarters, the Four Chimneys, a home owned by Alexander S. Grigsby. Johnston had used the Grigsby home as his headquarters since October, though he was also known to use another local home, known as Mt. Gilead, as his private quarters. Callaway did not specify, but the homes were almost next to one another.[53]

Johnston and Callaway did not meet for long. Giving his consent to the expedition, Johnston sent Callaway back into the night—or more accurately at this point, the very early morning. The Georgian spurred his horse towards the Stone Bridge, where J. E. B. Stuart eagerly anticipated his return.

It was Friday, December 20, 1861. The countdown had reached zero.

---

51 Callaway, *The Bloody Links*, 30.

52 R. Wade Brice to unidentified friend, Dec. 19, 1861, Brice, Waters, and Watson Families, USC.

53 Callaway, *The Bloody Links*, 30; Mary Stachyra Lopez, *Centreville and Chantilly* (Charleston, SC, 2014), 32-33.

Chapter Ten

"There They Come"

The Battle of Dranesville Begins

Lieutenant Colonel James B. Martin, the 36-year-old second-in-command of the 10th Alabama Infantry, knelt in prayer. Martin was a well-respected lawyer back in Talladega County, and in 1860 was elected as a judge to the circuit court. When the 10th Alabama was formed in the spring of 1861, Martin's popularity led to his election as lieutenant colonel. He had recently "obtained a leave of absence from the army to hold his courts," but refused to leave as his regiment prepared to depart in the chilly morning hours of December 20. As Martin finished his prayer he turned to a friend and "expressed the conviction that the last day of his life had dawned, and he was prepared for it."[1] Martin joined his commander, Col. John Forney, as the 10th Alabama formed up. Soldiers shuffled in the cold darkness—it was near freezing and sunrise would not be for another three hours.[2]

Stuart's infantry slowly made its way out of the camps and headed for a rendezvous on the road out of Centreville. It was "three or four miles," as Lt. John Bratton wrote, and just enough of a march for the soldiers to start warming up.[3]

The exhausted Felix Callaway was nearing the end of his long night, noting that "the road was filled with troops." He rode up to Stuart and reached for a slip of paper that Johnston had given him. Captain Allen Cutts "struck a match

---

1 W. Brewer, *Alabama: Her History, Resources, War Record, and Public Men, From 1540 to 1872* (Montgomery, AL, 1872), 543-544.

2 Krick, *Civil War Weather in Virginia*, 42.

3 Bratton, *Letters of John Bratton*, 50.

Lieutenant Colonel James B. Martin
10th Alabama Infantry
Courtesy of the Public Library of Anniston-Calhoun County, Russell Brothers Collection

and Stewart took off his cap and held it, so as to protect it from the wind," Callaway remembered.[4] Stuart and Cutts read the note from Johnston—which evidently no longer survives—before Stuart folded the piece of paper and put it in his pocket. Whatever else the note said, it gave Stuart permission to proceed. He turned in the saddle and gave the word for the column to set off. Before Capt. Cutts followed, he turned to Callaway and said, "I have some misgivings as to the outcome of this little affair."[5]

With four regiments of infantry, 150 cavalry troopers, and four guns under Cutts's command, Stuart commanded somewhere between 1,600-2,500 soldiers.[6] According to Pvt. Martin V. Moore, an orderly in the 1st North Carolina Cavalry, most of those soldiers did not share Capt. Cutts's pessimism. "The men were all in high spirits," he wrote, "All anxious to get away from the dull monotony of the winter quarters."[7]

At the front of Stuart's column rumbled, as he put it, "all the wagons of our army that could be spared." They numbered—depending on the sources—anywhere between 200 and 400 wagons. All were currently empty but, if the day went well, they would soon be stacked high with corn and hay.[8] Those wagons,

---

4 Callaway, *The Bloody Links*, 30.

5 Ibid., 31.

6 Stuart claimed in his official report that he led 1,600 soldiers during the day. *OR* 5, 490; Lieutenant J. Lawrence Meem, the adjutant of the 11th Virginia, guessed there were about 2,000 Confederates, while a newspaper correspondent in camp pegged Stuart at closer to 2,500; *Richmond Whig*, Dec. 27, 1861; *The Richmond Daily Dispatch*, Dec. 23, 1861.

7 *Atlanta Constitution*, Jul. 20, 1898.

8 *OR* 5, 490; *The Richmond Dispatch*, Dec. 23, 1861; *The Intelligencer*, May 1, 1901.

again according to Pvt. Moore, "seemed to insure the men with the spirit of fun and hilarity. . . . To most of the soldiers it looked like a holiday or frolic ahead."[9]

The Confederates started their 16-mile march towards Dranesville. In the Centreville camps, soldiers listened to the expedition's departure. "The tramp of infantry, the clatter of cavalry, the rumbling artillery, and the rattling of a long train of empty wagons jolting over the rough, hard frozen roads in the early dawn echoed through the dark forests," one of these soldiers wrote. The noise went "down the gloomy bottom and over the hills for miles away, arousing restless house dogs that barked and howled by turns."[10] Stuart's men "marched by stages of fifty minutes and rested ten," remembered a soldier in the Fincastle Rifles, Company D, 11th Virginia.[11]

The rests did not help Lt. John Bratton, whose feet were killing him. He later wrote to his wife that his "heels were blistered and sore from a march from picket a day or two before." He declared that his "miserable boots were already telling on my feet, and I threatened to turn back from that point." Bratton did not turn back, because he knew "some of my old boys . . . wanted me to be there in the hour of danger." He could not have faced himself if he allowed "my commrads to be subjected to more dangers and hardships than myself." Bratton kept walking.[12]

It was an uneventful march, the long column snaking its way out of Centreville and into the countryside. The most exciting moment came soon after the expedition set out. In the distance, "there was seen to shoot up in the northern sky a blazing rocket that went skimming along just above the horizon leaving a long comet-like tail behind for a few seconds and then suddenly disappear[ed] in darkness and gloom," an onlooker wrote. As the sparks faded back into the darkness, the Confederates figured the rocket "to be a sign between different camps of the enemy, stationed along the Potomac, apprising them of Stuart's advance in that direction."[13]

Stuart's whole column stretched close to four miles, guessed one wagon-driver. The road was, as the driver put it, "generally wide enough for teams to pass each other," but in other places, where the road crisscrossed over hills or through ravines, it was "not more than ten feet wide."[14] Lieutenant J. Lawrence Meem, the 11th Virginia's adjutant, wrote, "Our route lay on the Ox Road, crossing the Loudoun

---

9 *Atlanta Constitution*, Jul. 20, 1898.

10 Henry T. Owen Draft Article, Owen Papers, Library of Virginia.

11 Kessler, ed., *The Fincastle Rifles*, 5.

12 Bratton, *General John Bratton*, 51-52.

13 Henry T. Owen Draft Article, Owen Papers, Library of Virginia.

14 *Anderson Intelligencer*, May 1, 1901.

& Hampshire Railroad."[15] Sergeant O. B. Norvell, 1st Kentucky, remembered, "The roads [were] rough and hard frozen. I do not think any man who made that march and reached the field will ever forget it."[16]

Stuart's column closed on Dranesville from the south. His soldiers were guiding on the Centreville Road (modern-day Reston Avenue), which Sgt. Norvell called "a narrow country road, through a dense thicket of pine trees and undergrowth." Those pine trees soon proved to be the bane of the Confederate forces.[17]

Having left Centreville at 5:00 a.m., Stuart's men approached Dranesville just shy of noontime. They had marched close to sixteen miles, at an average pace of just above two miles-per-hour.[18]

Stuart wrote in his official report that he wanted to "take possession of the two turnpikes to the right of Dranesville, leading directly to the enemy's advanced posts, so as to prevent any communication of our movements reaching them." Those turnpikes were the Leesburg & Alexandria and the Leesburg & Georgetown pikes. Once he controlled the road network, Stuart would "take a position with two regiments and a section of artillery on each turnpike, also to the right of Dranesville, and close enough to their intersection to form a continuous line." With this blocking force in place, Stuart's wagons would have free reign of the farmlands west of town. As the Confederate column approached Dranesville, Stuart sent his cavalry forward to secure the town.[19]

The 150 troopers fanned out. As the Centreville Road approached Dranesville, the dense pine thickets gave way to open fields. Captain Andrew Pitzer, from the 2nd Virginia's Botetourt Dragoons, sent Pvt. James Figgat ahead to scout the town itself; the soldier spurred his horse forward and rode towards Dranesville. It was not very long, however, before he wheeled his mount and galloped back towards Pitzer. Federal soldiers were already in town, Figgat breathlessly reported. Pitzer instructed the private to find Stuart and relay what he had seen.[20]

Major James Gordon, 1st North Carolina Cavalry, spotted the Federal soldiers at almost the same time. There were multiple regiments coming from the direction of Washington, and some of them were beginning to wheel into lines of battle. Gordon told Martin Moore, his orderly, to report to Stuart. "By a very rapid ride

---

15 *Richmond Whig*, Dec. 27, 1861.

16 *The Atlanta Constitution*, Aug. 16, 1898.

17 Ibid.

18 *The Columbus Daily Sun*, Jan. 23, 1862.

19 *OR* 5, 490.

20 Michael G. Henkle, "The Botetourt Dragoons in War and Peace," University of Richmond Honors thesis (2000), 30.

I had succeeded in overtaking the general just as he was emerging from a skirt of woods south of the town," Moore wrote.[21]

Stuart, Moore said, "was apparently in a state of much agitation and deep concern." Between the couriers' reports and now seeing the scene for himself, Stuart realized his initial plan of blocking the two pikes would never work. He also realized that nearly all the army's wagons were now rumbling towards a town occupied by an enemy force of unknown strength. "Nothing lay between the enemy and the foraging parties, whom Stuart was bound to protect," wrote a staff officer. Stuart rattled off orders.[22]

First, Stuart needed to save the wagons. He sent Pitzer to recall the wagons and to secure the Leesburg & Alexandria Turnpike west of Dranesville. Pitzer's troopers were to stay with the wagons, keeping "between them and the enemy," as the drivers turned around and made their way to safety. Stuart wrote after the battle, "This duty was performed by Captain Pitzer and his gallant little detachment in the most creditable manner."[23]

While Pitzer and his 50 or so troopers dashed off after the wagons, Stuart instructed Maj. Gordon to deploy a small skirmish line to delay the Federals from coming south "until our forces could come up," a trooper wrote home. "This we did successfully."[24]

With his tiny cavalry screen deployed, Stuart then sent orders for his infantry, "still three fourths of a mile distant."[25] An orderly galloped down the Centreville Road in a flash of hooves. "A cavalryman was seen rapidly approaching," Maj. Thomas Woodward, 6th South Carolina, noted. "This, with an order to halt and load, was the first intimation we had that the enemy was near and a fight on hand." Fingers reached into cartridge boxes, teeth tore the ends of the paper off, and hands poured the powder down the muzzles of rifles. Ramrods hissed as they were drawn from their hoops and upended, thudding bullets down into barrels. Nimble fingers thumbed percussion caps on the firing cones.[26]

Once the rifles were loaded, a second order to "Fix bayonets!" rang out, recalled John Bratton. "The words sent a thrill through me that made me forget my heels and fatigue," he wrote his wife. "We advanced for some distance at double quick

---

21 *Atlanta Constitution*, Jul. 20, 1898.

22 Ibid.; Henry B. McClellan, *I Rode with Jeb Stuart: The Life and Campaigns of Major General J. E.B. Stuart* (1885; repr. Bloomington, 1994), 44.

23 *OR* 5, 491.

24 *Weekly State Journal*, Jan. 8, 1862.

25 McClellan, *I Rode with Jeb Stuart*, 44.

26 Woodward, *From Fort Sumter to Dranesville*, 24.

time, until we came in sight of the enemy's pickets." Ahead of them, the 11th Virginia, the first infantry to arrive, had already begun to deploy.[27]

The wagons were being sent to safety, the cavalry deployed in a screen, and the infantry coming up in haste. Now Stuart sent word for Capt. Cutts, at the rear of the column, to bring up his four guns. "We were not slow by any means in executing our order. We brought our pieces to 'action front,'" Sgt. Eli Bozemen wrote.[28]

Cutts's battery of four cannon consisted of one outdated 6-pounder, one 12-pounder howitzer, and two 3-inch Ordnance Rifles. The rifles had been borrowed for the day from the Jeff Davis Artillery to give Cutts a little more fire power.[29] Trying to unlimber in the confines of the Centreville Road and among the thick pines proved difficult for the Georgian gunners.

Meanwhile, at the front came the sharp crack of rifles as the skirmishers of both armies ran into each other.

* * *

Edward Ord's column had departed Camp Pierpont close to 6:00 a.m., about an hour after Stuart left Centreville. It consisted of Ord's entire brigade— the 6th, 9th, 10th, and 12th Reserves. The 1st Pennsylvania Rifles were also attached for the day, alongside Battery A, 1st Pennsylvania Artillery, led by Capt. Hezekiah Easton, and two squadrons of the 1st Pennsylvania Reserve Cavalry. As the bleary-eyed soldiers dragged themselves out of their quarters, they "had no time to get breakfast or rations," remembered Sgt. Charles Becker, 9th Reserves, before being ordered to form into marching columns.[30]

Ord arranged his regiments with the cavalry in front. Colonel George Bayard, who had raided Dranesville in November, was in Washington that morning, leaving Lt. Col. Jacob Higgins to command the two squadrons of troopers.[31]

Behind the cavalry were the 1st Pennsylvania Rifles—the "Bucktails"—who were astonished to find their lieutenant colonel, Thomas Kane, mounted and waiting. Kane, still extremely feverish, had demanded "promises from a friend and his surgeon to advise him should marching orders be received." In his zeal to get to the front, he "had nothing to eat or drink all day except a bite from a

27 Bratton, *Letters of John Bratton*, 51; *Richmond Whig*, Dec. 27, 1861.

28 *The Columbus Daily Sun*, Jan. 23, 1862. The identity of Bozeman is surmised in Speicher, *The Sumter Flying Artillery*, 49.

29 Speicher, *The Sumter Flying Artillery*, 39, 41; Lawrence R. Laboda, *From Selma to Appomattox: The History of the Jeff Davis Artillery* (New York, 1994), 12-13.

30 *OR* 5, 477; Sgt. Charles Becker quoted in Ent, *The Pennsylvania Reserves in the Civil War*, 30.

31 *The National Tribune*, Jul. 2, 1903.

pie", an orderly remembered. But Kane refused to miss a fight if his Bucktails would be there.[32]

After the Bucktails came, in order, the 9th, 10th, 6th, and 12th Reserves. Per McCall's orders, Capt. Chandler Hall, quartermaster for the division, oversaw the 38 wagons going along with the expedition, at the rear of the column. Once the column got moving, "Each regiment threw out two companies of flankers on each side of the column to scour the woods and prevent a surprise."[33]

Unlike Stuart's column, where one can only make educated guesses on the number of soldiers present, Ord's numbers are easily discernible. On December 12, Pvt. James Chadwick, 9th Reserves, copied in a letter home the returns from McCall's division, listing strengths for every regiment. Ord's brigade, Chadwick wrote, totaled 3,766 soldiers; each regiment averaged 940 men. Chadwick did not subtract from his numbers those men sick or on detached duty, but even factoring those, it would be fair to say Ord's brigade numbered over 3,000 men on December 20. Added to that were the 900 or so Bucktails, 500 cavalry troopers, and the 105 artillerists manning the four guns in Easton's battery—two 24-pounder howitzers and two 12-pounder Napoleons. In total, Edward Ord led an estimated 4,500 men out of Camp Pierpont. He outnumbered J. E. B. Stuart by, at best, 2,900 men, and at worst, a still-impressive 2,000 soldiers.[34]

As the cavalry and Bucktails marched, the 9th Reserves hitched rides in the wagons that Capt. Hall would soon fill with forage. Sergeant Charles Becker referenced "the pretty rough country ride," but the bumps were not enough to dampen the Pennsylvanians' spirits. Private Alexander Murdoch, of the Pittsburgh Rifles, said later the soldiers made, "the echoes ring with 'We'll hang Jeff Davis on a sour apple tree, We'll hang Jeff Davis on a sour apple tree, We'll hang Jeff Davis on a sour apple tree as we go marching on.'" General Ord galloped up beside the wagons and hushed the soldiers, saying, "Boys, you make too much noise; when you meet the enemy pounce upon him like a wildcat."[35]

---

32 Rauch and Thomson, *"Bucktails"*, 73-74; Kane Papers, Box 20, Folder 5, Item 26, BYU.

33 Sypher, *The Alleghanian*, 130; The number of wagons is given by McCall in *OR* 5, 476.

34 James Chadwick to his father, Dec. 12, 1861, Allegheny College. The specifics of the regiments were: 6th Reserves: 957, 9th Reserves: 977, 10th Reserves: 974, 12th Reserves: 858, 1st Rifles: 905 and 1st PA Cavalry: 897, though only half accompanied Ord. In his report, Col. John Taggart, 12th Reserves, wrote his regiment numbered 575 on the day of the battle, *OR* 5, 487. The strength of Easton's Battery comes from "Book Records of Volunteer Union Organizations, 1st Pennsylvania Light Artillery, Morning Reports, Companies A to H and Recruits, Volume 6," Morning Report Dec. 20, 1861, NARA. Easton's armament is given in Sypher, *Pennsylvania Reserve Corps*, 113.

35 Becker quoted in Ent, *The Pennsylvania Reserves in the Civil War*, 31; Alexander Murdoch, "The Pittsburgh Rifles and the Battle of Dranesville," in *The Western Pennsylvania Historical Magazine* 53, No. 3 (July 1970): 301-302.

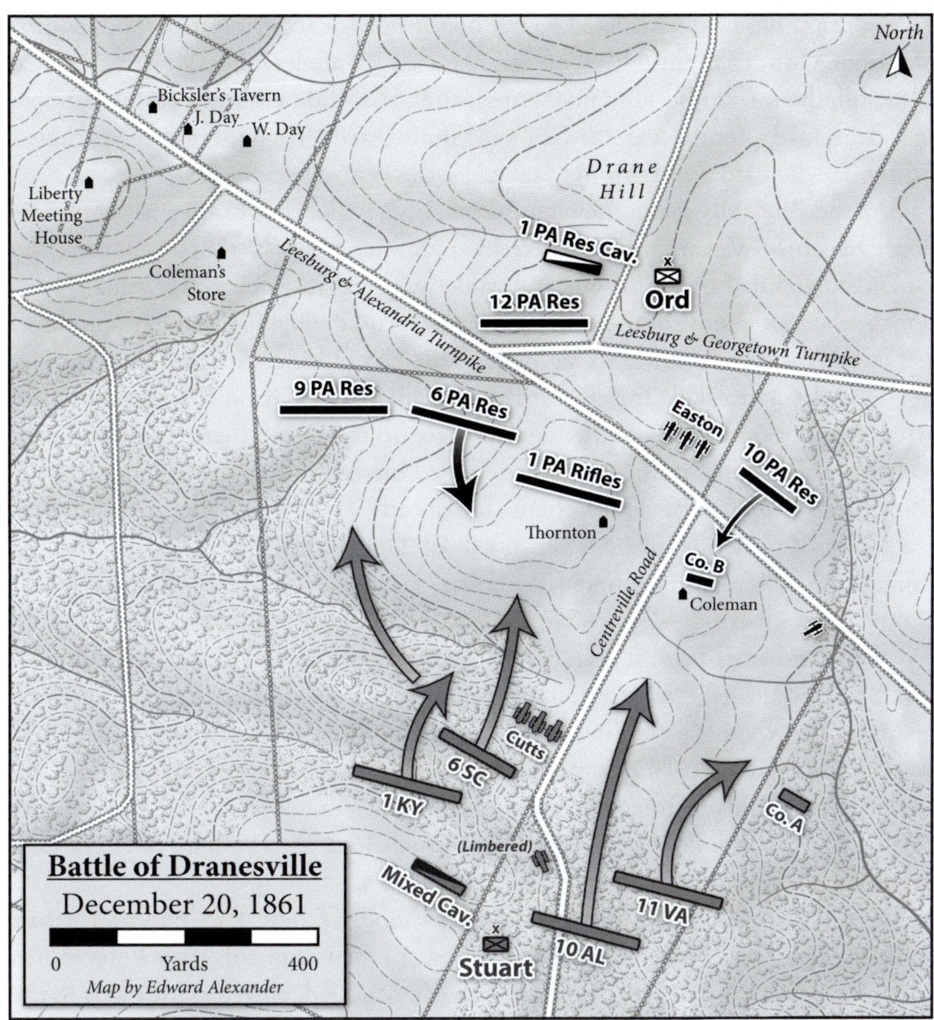

Ord's column made good time, arriving at John Gunnell's home without issue. Here, under the supervision of Capt. Hall, Ord left three companies of the 10th Reserves and some cavalry to help load the wagons. Two other companies from the 10th had stayed behind at Camp Pierpont on picket duty, and the 2nd Platoon of Company B, misunderstanding its orders, mistakenly stayed at Gunnell's as well. The rump of the 10th, just four and a half companies, continued with Col. John McCalmont towards Dranesville.[36]

36 *OR* 5, 478. The three companies of the 10th Reserves that stayed at Gunnell's were E, F, and G. The companies back on picket duty were H and K. That left 1st Platoon, Company B, and Companies A, C, D, and I to fight in the battle; *OR Supplement*, Pt. 2, Vol. 78, 582-583.

Continuing, Ord instructed Kane to veer north, "scouring the woods south" of Minor Crippen's, and checking for reported Confederate cavalry in the area. Although the Bucktails found no Confederates, they did not return empty handed. In a claim filed after the war, the Crippen family listed, "Bacon, Preserves, Sickkles, Butter, Fowls, Lard, [and] Honey" taken by the Pennsylvanians.[37]

As the Bucktails made their return to Dranesville, they also came across the home of James W. Farr, guided there by a familiar face—Nathaniel Hanna. The Unionist, who had fled his home and whose wife was threatened by William Day, now worked as a guide for the Federal army.[38] Accused of taking part in the ambush at Lowe's Island, Farr had thus far avoided the fate of his compatriots languishing in the Old Capitol Jail. But as the Pennsylvanians arrived on his property, they arrested Farr. Soon after, another courier rode up to Kane, ordering him to hurry to Dranesville. Kane, reading the note, "raised himself in his stirrups and gave the command: 'Forward, Bucktails, there's fun ahead.'"[39]

While Kane's riflemen scouted north of Dranesville, Ord's cavalry and the vanguard of his infantry entered the town. His men moved through town and climbed the small ridge on which the Liberty Meeting House sat. He borrowed a pair of field glasses from a staff officer and used them to scan the ground in front. Ord could see "the occasional appearance of a few mounted men on a slope behind some woods in a hollow to my left and front" and he "felt pretty sure there was a force there preparing some mischief." He directed his infantry to left face, which reformed his regiments from road column—four abreast—into a two-rank battle line. Now the Pennsylvanians were poised along the Leesburg & Alexandria Turnpike, facing south.[40]

Ord was still waiting for Easton's guns, and he only had two and a half regiments (the half being the few remaining companies of the 10th Reserves) in battle line. The 9th Reserves were further back, having deployed skirmishers in the pines straddling the Centreville Road. Feeling uneasy about the situation, Ord sent word for his regimental commanders to pull back through town and reform near the intersection of the Leesburg & Alexandria and Leesburg & Georgetown Pikes. At the same time, he directed one of his orderlies to go find Kane's Bucktails and bring them back to the town. It was probably this movement of troops that Capt. Andrew Pitzer and his troopers saw as they rode forward to scout the town.

---

37 *OR* 5, 481; Minor Crippen Southern Claims.

38 *OR* 5, 481; Castleman, *Reminiscences of an Oldest Inhabitant*, 17.

39 Rauch and Thomson, *"Bucktails"*, 75, Francis John King to unknown recipient, Dec. 26, 1861, Author's Collection.

40 *Carlisle Herald*, Jan. 1, 1886; *OR* 5, 478; *The Pennsylvania Daily Telegraph*, Dec. 25, 1861.

Captain Hezekiah Easton
Battery A, 1st Pennsylvania Artillery
LOC

Colonel Conrad Feger Jackson, commanding the 9th Reserves, pushed his Company A— the Pittsburgh Rifles—towards the thick pines surrounding the Centreville Road. Kane sent his Company E, under the command of Capt. Alanson Niles, to join the Pittsburghers on the skirmish line. The two companies fanned out into the woods, which Cpl. Levi Duff, 9th Reserves, explained consisted of the soldiers "following the next one in front not very closely but about five paces behind him." Private Alexander Murdoch gave more details, writing later that the company's formation consisted of "marching single file on a line parallel with, and about 300 yards from, the main body—with the men 2 to 3 yards apart." The Pittsburghers moved "as noiselessly as possible until within a mile of Drainsville we struck at right angles the road from Centerville, where we halted." Some soldiers then "threw ourselves down and put in the time attacking our haversacks, the frosty air and brisk exercise having sharpened our already good appetites." On their left, the Bucktails from Niles's Company E "were ordered to halt and preserve silence."[41]

Private George Dean, 9th Reserves, stood with another private, Alexander Smith. Dean wrote later, "I remember trading off a piece of corned beef for some salt pork that he had, and we were chatting and probably smoking."[42] It was a brief respite after a hard march through the thick, entangling pines.

Alexander Smith, 21-years-old, came from a prominent Pittsburgh family. His father, Hugh Smith, had been one of the first to successfully tow coal to markets past the rapids of the Ohio River. The audacious excursion made the Smiths

41 Levi B. Duff, *To Petersburg with the Army of the Potomac: The Civil War Letters of Levi Bird Duff, 105th Pennsylvania Volunteers, ed. Jonathan E. Helmreich* (Jefferson, NC, 2009); Murdoch, "The Pittsburgh Rifles and the Battle of Dranesville," 302; *Wellsboro Agitator*, Jan. 8, 1862.

42 George Dean, "Battle of Dranesville," 1, William Blake Dean Papers, MN Historical Society.

extremely wealthy.[43] Alexander Smith joined the Pittsburgh Rifles on July 22, "the last man to join the company before leaving Pittsburgh." And now, standing in the trees, he and George Dean snacked on corned beef and salt pork.

While most of the Pittsburghers ate a quick lunch, another soldier went forward on a personal reconnaissance. "I walked around a curve in the road, and saw a whole body of rebels advancing on us," he wrote. The Confederates were coming on quick, answering J. E. B. Stuart's call for the infantry to move at the double-quick. "I knew they were 'secesh' from their diversity in dress," the Federal soldier continued. He turned on his heels and sprinted back to the company.[44]

"*There they come! See them!*" screamed the Pennsylvanians as they dropped their food and grabbed their rifles.[45] "At this moment a number of shots were heard and bullets whistled by us," Dean remembered. Lieutenant James Beattie "gave the order to fall back to the turn-pike as rapidly as possible and rally on the regiment."[46]

"We were so intently watching the approaching column," Alexander Murdoch said, "That we forgot that the Boys in Gray could also deploy as skirmishers until zip—zip! Zip! Zip! The rifle balls came in upon us from both flanks." A Pennsylvanian wrote, "Bullets were barking the trees and cutting the limbs of trees rather too briskly to stand still." The Pittsburghers were armed with Sharps Rifles and started up a steady return fire, while simultaneously moving back through the woods and heading for the safety of the main column. Captain Niles's men also backstepped at the "double quick, with bullets whistling by us and tearing up the dirt at our feet."[47]

Not everyone made it. A bullet struck Alexander Smith in the neck, dropping him. His comrades figured he was dead "but there was no time to stop there." They left the young man among the debris of the pine trees. Nearby, Pvt. Nelson Geer, from the Bucktails, was wounded in the cheek.[48] George Cook, also from the Bucktails, had a sadder fate. Earlier that morning Cook had been "on guard duty when we marched out," one of his comrades wrote. "He was anxious to be along with the regiment, and hired another man to do duty for him in his absence. He

43 George H. Thurston, *Pittsburgh's Progress: Industries and Resources* (Pittsburgh, 1886), 122; No Author, *Iron Age*, Vol. 62 (New York, 1898), 22; "Obituary of Andrew D. Smith," in *American Manufacturer and Iron World*, Oct. 28, 1898.

44 *The Daily Pittsburgh Gazette*, Dec. 27, 1861.

45 Murdoch, "The Pittsburgh Rifles and the Battle of Dranesville," 302.

46 Dean, "Battle of Dranesville," 1.

47 Murdoch, "The Pittsburgh Rifles and the Battle of Dranesville," 302-30; *The Daily Pittsburgh Gazette*, Dec. 27, 1861; *Wellsboro Agitator*, Jan. 8, 1862.

48 *The Daily Pittsburgh Gazette*, Dec. 27, 1861; *Warren Ledger*, Jan. 4, 1862.

was thus able to be in the fight, but was shot through the head, almost at the first fire," and died instantly.[49]

It was a little after noon; the battle of Dranesville had claimed its first casualties.

*   *   *

The Pittsburgh Rifles had tangled with Companies A and D of the 11th Virginia Infantry. Both Confederate companies were pushed forward by Col. Samuel Garland, and as they advanced, they straddled the Centreville Road, with Company A on the right and D on the left. As the infantry came up, the thin screen of Maj. Gordon's cavalry happily gave way, moving back down the Centreville Road where Capt. Cutts unlimbered his battery.[50]

Soldiers from Company D found the wounded Alexander Smith. "They raised a great cheer when they got his rifle," a soldier wrote. Another Confederate stripped the wounded Pennsylvanian's cartridge box off.[51]

The infantry skirmish quickly ended, and now the only shots were the opening artillery salvos from the Sumter Flying Artillery. "We took position in a narrow country road walled in by a dense pine grove," a gunner in the battery wrote. "The road was so narrow and the forest so thick, that there was no room to work but three guns." One remaining gun had to stay limbered-up.[52] The Georgians made the most of the limited space, pushing their cannon "behind a slight swell of ground, the muzzles of the guns just clearing this slight elevation."[53]

Cutts's shells screamed through the air and exploded by the Federal regiments. George Dean later remembered what it was like to be under artillery fire for the first time: "I must say it certainly was terrifying, as the shells whizzed and tore through the trees and air." Nearby, Pvt. Angelo Crapsey, one of Kane's Bucktails, wrote, "Slam bang went the cannon. I could see into the muzzle of it. The fire rolled out of it with a tremendous howl. The shell passed over our heads saying 'Secesh' and struck in a field just beyond and burst."[54]

49 Wallace M. Moore to William O. Bourne, Apr. 27, 1868, William O. Bourne Papers, 2nd ser., no. 114, LOC.

50 Kessler, ed., *The Fincastle Rifles*, 5; *Weekly State Journal*, Jan. 8, 1862.

51 John McQuaide to William McQuaide, Dec. 23, 1861, *Civil War Times Illustrated Collection*, USAHEC; *Pittsburgh Gazette*, Dec. 27, 1861.

52 James M. Folsom, *Heroes and Martyrs of Georgia: Georgia's Record in the Revolution of 1861* (Macon, GA, 1864), 111.

53 William S. Hammond, "The Battle of Dranesville," in *Southern Historical Society Papers*, Vol. 35, ed. R. A. Brock (Richmond, 1907), 75.

54 Dean, "Battle of Dranesville," 2; Crapsey quoted in Dennis Brandt, *Pathway to Hell: A Tragedy of the American Civil War* (Lincoln, NE, 2010), 65.

The Sumter Artillery's opening shots came before the Federal regiments "had got fairly into position," Col. John Taggart, commanding the 12th Reserves, wrote. He referred to the "heavy fire of shot and shell, which fell thick and fast in the vicinity of the left of the regiment." Though certainly an impressive display of fireworks, the Confederate guns did not cause much damage. "The shells at first exploded in our rear, tearing up the ground and splintering the fences in every direction, but fortunately did no damage to the men under my command," Taggart reported.[55]

In these hectic few moments, J. E. B. Stuart had to decide what to do. With Capt. Pitzer still getting the wagons to safety, Stuart figured if he did nothing "our wagons would have fallen an easy prey. . . . I saw at once that my only way to save them was to make a vigorous attack upon [the enemy's] rear and left flank and to compel him to desist from such a purpose."[56] Stuart was thinking on the fly—he had no other option.

Dranesville stands as a clear example of a meeting engagement. Antoine Henri Jomini, a staff officer in the Napoleonic period, wrote *Summary of the Art of War,* a text of which cadets at West Point such as J. E. B. Stuart and Edward Ord would have been at least aware. Concerning the unpredictability of meeting engagements, Jomini cautioned, "The accidental and unexpected meeting of two armies on the march gives rise to one of the most imposing scenes in war. . . . A great occasion of this kind calls into play all the genius of a skillful general and of the warrior able to control events." With his decision to send forward his infantry, Stuart was trying to control the rapidly unfolding events.[57]

Stuart ordered Col. Samuel Garland to take his 11th Virginia and file to the right (east) of the Centreville Road and gave similar instructions for Lt. Col. Andrew Secrest to take the 6th South Carolina left (west) of the road. The 10th Alabama and 1st Kentucky moved up closely behind to support the two regiments in front of them.[58]

---

55 *OR* 5, 487.

56 Ibid., 490-491.

57 United States Army, *Army Doctrine Publication, 3-90: Offense and Defense* (Washington, 2019), 2-14; Antoine Henri Jomini, *Summary of the Art of War,* trans. G. H. Mendell and W. P. Craighill (1862, repr. Philadelphia), 207-208. Historians of the Civil War have debated back and forth regarding Jomini's importance to the tactical mindset of generals in the 1860s; see Carol Reardon, *With a Sword in One Hand and Jomini in the Other: The Problem of Military Thought in the Civil War North* (Chapel Hill, 2012) for an overview of Jomini's importance, or not, on Civil War generals.

58 *OR* 5, 491.

The battle unfolded simultaneously east and west of the Centreville Road, but for narrative's sake, the events east of the road will be relayed first. The next chapter will discuss what transpired west of the road.

Adjutant Meem of the 11th Virginia wrote that the regiment "formed into line of battle just along a thicket of pines" and began to advance towards the Federals. Company G's Pvt. William P. Holland wrote of seeing his enemy in the distance: "They came up in such numbers that it seemed to me that the whole earth looked blue."[59]

*   *   *

J. E. B. Stuart had done what he could to get his infantry into line as quickly as possible, but his counterpart was working just as hard. After directing his infantry to reform their battle lines facing toward the new threat, Edward Ord raced back for his own artillery. The Confederate shells were bursting behind his lines, and Ord wanted to get Capt. Easton's battery up to return the fire.

Captain Ira Ayer, commanding the 10th Reserves' Company I, remembered Ord riding up. "'Make way for my artillery,' he shouted, and without slackening his speed, dashed by, while his 'war-dogs' followed close behind," Ayer wrote. "The scene was, I think, the most animated that I witnessed during the war. He was mounted on a beautiful bay, and as he rode up, his eyes flashing fire and every lineament of his countenance betokening courage, his presence inspired all with confidence." William Burgess, 6th Reserves, remembered Ord "riding about with the oil clothing covering of his cap hanging down his back."[60]

The 1st Pennsylvania Artillery's Battery A seemed to fly down the turnpike; the repeated trips to Dranesville were paying off. The Pennsylvanians knew the area intimately—Easton specifically referred to the Confederate infantry coming down the road between "Thornton's and [Robert] Coleman's houses."[61]

Easton's guns were moving too quickly, as it happened. They "went at a run," Ord wrote, "capsizing one of their pieces." It was one of the two 24-pounders, and "horses, wheels, and even the riders turned over," a witness wrote. No lasting damage resulted from the capsize and no one was wounded or killed; the gunners quickly righted the piece and went back into action.[62]

---

59 *Richmond Whig*, Dec. 27, 1861; Holland, *Recollections of a Private*, 8.

60 Samuel P. Bates, *Martial Deeds of Pennsylvania* (Philadelphia, 1876), 818; William Burgess to William D. Dixon, Aug. 24, 1886, Virginia Tech Special Collections and University Archives.

61 *OR* 5, 489.

62 Ibid., 478; *Philadelphia Press*, Dec. 24, 1861.

Three of the Federal guns unlimbered on a rise known locally as Drane's Hill. It had been here, decades earlier, that Washington Drane had opened his Mountain View Hotel. From Drane's Hill, Easton's battery had a clear view down into the pines and the opening of the Centreville Road. As the gunners finished unlimbering and wheeling their artillery into position, they could see the 11th Virginia and 6th South Carolina advancing towards them.[63]

"Our cannoniers and limber-men pulled off their coats and went to work in earnest," a Pennsylvanian remembered. "Having nothing to indicate the position of the enemy but the smoke of their guns, I opened a brisk discharge of shells into the woods occupied by the enemy," Capt. Easton reiterated.[64]

Once the Pennsylvanians wheeled their artillery into place, they transformed Drane Hill into a nearly impregnable position. Though a brigadier general, Ord acted the role of a battery commander, essentially making Easton his second. Dranesville was his first substantial engagement, and his first battle in charge of so many soldiers. Thus, Ord reverted to what he knew: artillery. His service as a battery commander and his experience as superintendent at Fort Monroe for the gunnery school, now proved dividends. Second Lieutenant A. B. Sharpe, serving on Ord's staff, later remembered the general "ordered Captain Easton, who was standing near him . . . to load with shells." Sharpe added, "He pronounced shell broadly, as if it was written shall. I can see and hear him now turning and saying to quiet, noble Easton, in a loud tone: 'Load with shall.'"[65]

Ord consistently called out encouragement to his artillerists. As he watched the shells slicing through the rebel infantry, he shouted to his gunners, "Keep at that!" He called out, "Give it to 'em, boys! That's a good shot!"[66]

Soon after, Kane's Bucktails arrived on the battlefield at the double-quick. They crossed over the Leesburg & Alexandria Turnpike and filed right, shaking out from column into a battle line. The 1st Pennsylvania Rifles became Ord's center, forming below the base of Drane Hill. Kane's deployment put his left flank by the imposing brick Thornton House. He shouted orders for Lt. Bruce Rice from the regiment's Company I to detail men to fortify the home. About twenty soldiers rushed inside and began to fire from the home's windows. Back in October, the Thornton House had been George McCall's headquarters, and now it sheltered his soldiers. Kane later said he "perceived we held the key of the position against

---

63 Ron Baumgarten, "A Splendid Little Affair: The Battle of Dranesville," *Civil War Trust* (Dec. 2011); Hammond, "The Battle of Dranesville," 74.

64 *Lebanon Evening Express*, Dec. 26, 1861; *OR* 5, 489.

65 *Carlisle Herald*, Jan. 1, 1886.

66 *OR* 5, 479; Hill, *Our Boys*, 173.

Colonel John McCalmont
10th Pennsylvania Reserves
LOC

the enemy."[67] He was right. The fortification of the Thornton House created a devastating obstacle to the Confederate infantry's advance.

On Kane's left came up the 10th Reserves. Colonel John McCalmont led his four and a half companies into battle, shouting, "Ba—tal—ion, At-ten-tion! Right-face! Forward—double quick—March!" As the soldiers ran down the turnpike and came perpendicular to what was rapidly becoming the front line, McCalmont ordered his men to file left. This swung them into a battle line. Seeing a fence line blocking the path ahead, he sent a detachment of men to knock it down. As the regiment kept marching, the color bearer, Frank Alexander, pulled the leather sheath off the Stars and Stripes. "Scarcely had it straightened in the breeze," a 10th Reserves soldier remembered years later, "when a rebel shell came screaming over our heads and burst away off on our left, and though the shell passed probably seventy-five or a hundred feet over our heads, I never before or since saw such dodging." With a touch of humor, the soldier added, "We had not yet learned that the balls one hears, or sees, are the ones he may laugh at."[68]

With the 10th Reserves formed in line, McCalmont sent Capt. Thomas McConnell, Company B, ahead with a platoon of soldiers to make a small skirmish line. The platoon spread out and soon joined the fray.[69]

From a bird's eye view, the battle east of the Centreville Road, on the Confederate right, Federal left, looked as such: the 10th Reserves formed Ord's left, linking with Kane's Bucktails in the center of the line, while Easton's and Cutts's batteries were trading shots from about 500 yards away. Coming straight at the Pennsylvanians

---

67 Bard, *John Bard's History of the Old Bucktails*, 18; Kane Papers, Box 23, Folder 4, Item 31, BYU.

68 *OR* 5, 483-484; Ernest A. Smith, *Allegheny—A Century of Education* (Meadville, PA, 1916), 170. The color bearer's identity as Frank Alexander comes from *The Middlebury Register*, June 6, 1908.

69 *OR* 5, 485.

Colonel Samuel Garland
11th Virginia Infantry
LOC

was the 11th Virginia, while the 6th South Carolina was just about to contact Ord's right flank.

Colonel Samuel Garland's Virginians advanced. Chiswell Dabney, one of Stuart's staff officers, relayed the general's orders, telling Garland, "The general says there are about 2,000 Yankees down here in the pines, and he wants you to . . . drive the Yankees out."[70]

The soldiers of the 11th came mostly from the Piedmont region of Virginia, with the nucleus of the regiment hailing from the city of Lynchburg with company names such as the Southern Guards, Fincastle Rifles, and the Valley Regulators.[71]

At the 11th's head was Col. Samuel Garland, a Lynchburg native and a graduate of both the Virginia Military Institute and the University of Virginia. After practicing law in Lynchburg with his uncle, Garland helped raise a militia company in 1859 in response to John Brown's raid on Harpers Ferry. With war's onset in 1861, he again helped raise troops and was elected the 11th's colonel.[72] Garland's Company A, which had skirmished with the Pittsburgh Rifles a little while earlier, extended too far to the right into the pines. It was extremely difficult to see through the trees, and Garland lost contact with the company. To try and reconnect, Garland moved his regiment to the right, sending another company to fill the gap made by the departing Company A. Garland instructed the regiment's adjutant, Lt. Meem, to find the missing company, but even after three forays into the pines, Meem could not do so. Meanwhile, Garland gave the order for the rest

---

70 Holland, *Recollections of a Private*, 8.

71 Robert Thomas Bell, "The 11th Virginia Infantry Regiment, C.S.A," Master's thesis (Virginia Polytechnic Institute, 1968), 16.

72 Ezra Warner, *Generals in Gray: Lives of the Confederate Commanders* (Baton Rouge, 1959), 98; Aubrey Wiley, "Garland's Men: Lynchburg's Home Guard," Jones Memorial Library, Lynchburg, 2; Susan R. Beardsworth, "Three Lynchburg Generals of 1861-1865," Jones Memorial Library, Lynchburg, 3.

of the regiment to advance; as it did, the Federal fire began to take its toll, and soldiers dropped from the ranks.[73]

"The Yankees opened on us with their small arms and soon brought their artillery to bear on ours," wrote Pvt. Philip Franklin. Still ensconced in the pines, Franklin told friends, "Our Regt did'nt do much firing from the fact that we were in about two hundred yards of their battery and they could have slaughtered every one of us with canister if we had shown ourselves." Franklin described the constant musketry and its effect: "Their balls flew so thick that the pines fell like rain."[74]

Private James Old, in the 11th's Company B, had a close call. "I was shot through the hat with a piece of a bum shel it strick my hat . . . brim in front cuting a hole about 4 inches long and brushed my right eye," he wrote his brother. "It was a verry narrow risk of my life if it had strick a half of an inch lower it would have blowed my skull off." Old added, "I hope you will [not] have to come to war for it is awful."[75]

Not all of Garland's men were so fortunate. "A party of their picked sharpshooters annoyed us considerably firing from the windows of a large house on the pike," Adjutant Meem wrote, alluding to the Bucktails in the Thornton House. "The firing now of cannon and musketry was terrific," Meem continued. "There was no intermission and shell, grape, and shot were poured into us at a rapid rate, doing tremendous execution." Captain Albert Yeatman, commanding the 11th's Company K, was wounded with a "shell contusion over the left eye."[76] The casualties suffered in the 11th were not all the result of Federal fire, either. Twenty-one-year-old John Henry from Lynchburg was killed "by the accidental explosion of his own gun as the ball entered under his jaw & passed through the top of his head."[77]

In the middle of the firefight stood J. E. B. Stuart, surrounded by his staff. Private William Holland, 11th Virginia, was standing close enough to Stuart that the general put his arm on Holland's shoulder and shouted, "Stand your ground. Die!"[78]

---

73 *OR* 5, 491; *Richmond Whig*, Dec. 27, 1861. Eventually the missing Company A reunited with the regiment, but for the remainder of the battle "Layed in the hollow" for safety. A.H. Benson to his uncle, Jan. 11, 1862, Austin-Twyman Papers, Folder 140, Special Collections, College of William & Mary.

74 Philip Franklin to his father, Jan. 3, 1862, VMHC.

75 James Old to his brother, Dec. 25, 1861, VMHC.

76 *Richmond Whig*, Dec. 27, 1861; Albert Yeatman CSR, *Company K, 11th VA Infantry*, NARA.

77 William King to his wife, Dec. 21, 1861, King Family Papers, Albert & Shirley Small Special Collections, University of Virginia.

78 Holland, *Recollections of a Private*, 8.

Amongst the maelstrom sat the home of Robert Coleman. The schoolteacher Coleman was one of the few men remaining in town. He and his family scurried into the cellar of the home, where "two shots passed through the building." And that was just in the cellar. Robert's wife Ann later testified that "eleven cannon balls shot through the house and two shells exploded. House was badly damaged; the furniture almost destroyed." The battle of Dranesville, whose genesis lay in the activities of civilians, now put those civilians directly into the line of fire.[79]

Coleman's home sat across the Centreville Road from the Thornton House, at the edge of the pine trees. The clearing around the home became a no-man's-land between the Federals on the turnpike and the attacking Confederates. Garland's Virginians stalled as soldiers found shelter among the pine trees. They knew that to leave the cover and advance across the open fields meant certain death, and the soldiers settled in to exchange musketry volleys back and forth. From behind and to their left came their support, the 10th Alabama Infantry, led by Col. John Forney.

Forney's men were going into their first battle. Having missed Manassas, the soldiers had suffered through abysmal camp diseases near Bristoe Station, leaving at least 60 buried back in their former camps. Federal musketry and artillery now added to that casualty count.[80]

Unlike the 11th Virginia, the 10th Alabama stormed into the clearing outside Robert Coleman's home. The advance was made "incautiously," Pvt. Bailey George McClelen of the 10th Alabama wrote in his diary.[81] In front of them was Capt. Thomas McConnell's platoon from the 10th Reserves. The Pennsylvanians were "secreting ourselves in some deep gullies or trenches, natural rifle pits," McConnell wrote as the Alabamians came out.[82] Behind the platoon, up near Easton's battery, were the rest of the 10th Reserves, which could deploy if needed.[83]

"The Tenth Alabama," J. E. B. Stuart wrote, "rushed with a shout in a shower of bullets." Those bullets were mostly delivered by McConnell's platoon. As the Pennsylvanian wrote, "I then ordered all to fire, which order was so well obeyed that the enemy were instantly thrown into confusion."[84]

---

79 Ann Coleman Southern Claims, 1, 4.

80 "Confederate Deaths Near Bristow Station, Virginia, Prince William County, 10th Alabama," 10th Alabama Regimental File, Confederate Regimental File, AL Department of Archives and History. The cemetery where the dead from the 10th AL are buried from their summer and fall stay in 1861 is now preserved as part of the Bristoe Station Battlefield Park.

81 Diary of Bailey George McClelen, 10th Alabama Regimental File, Confederate Regimental Files, AL Department of Archives & Manuscripts, 26.

82 *OR* 5, 486.

83 Smith, *Allegheny*, 171.

84 *OR* 5, 491; *OR* 5, 486.

The volley slammed into the 10th Alabama like a strong gale, staggering the men. Bailey George McClelen wrote, "The battle waxed warm and fierce, the missiles of death flew thick and fast and had no respect for persons with whom they came in contact."[85]

Among those killed was Lt. Col. James B. Martin. His premonition that this day would be his last came true as "He fell at the head . . . cheering the men on to victory or death," an officer in the 10th Alabama wrote. "He died like a man at his post."[86]

Martin was not the only officer to fall. Colonel Forney "rode backward and forward in front of the line, encouraging his men." As he did so, he "was wounded in the arm four inches below the shoulder, and the ball passed through the musel of his shoulder back of his arm," wrote an Alabamian. A family historian later wrote, "The ball that wounded [Forney] passed through his right arm, badly shattering the bone." John's brother Captain William Forney, commanding the 10th's Company G, also went down, shot "about half way from his foot to his knee."[87] One of William Forney's lieutenants, George C. Whatley, had a close call. He wrote to his wife about finding "my overcoat with a bullet shot in it."[88]

In a matter of moments, the 10th Alabama was shot to pieces. Their colonel was wounded, their lieutenant colonel killed, and company-grade officers knocked down as well. Major John Woodward (not to be confused with Maj. Thomas Woodward of the 6th South Carolina) assumed command "on one side of the road, and the senior Captain on the other," a newspaper correspondent to the *Richmond Dispatch* reported. That senior captain was John Caldwell, commanding the regiment's Company A. "Caldwell took charge of the right wing and stood up like a 'Pea Cock,'" another Alabamian remembered.[89]

The Alabamians were unable to stand the unrelenting fire for long. They were also being enfiladed by the 24-Pounder howitzer that had earlier capsized. Once righted, the howitzer was wheeled into position to the left of Drane Hill, firing down the length of the Confederates' line. It was soon joined by two other guns,

---

85 McClelen, *I Saw the Elephant,* 21.

86 James P. Pate, ed., *When This Evil War Is Over: The Correspondence of the Francis Family, 1860-1865* (Tuscaloosa, AL, 2006), 62.

87 Ibid.; Annie Forney Daugette, "Life of Major General John H. Forney," in *The Alabama Historical Quarterly* 9, No. 3 (Fall 1947): 371.

88 George C. Whatley to his wife, Jan. 16, 1862, 10th Alabama File, Confederate Regiments File, AL Archives & Manuscripts.

89 Pate, ed., *When This Evil War Is Over,* 62.

A woodcut from the January 11, 1862, edition of Harper's Weekly. In the foreground is Easton's battery firing towards the Sumter Light Artillery, marked by the plumes of smoke in the background. On the right is the Thornton House, and opposite it, the Robert Coleman House. *LOC*

sent by Ord to turn up the pressure. The three artillery pieces raked the Alabamians, sending jagged pieces of iron into men's bodies.[90]

Major Woodward and Capt. Caldwell led their men back into the safety of the pine trees, where they "engaged us warmly during the remainder of the battle," Capt. McConnell wrote.[91] But the damage had been done, and it had been decidedly one-sided. In their brief charge, the Alabamans suffered 67 casualties. It was the highest loss of any of Stuart's regiments at Dranesville. The 11th Virginia, which had stayed in the shelter of the pines, had lost just 21. Opposing them, the 10th Reserves did not have a single casualty. Remembering the fight years later, John Rhodes, who had fought in the 10th Alabama's Company E, wrote, "We were ambushed at that fight and did not have a fair showing."[92]

The fighting on the east side of the Centreville Road settled into both sides trading musket volleys back and forth, with nothing more substantial occurring.

90 *OR* 5, 479.

91 Ibid., 486.

92 In his report Stuart tabulates the 10th AL's losses as totaling 66, but independent research has revealed four more. The names of the casualties are printed in Appendix 3. *OR* 5, 489, 494; *Our Mountain Home*, Oct. 10, 1900.

Between the 10th Alabama and 11th Virginia, close to 90 Confederates now lay dead or wounded, while the Reserves had come out nearly unscratched. On the west side of the road, however, it was an entirely different matter. As the fighting on the east side sputtered out, the fighting west of the Centreville Road crackled and roared with a tenacity that showed no signs of stopping.

Chapter Eleven

"Men & Horses Fell Around Me Like Ten-Pins"

Fighting Continues

When the 11th Virginia and 10th Alabama veered to the right of the Centreville Road, Stuart pushed the 6th South Carolina and 1st Kentucky to the left. Captain Cutts's guns were still firing shot and shell towards the Federal lines. The actions on Stuart's left, which proved to be the bloodiest of the battle, began to unfold.

Seeing the Confederates approach, Lt. Col. Thomas Kane's 1st Pennsylvania Rifles opened fire. Kane later wrote of a fence by the Thornton House "which prevented our marksmen from having [the Confederates] distinctly in view." Kane continued, "I was obliged to call for volunteers to my assistance." Eight men dashed forward, tearing down the fence and clearing the field of fire. While doing so, Pvt. George Raup was killed instantly; Kane eulogized him as "one of the best soldiers in the regiment."[1]

Corporal Samuel Galbraith, in the Bucktails' Company B, was killed around the same time—one account even suggests he and Raup were struck "by the same grape shot" coming from the Confederate artillery.[2] The fact that the Bucktails were now coming under artillery fire meant that the Sumter Flying Artillery had switched to deadly grapeshot and canister. The Confederate canister was described by Kane as "particularly severe in this place."[3]

---

1 Kane Papers, Box 23, Folder 4, Item 31, BYU.

2 *Philadelphia Inquirer*, Dec. 23, 1861.

3 Kane Papers, Box 23, Folder 4, Item 31, BYU.

Corporal Angelo Crapsey, in Kane's Company I, agreed. "The bullets flew like hail & those big bull dogs barked & howled as if they were bound to bite some of us & they threw lots of little shot called grape & canister," he wrote. "The cannon balls came whirring through the air & smashing down everything that was in range except a tree about 3 feet in diameter & that got a hole popped into it as large as your head & went more than half way through it." With a final flourish, Crapsey noted, "Them tormented shells! Col. Kane said he did not think that they were oyster shells."[4] The Bucktails were "ordered to lie down" to avoid the artillery fire, another soldier wrote.[5]

Bucktails inside the Thornton House tried to eliminate the enemy artillery crews. Corporal W. W. Brewer wrote to his father, "We could see them plain where they worked their guns, and when they would commence to load we would give them some from the windows." The Georgians tried to swat away the Bucktails as if they were pesky flies. "They aimed their fire at the house," Brewer went on. "There was several cannon balls come in the house and one of them come through the wall about a foot from where I stood and scattered the brick."[6]

The Sumter Artillery's reign over the battlefield was short-lived. J. E. B. Stuart was an excellent cavalry officer, and he had so far handled the deployment of his infantry well, but he fell short of deploying the artillery with skill. Perhaps thinking of his easy victory at Lewinsville three months earlier, Stuart brought Capt. Cutts's battery to within 500 yards of the Federal line. He forgot how his artillery dispositions had caused concern among his superiors who, while impressed with Stuart's performance, worried about his cavalier use of artillery. Stuart now made the same choice as he had at Lewinsville, bringing artillery dangerously close to the firing line. But this time, Edward Ord made him pay.

Sergeant Eli Bozeman, fighting in the Sumter Artillery, described what happened. "Their shot and shell went over us, but by this time they were getting our range very accurately, and our men began to fall rapidly." The Georgians stood to their guns, and sergeants stepped in when crewmembers were killed or wounded. Within just a few minutes of Easton's guns opening, disaster struck the Confederates. For soldiers and officers seeing combat for the first time, the fate of the Sumter Flying Artillery was a gruesome introduction to war.[7]

4 Crapsey quoted in Brandt, *Pathway to Hell*, 65-66.

5 *Philadelphia Press*, Dec. 27, 1861.

6 W. W. Brewer, *Corporal Brewer: A Bucktail Survivor*, Vol. 1, ed. William Means (Edmonton, ALB, 1997), 210.

7 *The Columbus Daily Sun*, Jan. 23, 1862.

"Many had been wounded and fell nearby; but the worst sight of all—the most heartrending scene was soon to occur," Bozeman wrote. "My gunner, John McGarrah, acting No. 1, and Williams, acting No. 3—No. 3 being just in the rear of No. 1, were standing the galling fire like men, when in an instant a solid shot had severed their heads from their bodies, and the two lifeless corpses lay on the ground—their brains bespattering all who were near." With no one left to help man the cannon, Bozeman himself stepped up and grabbed the sponge-rammer, which was "gory with blood and brains." Even Maj. James Gordon, sitting astride his horse in reserve nearby, saw the devastation. "There were two men standing near each other & both their heads were taken off with a cannon shot. Many of them were badly mutilated," he wrote.[8] A day later, a Confederate soldier saw the corpses and noted, "The head of one of them was entirely severed from the body, that of the other cut off just above the nose."[9] Washington Franklin Williams was 16-years-old when his life came to its gruesome end.[10]

McGarrah and Williams had been crewing one of the borrowed 3-inch Ordnance Rifles from the Jeff Davis Artillery. Their grisly deaths splashed their fellow crewmates, their tools, and their cannon with gore. When the cannon was returned, the other battery found it "bespattered with the brains and blood of an artilleryman."[11]

It got worse for the Georgians. "Every shot of the enemy was dealing destruction on either man, limber, or horse," Stuart wrote in his official report.[12] One of Easton's guns scored a lucky shot on a caisson, exploding the ammunition chest in a fiery display that killed and wounded more crew members. A Pennsylvanian, seeing the damage after the battle, wrote of the casualties, "legs and arms were strewn all over the ground."[13]

Captain Cutts's battery suffered 17 killed or wounded out of "forty cannoniers and drivers at the guns." The battery also had 25 of its horses killed, a limber destroyed, a caisson exploded, and another caisson left behind. "Never again during the war would the battery suffer that many men killed in one battle," their historian wrote.[14]

8 Ibid; James B. Gordon to his mother, Dec. 23, 1861, North Carolina State Archives.

9 *Richmond Dispatch*, Dec. 30, 1861.

10 Speicher, *The Sumter Flying Artillery*, 56.

11 Laboda, *From Selma to Appomattox*, 13.

12 *OR* 5, 492.

13 *Warren Ledger*, Jan. 1, 1862.

14 Folsom, *Heroes and Martyrs of Georgia*, 111; Speicher, *The Sumter Flying Artillery*, 56.

Meanwhile, Capt. Easton's battery sustained zero casualties. Artillerist John Shireman wrote, "One of our drivers had the heel knocked off of his boot, and another his leg slightly bruised by a piece of shell, but otherwise they all escaped with a sound skin." Easton wrote happily, "There was not a man or horse lost and no injury done my guns."[15]

Edward Ord offered a scathing review of his opponent. In a letter to his wife he wrote, "My artillery slaughtered them—while they were cooped up & jammed in a road which I raked. It was the old story—they had an ignoramus for a general, a fool for an artillery capt'n, took it for granted we would run, made no reconnaissance, posted their artillery just where I would have placed it to smash it soonest."[16] The Federal artillery blasted Cutts to pieces, in Easton's words, "by our third fire." With the Georgians no longer a threat, the Pennsylvanians could focus their attention and remaining rounds against the Confederate infantry pushing out of the pine trees.[17]

Kane's Rifles, still holding at the Thornton House, made up Ord's center. To their left, elements of the 10th Reserves were facing off against the 11th Virginia and 10th Alabama (as told in the last chapter). On Kane's right came Lt. Col. William Penrose's 6th Reserves, and to their right, Col. Conrad Jackson's 9th Reserves finished the battle line. Up by Easton's guns still sat in reserve Lt. Col. Higgins's two squadrons of cavalry and Col. John Taggart's 12th Reserves.

Lieutenant Colonel Andrew Secrest's 6th South Carolina advanced towards the front. Colonel Thomas Taylor moved his 1st Kentucky at the same time, "taking position about seventy yards" behind Secrest's men. The Kentuckians overlapped the Carolinians by "about half a regimental front to our left." Both regiments struggled through the woods.[18]

Major Thomas Woodward, the 6th South Carolina's second-in-command, remembered "Bill McAlily bore our colors well up."[19] Thus, for the first time, a Confederate battle flag, with its distinct and tilted cross, was unfurled on a battlefield. The flags had been distributed to regiments in the Confederate army starting back on November 28, in an elaborate program witnessed not only by

---

15 *Weekly Mariettian*, Jan. 11, 1862; *OR* 5, 489. The artillerist lightly bruised by a piece of shell is identified in Easton's report as Charles Osborn. He was killed at the battle of Antietam.

16 Edward Ord to his wife, Dec. 24, 1861, Edward Ord Papers, Box 1, Folder 3, Item 12, Stanford University.

17 *OR* 5, 489.

18 Woodward, *From Fort Sumter to Dranesville*, 24.

19 Ibid.

generals and other high-ranking officers, but also by Jefferson Davis. Thomas Blackwell, a soldier in the 6th South Carolina, called it "quite a military scene."[20]

J. E. B. Stuart rode up to Maj. Woodward. "Tell your Colonel to advance as he now faces," he directed. "You will encounter the enemy in the thicket before you; engage him briskly, and drive him out." Woodward sent the message to Secrest, and years later remembered "the sharp, shrill tones of [Secrest's] well-known voice, the commands: 'Battalion, forward, guide centre-march!'"[21]

The entirety of the 6th South Carolina was not on the field. Half of the regiment was back at Centreville on "detail duty, cutting logs for our winter quarters," Woodward remembered. When orders for the expedition had gone out the previous evening, "a detachment of 334 men, rank and file, consisting of details from each company" was assigned to the column.[22]

South Carolinian Pvt. John M. Brice wrote his father, "We had as bad a position as we could possibly have had, being in the midst of a thicket of shrub pines, where we could not see well what we were doing, whilst the Yankees had splendid positions & scattered the shot at us in all directions." Major Woodward, still mounted on his horse, rode forward "with the reins of my bridle over my horse's neck, both hands engaged in warding the limbs and brush from my face." Years later, he recalled it as "the greatest trial of my life."[23]

That trial got worse before the Carolinians got very far. It is unsurprising that the Confederate units operating in the thick trees got disoriented and mistook friend for enemy. Major Woodward remembered, "In a clear, ringing, military voice, I heard the commands: 'Ready, aim,' and looking in the direction, I saw the Kentuckians in the kneeling position, with their rifles well leveled on us." Before he could do anything, "there came a solid, crashing volley." The Kentuckians' shots killed Privates James McKeown and J. W. Smith and further wounded Privates R. W. Lipsey and C. A. Boyd. That volley "threw the company into some confusion," a South Carolinian recalled. Woodward said the five killed and wounded soldiers were "victims of somebody's egregious and most criminal stupidity."[24] Some of the Carolinians returned fire, and Cpl. John M. Johnson, in

---

20 John M. Coski, *The Confederate Battle Flag: America's Most Embattled Emblem* (Cambridge, 2005), 10-11; William S. Connery, *Civil War Northern Virginia 1861* (Charleston, SC, 2011), 27-20; Thomas Blackwell to his wife, Nov. 29, 1861, Blackwell Papers, South Carolina Historical Society.

21 Woodward, *From Fort Sumter to Dranesville*, 25.

22 Ibid., 26; *OR Supplement*, Vol. 64, 609.

23 John M. Brice his father, Dec. 21, 1861, Walter Brice Collection, VMHC; Woodward, *From Fort Sumter to Dranesville*, 26.

24 Woodward, *From Fort Sumter to Dranesville*, 24; *OR Supplement*, Vol. 64, 643.

the 1st Kentucky's Company E, was killed instantly.[25] Overcoming the chaos of the friendly fire, Confederates pressed for the tree line. The Pennsylvania Reserves were waiting for them.

"Then came the tug of war," Sgt. John Lewis, Company C, 6th Reserves, wrote. "We opened on the rebels with our musketry. . . . They then returned the fire." Another Pennsylvanian called it "an unbroken line of living fire."[26] A South Carolinian guessed the two sides were no more than 100 yards away from each other.[27]

In the middle of the exchanged volleys was Lt. Benjamin Ashenfelter, 6th Reserves. "We was ordered to lye down upon our faces which we did," he wrote his parents. "We laid in that position about 15 minutes, them shooting at us all the time." Having just bought a sword in Washington the day before, Ashenfelter now found it sorely overrated. "Picked up a secesh musket and went to work with that," he matter-of-factly stated.[28]

Being shot at for the first time, Lt. Col. William Penrose, commanding the 6th Reserves, panicked and froze in place. Private William Jayne wrote that Penrose "seemed to forget that he was an officer, and gave no commands whatever." Adjutant Henry McKean began to shout orders, taking Penrose's place. Watching the event unfold, Ord stepped in and directed Thomas Kane to command both his Riflemen and the 6th Reserves. Kane ran to converse with the 6th, leaving Capt. Hugh McNeil in charge of the Bucktails for the time being. Soon Ord rode up to the 6th Reserves to help Kane.[29]

"Boys, I want you to occupy that wood to the right of the brick house," Ord cried out, pointing at the Thornton House, still swirling in smoke from the Bucktails fortified inside. "The 6th with a shout advanced to the wood, scrambling over fences and forming quickly in line," Sgt. George Merrick wrote home. "Our Minnie's poured forth a fire that, borne off by the breeze, was plainly heard by our pickets ten miles away. The fire of musketry was deafening and incessant," Merrick recounted vividly. "Crack, crack, crack, went the reports of our rifled muskets, with occasionally the clanging of several hundred going off simultaneously, and the loud roar of the heavy guns literally shook the ground." After the battle, the soldiers in the 6th Reserves looked over themselves. "A number of the boys have holes through their clothes where bullets passed through them," Sgt. John Lewis

25 John M. Johnson CSR, Company E, 1st KY Infantry, NARA.

26 *Honesdale Democrat*, Jan. 9, 1862; *Wellsboro Agitator*, Jan. 8, 1862.

27 Frank Moore, ed. *Rebellion Record: A Diary of American Events*, Vol. 3 (New York, 1864), 503.

28 Benjamin Ashenfelter to his mother, Dec. 31, 1861, and Jan. 3, 1862, USAHEC.

29 *Honesdale Democrat*, Jan. 9, 1862; Thomas Kane Papers, Box 23, Folder 4, Item 31, BYU.

wrote.[30] What could have been a devastating moment for the 6th Reserves when Lt. Col. Penrose froze was saved by Ord's and Kane's leadership. These men, under fire for the first time, proved themselves up to the task. The Federal battle line never buckled.[31]

Like the 10th Alabama on the east side of the road, the 6th South Carolina pushed out of the woods, trying to close on the enemy. The Pennsylvanians' volleys rocked its line, causing men to drop. Color bearer William McAlily went down, shot in the hand. A second color bearer grabbed the flag but was shot too. Bucktail John Bard said, "The flag of the regiment in our front went down several times from the time they left the woods until they returned to it."[32]

One of the men that grabbed the Carolina flag was Capt. Obadiah Harden, commanding Company E. Harden was a successful farmer from Chester County. When the war began, Harden had five children, and enslaved 13 people. The fear of losing those slaves terrified him. "I had a very bad dream last night," he wrote to his wife Paulina in the summer of 1861. "I dreampt that all the abolitionists were marching down through our country and that I had not joined the army to keep them back." But of course, Harden had joined the army. And now he reached for the 6th South Carolina's battle flag. He didn't hold it long before he too was shot down. He died 12 days later, on New Year's Day, 1862, just two days after his 34th birthday. Nearby, Harden's younger brother Thomas was killed instantly. The 6th South Carolina was being ripped apart as it advanced.[33]

The South Carolinians came to a fence bordering the thicket and tried to climb over it. It was a difficult task with the soldiers' equipment and bulky muskets, made even worse by the Federals' fire. Corporal L. S. Douglass "was hurt in the ear by the bayonet of one of our men in crossing a fence," John M. Brice wrote his father.[34]

Once over the fence, the Carolinians dove for cover to escape the musketry. "The order was given to fall to the ground," John Bratton wrote to his wife. "I gave it if nobody else did." Still, casualties mounted. Bratton was lying on his face when his cousin, Capt. Edward Means "called out to me to come [and] that Frank and Bev were shot." After hesitating a moment in the face of the gunfire, Bratton got up

---

30 *Wellsboro Agitator*, Jan. 8, 1862; *Honesdale Democrat*, Jan. 9, 1862.

31 William Penrose resigned his commission and left the army on Dec. 21, the day after the battle; Samuel P. Bates, *History of Pennsylvania Volunteers, 1861-65*: Vol. 1 (Harrisburg, PA, 1869), 701.

32 William McAlily, CSR, 6th SC Infantry, NARA; Bard, *John Bard's History of the Old Bucktails*, 19.

33 Chester County, SC, 1860 Census; 1860 Slave Schedule Chester County, Harden; J. Edward Lee, and Ron Chepesiuk, eds, *South Carolina in the Civil War: The Confederate Experience in Letters and Diaries* (Jefferson, NC, 2000), 14, 18; Thomas Harden CSR, Company E, 6th SC Infantry, NARA.

34 John M. Brice to his father, Dec. 21, 1861, VMHC; L. S. Douglass CSR, Company G, 6th SC Infantry, NARA.

Captain Obadiah Harden was mortally wounded as he carried the flag of the 6th South Carolina forward. *Courtesy of the Louise Pettus Archives & Special Collections at Winthrop University*

to go look. He found Frank English bleeding out and Frank's uncle, Capt. Means, desperately trying to stanch the blood flow. Bratton told Means, "He was wasting time with him, that nothing could be done for him." Nearby, another of Frank's uncles, Beverly Means, lay wounded. The 17-year-old Frank English, who wanted so desperately to go home to resume his studies, and to leave the war behind him, breathed his last amongst the pine trees. [35]

English died without ever knowing that his father had tried to move heaven and earth to get him out of the army. Five days later, on Christmas Day, Mary Chesnut, wrote in her diary, "Frank English was killed. His father wrote to Mr C[hesnut] to get a discharge for him—his health was so feeble. He is discharged now, poor boy, from this earth and its troubles."[36]

There would be time later, a lifetime's worth, to mourn. For now, the 6th South Carolina still found itself facing off against three regiments of Pennsylvania Reserves. Bratton wrote, "I had a feeling that I would be killed, but I dare say all had that."[37]

Stuck in the woods, they could "only occasionally. . . see the enemy," wrote Carolinian William Coleman. "Consequently they had to fire a great measure at random." Major Thomas Woodward later said, "Our situation was getting desperate." But help was coming.[38]

---

35 Bratton, *General John Bratton*, 52. In this section of Bratton's letter, the text says he "found poor Frank Gaillard dying…" It is unclear if "Gaillard" was Frank English's middle name; there was certainly no Frank Gaillard in the 6th SC. In fact, the only person with the first name of Frank killed or wounded in the 6th was Frank English. This, in conjunction with Edward Means's reaction, makes it clear that Bratton was talking about Frank English.

36 Chesnut, *Mary Chesnut's Civil War*, 269.

37 Bratton, *General John Bratton*, 53.

38 William Coleman to his mother, Dec.23, 1861, USC; Woodward, *From Fort Sumter to Dranesville*, 26-27.

Once the 1st Kentucky had stopped firing at the Carolinians, it moved further to the left and then advanced straight for the edge of the woods. Opposing them was Col. Conrad Jackson's 9th Reserves. It had been the 9th Reserves' Company A—the Pittsburgh Rifles—that had fired some of the first shots of the battle, and now those soldiers rejoined the regiment. One of them, Pvt. Ell Torrance, remembered Edward Ord meeting them and calling out, "Come down on them boys, like the wild-cat in the mountain."[39]

Before the 9th Reserves could fire, its colonel hesitated. Conrad Jackson had been raised by an uncle from a young age within the Society of Friends. Jackson threw aside Quaker pacifism to become an officer in the 9th Reserves, and now found himself staring into the foreboding woods in front. Off to his left the whole earth seemed to be splitting open with the sounds of musketry and cannonading.[40]

"Don't fire on us," a voice called from the woods. "We are the Bucktails; don't fire." Jackson believed the ruse and did not unleash his rifles. Some of Jackson's officers saw through the lie, and Capt. Robert Galway, commanding Jackson's Company D, "assured [Jackson] in the most emphatic manner they were rebels." Before Jackson replied, the 1st Kentucky fired. The volley sliced through the 9th Reserves, thrashing men out of the line, including Capt. Galway, hit in the left leg.[41]

Ell Torrance remembered watching one soldier "rise on his knee to fire." Before the soldier had time to shoot "a bullet struck him in the neck, cutting the jugular vein, and the hot, red blood gushed out in a great stream." The firing continued, Torrance guessed, "at pistol range."[42] So many bullets flew through the air that one "broke his bayonet off," wrote Pvt. Thomas Dunlap.[43]

"We were within 30 yards of them before we knew it," Pvt. William Leslie wrote. "They fired on us first and the bullets came like hail stones over our heads."[44] Privates John Sexton and Joseph Stockdale were killed instantly; others fell out of line with grisly wounds.

The 1st Kentucky, while lucky to get the first shot off, soon fell into the same problem as its Confederate counterparts. The regiment found it difficult to maneuver through the trees, and casualties mounted. It had the additional

<hr>

39 Ell Torrance, "The Pennsylvania Reserves," in *Glimpses of the Nation's Struggle: Papers Read Before the Minnesota Commandery of the Military Order of the Loyal Legion of the United States, 1889-1892* (New York, 1893), 66.

40 Sypher, *Pennsylvania Reserve Corps*, 416.

41 *OR* 5, 483; *Executive Documents Printed by Order of the House of Representatives During the Second Session of the Thirty-Seventh Congress*, Vol. 5, Ex. Doc 59, 5.

42 Torrance, "The Pennsylvania Reserves," 66-67.

43 Thomas Dunlap to his parents, Dec. 21, 1861, Author's Collection.

44 William Leslie to friend Emma, Jan. 17, 1862, Library of Virginia.

Colonel Conrad F. Jackson
9th Pennsylvania Reserves
Courtesy of USAHEC

problem of a colonel who abandoned the regiment. Or at least that is what some of the Kentuckians thought. Colonel Thomas Taylor had led the regiment since its organization, and had directed them into combat atop Mason's Hill on Sept. 28. But at Dranesville, according to Lt. David Thomson, Taylor fled "about five minutes" after the shooting started. In the thick of the woods, Taylor got detached from the regiment. He would not rejoin his regiment until the next day; many assumed he had been killed until he walked back into camp. While Thomson may have thought Taylor fled, others wrote the colonel "rode to the right to see what disposition had been made of his neighbors, and on returning found the regiment gone." Regardless of how Taylor got separated from the regiment, it left the 1st Kentucky without a commander.[45]

The 1st Kentucky Infantry served with the Confederate army in Virginia from its arrival in August through the Siege of Yorktown in April 1862. After that, it returned to the Bluegrass State and disbanded, its members joining other Kentucky regiments and serving out the rest of the war.[46] Because of their limited service, there is a dearth of diaries, manuscripts, and letters from the soldiers' time in the 1st Infantry. Those limited resources leave several puzzling questions unanswered, especially regarding the Kentuckians' actions at Dranesville.

One of those questions is that even if Col. Taylor was missing, where was the rest of the regiment's command staff? The Kentuckians' lieutenant colonel was William Preston Johnston, son of Gen. Albert S. Johnston, and according to Johnston's service record, he was present with the regiment in December 1861. And yet, he appears nowhere in the admittedly limited records concerning the 1st Kentucky at Dranesville. The same applies for the regiment's major, Edward Crossland, who,

45 David Thomson to Jefferson Davis, Nov. 2, 1862, Jefferson Davis Papers, NARA; *Richmond Dispatch*, Dec. 23, 1861.

46 *The Courier Journal*, Mar. 5, 1882.

Colonel Thomas Taylor, 1st Kentucky Infantry, whose role in the battle of Dranesville remains unclear nearly 160 years later. *LOC*

according to his service record, was likewise present at Dranesville but appears in virtually no sources. The only exception is a throwaway line in Stuart's report, where he refers to "the gallant Taylor," and "the intrepid Major Crossland." But even then, no concrete evidence elaborates on the role those two officers played during the fight.[47]

If it wasn't Taylor, Johnston, or Crossland, who led the Kentuckians after Taylor's departure? Lieutenant Thomson claimed it was Capt. Joseph Desha, who went into the fight at the head of the regiment's Company C.[48]

Desha, 28-years old, came from a well-off Kentucky family. His grandfather, for whom he was named, had been governor of Kentucky from 1824 to 1828. In 1861, Desha helped raise a company for the 1st Kentucky, and went off to war with his soldiers. Now, as the 1st Kentucky traded blows with the 9th Pennsylvania Reserves, it seems Capt. Desha took command of the whole regiment.[49]

Stuart took the Kentuckians' Company B and put them by Cutts's battery, or at least what was left of it. One of the Kentuckians remarked that he found "many of the gunners and almost every horse shot." The rest of the regiment advanced further into the woods.[50]

One of the advancing Kentuckians was Private William Phelps, a soldier in Desha's Company C. The city attorney of Covington, Kentucky, he had eagerly joined the 1st Kentucky. As the firing continued, a bullet hit Phelps in the left hand and continued through his wrist, shattering the bone.[51]

---

47 William Preston Johnston CSR, 1st KY Infantry, NARA; Edward Crossland CSR, 1st KY Infantry, NARA; *OR* 5, 493.

48 David Thomson to Jefferson Davis, Nov. 2, 1862, Jefferson Davis Papers, NARA.

49 W. R. Rogan, "Capt. Jo Desha," in *Confederate Veteran* 10, No. 8 (1902), 370.

50 *Atlanta Constitution*, Jul. 16, 1898.

51 John L. Johnson, *The University Memorial: Biographical Sketches of Alumni of the University of Virginia Who Fell in the Confederate War* (Baltimore, 1871), 80-81.

Further down the line, the Kentuckians' Company K made its own way through the pines. Helping lead them was 1st Lt. David Todd, a half-brother to Mary Todd Lincoln. Todd fought through the ever-increasing musketry coming from the Federal lines, though his company was largely protected by the heavy trees, suffering only two casualties.[52]

The 9th Reserves had recovered from the Kentuckians getting the drop on them. Private Alexander Murdoch remembered officers shouting out, *"Fire at will[,] Fire!"* The Pittsburgh Rifles "astonished those Johnnies with the rapid handling of our Sharpe's Rifles." The cacophony of battle rose and fell. "Whiz-bang-zip, intermixed with the groans of the wounded and the roar of artillery on our left made what we then thought was a fearful racket," Murdoch went on.[53] While the 9th Reserves traded volleys with the rebels, its major, James Snodgrass, "had his horse shot under him."[54]

The battle, which had started a little after noon, had been going on for more than an hour. Right about then, as Edward Ord was off personally directing infantry regiments to advance, Maj. Gen. George McCall arrived. Earlier in the morning, Ord had sent his division commander a note, updating the general on his progress and noting the rumored presence of Confederate forces near Hunter's Mill and Herndon. McCall received Ord's note "At 10.30 a.m.," about an hour and a half before the battle started. "I immediately mounted my horse, and with my staff and an escort of cavalry moved rapidly forward to overtake, if possible, Ord's brigade," McCall wrote.[55]

Still a few miles from Dranesville, McCall reined in at Difficult Run to talk with John Reynolds. The two conversed about Reynolds's role in case anything happened, and then McCall spurred on again. "When within about 2 miles of Dranesville I heard the first gun fired by the enemy," McCall said. He hurried on to get to his men, under fire for the first time.[56]

McCall was not the only one to hear the firing. At Camp Pierpont, eager and anxious Pennsylvanians began to catch earfuls of the noise in the distance. Private Vernon Henderson, a soldier in the 6th Reserves, but on detached duty at

---

52 David Todd, Company K, 1st KY Infantry, CSR, NARA; See Appendix 3 for casualties in the 1st KY; Stephen Berry and Angela Esco Elder, eds., *Practical Strangers: The Courtship Correspondence of Nathaniel Dawson and Elodie Todd, Sister of Mary Todd Lincoln* (Athens, GA, 2017), 276.

53 Murdoch, "The Pittsburgh Rifles and the Battle of Dranesville," 303. Emphasis in original.

54 *Philadelphia Press*, Dec. 23, 1861.

55 *OR* 5, 474.

56 Ibid.

Langley, wrote, "Heavy firing was heard in the direction they had taken. We waited impatiently until dark for news."[57]

Other soldiers were not so keen on waiting. "Boom! came the sound of [a] gun," Frank Holsinger of the 8th Reserves wrote. Holsinger, grabbing his gun and gathering his equipment with other soldiers, began to "scamper toward the sound of cannon." As Holsinger got closer, he came across "a wounded corporal of the Sixth Regiment Reserves. He was the first soldier I had seen coming from the field wounded." He and his comrades rushed past the wounded man, still eager to get to the fighting. George Meade also heard the firing. "Without waiting for orders, I started with the brigade," he wrote, but arrived too late to participate.[58]

Even at Camp Griffin, 11 miles from Dranesville, the Federals heard the gunfire. Winfield S. Hancock wrote to Gen. McClellan's chief of staff, explaining that two brigades and two artillery batteries had already left camp for the sound of the firing. "My brigade is here under arms. I shall go out to the turnpike myself immediately."[59] Hancock's men departed around 1:00 p.m. and "marched at a rapid pace," trying to get to the aid of their comrades. "We marched on double quick four miles," a New Yorker wrote. "I tell you, it made some of the boys puff." They came to a burned bridge near Hunter's Hill and were forced to halt.[60]

Reinforcements were rushing to help Stuart, too. Just as the rolling noise of cannon and muskets could be heard at Langley and Lewinsville, so too it was audible at Centreville. William McClendon, a soldier in the 15th Alabama, remembered years later: "We heard the report of cannon in fast succession and a dull roaring sound resembling the muttering sound of distant thunder, which we took to be the sound of small arms." Reaching the decision to go help Stuart, "We raised the 'Rebel yell' and quickened our step." They, like their Federal counterparts, did not make it to the battlefield in time.[61]

But at least one reinforcement did. Lieutenant C. L. Jackson was a volunteer aide to Brig. Gen. Sam Jones. "He was on his way to join [Jones]," a postwar newspaper read. "When passing through Drainesville, he saw the terrible battle in progress, and without reporting to General Stuart, he immediately threw himself into the thickest of the fight." Jackson and his "gray horse . . . were everywhere

---

57 Vernon Henderson Diary, Entry Dec. 20, 1861, USAHEC.

58 Frank Holsinger, "How Does One Feel Under Fire?" in *War Talks in Kansas: A Series of Papers Read Before the Kansas Commandery of the Military Order of the Loyal Legion of the United States* (Kansas City, 1906), 292; Meade, *The Life and Letters of George Gordon Meade*: Vol. 1, 237.

59 George Brinton McClellan Papers: Correspondence I, 1783-1888, 1861; Dec. 14-23, 149.

60 *Vermont Journal*, Jan. 4, 1862; *Jamestown Journal* (NY), Dec. 27, 1861.

61 W. A. McClendon, *Recollections of War Times By An Old Veteran While Under Stonewall Jackson and Lieutenant General James Longstreet* (Tuscaloosa, AL, 2010), 49.

conspicuous in the midst of shot and shell." The volunteer aide did well enough not only to gain recognition in Stuart's report, but also grabbed the attention of Thomas Kane. After the battle, Kane passed a note through the lines, extending "his compliments to the commander of the Southern forces this afternoon, and desires to speak in terms of commendation and praise of the gallant conduct of the officer who rode the gray horse."[62]

While Lt. Jackson was rallying soldiers, the Confederate attack began to wane. All four of Stuart's regiments had been stopped at the wood's edge, and his artillery had been blasted to pieces. When the action began, Stuart showed initiative and tackled the principles of a meeting engagement well. However, the battle had spiraled out of his control as soon as Edward Ord deployed his artillery and blasted the Sumter Flying Artillery off the map.

Stuart was left with nothing to do but continue to press his infantry forward. Ever since the first shot had been fired, it was Stuart's intention to buy time for his wagon train to retreat to safety, and he had done so. The wagons, though empty of the forage that had been the sortie's objective, were nonetheless safe, and every extra minute just racked up the butcher's bill. Throughout the fight, Stuart remained in the thick of it. "I was never in greater personal danger," he wrote his wife Flora. "Men & horses fell around me like ten-pins, but thanks to God to whom I looked for protection, neither myself nor my horse was touched."[63]

Plenty of others were going down, though. Major Thomas Woodward figured the 6th South Carolina had just fired its twentieth volley when "my horse received his death wound in his flank . . . and finding that he was rapidly sinking under me, I sprang to the ground." Woodward had just cleared his dying animal "when a shot from the window of the brick house . . . passed through the upper third of my left thigh, spinning me round like a top." Pennsylvanians in the Thornton House were finding their marks. Carolinians George Ladd and Alexander Douglass sprang to their wounded major and tried to help him out of the pines. Woodward passed word to Lt. Col. Secrest, "giving him the admonition that 'the sooner he got out of there, with what men were left, the better it would be.'" Some soldiers from the 11th Virginia helped the wounded Woodward "in an ambulance and cover[ed him] up with blankets."[64]

Around this time, too, Capt. Joshua Desha was hit. A projectile hit him "in the shoulder, his left arm crushed below the elbow, rendering it almost useless the rest

---

62 *The Daily Picayune*, Nov. 5, 1893. A reprint of the article is published in *Southern Historical Society Papers* 21, ed. by R. A. Brock (Richmond, 1893), 301; *OR* 5, 494.

63 J. E. B Stuart quoted in Thomason, *Jeb Stuart*, 126-127.

64 Woodward, *From Fort Sumter to Dranesville*, 27; Holland, *Recollections of a Private*, 9.

of his life." Desha's soldiers carried him to the rear. In their fight the Kentuckians suffered 27 casualties.[65]

Stuart knew it was time to leave. His wagon train had escaped safely back to Centreville, in part because of some rather ingenious driving. One of the drivers, Jim Wilkerson, said "that he turned his team in an eight-foot cut and passed two more in a ten-foot cut and had liked to have beat the whole train to camp." Fellow comrades claimed, "His driving was like the driving of Jehu, for he drove furiously." Another driver, Jacob Dove from the 1st North Carolina Cavalry, claimed to have taken his wagons out of danger and "even made them jump fences." The dramatic escapes prevented their capture. "We had fought to protect some of our wagons," Private William Holland in the 11th Virginia succinctly explained. "The wagons had to come back without the forage, but we kept the Yankees from capturing them."[66]

The wagons were gone, and Stuart's priority now was Capt. Cutts's broken battery. Nearly all the Georgians' horses had been killed, so Stuart called on nearby infantry to help drag the cannon out by hand. Soldiers who, a few minutes earlier, had been trading shots with the Federal infantry, now shifted their focus to grabbing ropes and began to drag the guns out of harm's way. A Virginian wrote "The boys took hold with a hearty will." Another, Theodore Hammond, "pulling the horse, thus showing himself possessed of great strength as well as great courage, and thus the battery was saved." Sergeant O. B. Norvell, from the 1st Kentucky, noted, "Company B staid with the wreck of the battery until the repulse of our line and then helped the artillerymen to drag the guns by hand."[67]

The infantrymen did not take everything. They left the battery's debris, including the dead men and the exploded caisson. One of J. E. B. Stuart's staff officers passed along a story of the general himself riding back with the battery. "Over his horse's neck hung a quantity of harness which he had stripped from some of the dead artillery horses." But as Stuart biographer Emory Thomas points out, "It is worth asking why Stuart, the general commanding, was carrying off that artillery harness. Surely he had more important things to do." Thomas continues: "The harness hanging from Stuart's horse certainly bore witness to his energy and

---

65 W. R. Rogan, 370; *OR* 5, 494; A tally of the 1st KY's losses tabulate to twenty-seven, not the twenty-six that Stuart reported. The names of the casualties are in Appendix Three.

66 *Anderson Intelligencer*, May 1, 1905; Rufus Barringer, "First Cavalry," in *Histories of the Several Regiments and Battalions from North Carolina, In the Great War 1861-'65*, Vol. 1, ed. by Walter Clark (Raleigh, 1901), 419-420; Holland, *Recollections of a Private*, 9. The reference to Jehu comes from 2 Kings, 9:20 (KJV): "And the watchman told, saying, He came even unto them, and cometh not again: and the driving is like the driving of Jehu the son of Nimshi; for he driveth furiously."

67 Kessler, ed., *The Fincastle Rifles*, 5; *Richmond Whig*, Dec. 27, 1861; *Atlanta Constitution*, Jul. 16, 1898.

attention to detail. But it was also evidence that Stuart had lost control of events." Now, he was "literally picking up the pieces of a shattered day."[68]

Stuart's infantry began to fall back the same way they came. It was close to 2:00 p.m. The battle, which had lasted two hours, was in its closing moments. Edward Ord, seeing the rebels in front of him retreating, started to organize a counterattack. He rode up to the 6th Reserves and called out, "What regiment is this?" A lieutenant shouted back, "*The bloody Sixth.*" Pointing at the retreating Confederates, Ord directed the Pennsylvanians after them.[69] Though the brigadier general was right in the middle of the firing, he showed no trepidation. Placidus Ord, serving on his brother's staff, later wrote that his sibling "wears the *medal* of the Virgin Mary ever around his neck, still believing that relying on her, he feels safe from the balls of the enemy."[70]

As Ord began his pursuit, he received word that his division commander, George McCall, had arrived. "As I was very busy urging the men forward, and they required all my attention to keep them to their work, I did not at once report, but when we reached the ground occupied by the enemy's battery I reported to him." Rather than trying to command Ord, McCall "was so kind as to direct me to continue the pursuit in the same order and to continue my dispositions, which I did."[71]

Or at least he tried to. Ord later told George Meade in confidence that the soldiers acted "better than he expected, but not so well as they ought." When he tried to order his regiments to counterattack, the Pennsylvanians were hesitant to follow the Confederates into the same thick pine trees that had just proven such an obstacle. Meade wrote to his wife, "Ord says if they had charged when he first ordered them, he would have captured the whole battery and lots of prisoners."[72]

In an especially surprising tale, Surgeon S. D. Freeman of the Bucktails entered the Thornton House during the action. While most of the soldiers were firing out of the windows, Freeman found Pvt. Eli Seamans "standing before a mirror, oiling his hair." A shocked and stunned Freeman shouted at the soldier, "Shoot down the rebels," before Seamans went back to it.[73]

---

68 McClellan, *I Rode with Jeb Stuart*, 45-46; Thomas, *Bold Dragoon*, 100.

69 William Burgess to William D. Dixon, Aug. 24, 1886, Virginia Tech Special Collections and University Archives. Emphasis in original.

70 Placidus Ord quoted in Cresap, *Appomattox Commander*, 363. Emphasis in original.

71 *OR* 5, 479.

72 Meade, *The Life and Letters of George Gordon Meade*: Vol. 1, 237-238.

73 M. A. Leeson, *History of the Counties of McKean, Elk, and Forest, Pennsylvania, with Biographical Selections Including Their Early Settlement and Development* (Chicago, 1890), 136.

Some of the Pennsylvanians did, in fact, charge forward. After having spent the whole battle in reserve, the 12th Reserves stormed down from the turnpike and rushed forward. During its brief pursuit, the 12th suffered its only casualty when Pvt. William Fox was struck in the leg. But Fox was lucky—the bullet hit his wallet "and a $2.50 gold piece in it was bent nearly double."[74]

Others were not so fortunate. Kane's Bucktails led the counterattack and the Keystoners charged ahead with a cheer. At the front was Capt. Alanson Niles, whose skirmishers had been pushed back at the very beginning of the fight. Kane wrote about Niles, "although his tall figure rendered him conspicuous and marked for the enemy's sharpshooters, he did not cease exposing himself to cheer on his men." During the pursuit, "while in the act of firing a gun which he picked up from the ground near him," Niles was shot through the side. The "bullet, piercing his lung, made him drop to the ground." Though at first feared a mortal wound, Niles eventually recovered and was with the regiment until 1864.[75]

Thomas Kane was shot soon thereafter. Though still stricken with fever, from all accounts Kane rose to the occasion and commanded his regiment ably. He led them forward, guiding along the Centreville Road, but Stuart's regiments were not going easily. Some of the Confederates staged a fighting withdrawal, firing as they went. A friend of Kane wrote to Brigham Young, the Mormon leader, after the battle, describing what happened next: "The buckshot pass[ed] through the cheek, and fractur[ed] a tooth. . . . There is another small opening through the cheek near the angle of the mouth." Kane reeled from the wound, but "A moment's halt, just sufficient to tie a bandage of some sort, and he again, despite the pain and loss of blood, resumed his position at the lead of his men." The wound bothered Kane for years.[76]

Ord's pursuit ended before it got under way. His men, the ones he could get to go forward at all, were bone-tired and low on ammunition, and their adrenaline was giving way to exhaustion. They had woken nearly 11 hours earlier, marched close to 12 miles, and then fought for at least two hours. With the Confederate rearguard proving not so willing to break and run, it was time to stop, regroup, and take stock of the situation.

The Confederate rearguard was led by James Gordon and his North Carolinian cavalry. They were the same troopers who had deployed first into an extended

---

74 *OR* 5, 488.

75 Kane Papers, Box 23, Folder 4, Item 31, BYU; *Wellsboro Agitator*, Jan. 8, 1862; Rauch and Thomson, *"Bucktails"*, 77. Niles was wounded again at Gettysburg.

76 John Bernhisel quoted in Matthew J. Grow and Ronald W. Walker, *The Prophet and the Reformer: The Letters of Brigham Young and Thomas L. Kane* (Oxford, 2015), 371; Rauch and Thomson, *"Bucktails,"* 77.

skirmish line, and now they were forming the last battle line. "The enemy came near enough to fire upon them once," Gordon wrote his wife. Those cavalry shots were the last of the battle.[77]

"We had a hard-fought battle here," Stuart wrote to D. H. Hill the next day. "I had four pieces and four regiments, say 1,200 strong. The enemy had from five to ten regiments, six or seven pieces artillery. They said 3,100," Stuart wrote. "Finding heavy re-enforcements arriving, I withdrew my command in perfect order from the field, carrying off nearly all the wounded. The enemy's loss was over 50 killed; our killed 27. They evacuated at dark." Stuart's interpretation of the events of December 20 did not align with reality, but for the moment, he was trying to mitigate the setback his force had just suffered.[78]

George McCall alerted his army commander of the fight, writing a dispatch from Dranesville. Dated 4:00 p.m., McCall briefly outlined the fight, and wrote, "We have found forty killed of the enemy + ten wounded on the field. Our loss two killed + three wounded. We have taken two caissons with the harnesses, the horses having been killed." McCall's casualty estimates for the Federal forces were woefully low of reality, but his dispatch highlights what the army knew, and when.[79]

One thing was especially clear, if the casualty counts were not: Ord had won the battle. After the failure of Manassas, and the defeat at Ball's Bluff, the soldiers of the Federal Army of the Potomac had finally, *finally*, won a victory. But they would have to wait to celebrate. Because now that they had won, the Federals had a bloody battlefield to pick up, scattered with the bodies of the dead, dying, and wounded.

The battle of Dranesville was over, but the recovery was just beginning.

<hr>

77 James B. Gordon to his mother, Dec. 23, 1861, NC State Archives.

78 *OR* 5, 490.

79 George Brinton McClellan Papers: Correspondence I, 1783-1888; 1861, Dec. 14-23, 156.

Chapter Twelve

"The Camps Are Filled With Trophies"

The Battle's Aftermath

For the first time in northern Virginia, a Federal force had won. There were other Union victories in western Virginia (Philippi, Rich Mountain, and Carnifex Ferry, to name a few) but never in front of Washington. Every time that blue fought gray, it seemed, it was the Confederates holding the field at the end of the fighting. But not today. Not at Dranesville. Around 2:30 p.m., as the firing stopped, it was the regiments of the Pennsylvania Reserves under the command of Brig. Gen. Edward Ord who had possession of the field.

The Pennsylvanians, after their brief pursuit, returned to the turnpike and formed back into a battle line. They waited to see if the Confederates would launch another attack, but none came. Alexander Murdoch, Pittsburgh Rifles, reached for "the solid comfort he had in his old stone pipe loaded up with 'Killikenick' tobacco." He shared it with a comrade, who returned the pipe with a sigh, "I tell you that is good." After it became clear the Confederates were not coming back, the regiments began to scour the battlefield.[1]

To the victors went the spoils. "The rebels threw down guns, blankets, knapsacks, cartridge boxes and took to their heels as fast as they could," James Chadwick, 10th Reserves, wrote. "Our men have brought in a great many relics. . . . They are here before me, and one of them all stained with blood." Watching his soldiers rifling through the pockets of a corpse, Ord snapped and "severely reprimanded some of the soldiers whom he saw cutting the buttons off the coat of an Officer who was lying dead," Chadwick went on. "He said,

1 Murdoch, "The Pittsburgh Rifles and the Battle of Dranesville," 303.

'Let him alone! He was a brave man though he was fighting in a bad cause.'"[2] Angelo Crapsey, 1st Rifles, added to a friend, "There was a general time a plundering. . . . [E]verything of account had been taken such as revolvers & Southern money or script & officers trappings, swords, &c."[3]

The Pennsylvanians also had a bloody battlefield to tend to. Ord's brigade suffered 74 casualties, 10 of whom were either killed outright or would soon die of their wounds. The losses were heaviest in the 1st Rifles (34 casualties) and the 9th Reserves (22), while the 6th Reserves followed with 16, and the 12th had just one wounded (William Fox, the soldier with the dented gold coin). The 10th Reserves and the 1st Pennsylvania Reserve Cavalry both suffered no casualties of which to speak. Easton's battery had some bumps and bruises.[4]

Opposite Ord, the Confederates suffered nearly three times as many losses. On the battlefield lay close to 60 dead Confederates and even more wounded. Although Stuart's regiments took many of their wounded with them, there were still others scattered about, some too seriously wounded to be moved, and others overlooked in the pines. They were now Ord's responsibility.[5]

As the battle ended, John Reynolds arrived with his brigade, followed by George Meade about an hour and a half later. With the entire division now around Dranesville, McCall oversaw the clean-up of the battlefield. The Pennsylvanians fanned out.

"The scene beggars description," one Pennsylvanian wrote. "In the direction of which we fired into the woods, were the dead and dying, completely riddled by our bullets, some had half dozen balls in their bodies." Walking up to where Cutts's battery was posted, he described, "Many without heads, others without limbs, which were scattered to some distance from where their bodies lay: everything indicating a frightful explosion of their magazine had taken place. Quite a number of horses were killed, and mingled with the dead rebels."[6] Sergeant George Merrick, seeing the devastation wrought by Easton's battery, wrote, "I saw not a tree which showed that their range had exceeded the width of the road, farther than several feet on a side. One large oak was pierced and shattered by three different shells,

2 James Chadwick to his mother, Dec. 20, 1861, Allegheny College.

3 Crapsey quoted in Brandt, *Pathway to Hell*, 67.

4 The losses presented here do not match up in totality with the casualties as tabulated in the *OR* 5, 489. See Appendix Three for a listing of all the casualties.

5 *OR* 5, 494.

6 *Pittsburgh Gazette*, Dec. 27, 1861.

and horses, overtaken in their flight by the death dealing missiles, lay in and near the road, the distance of half a mile."[7]

The Pennsylvanians set out, picking up both the Confederate casualties and their own. They decided to bring them to a few private homes along the turnpike. Ord reported, "The enemy left 21 of their most desperately wounded on the field . . . who were taken up, carried to houses, and their wounds dressed by our surgeons; but they will nearly all die."[8] Before they marched back to Dranesville, the Federals left behind "a good many bandages, so as to be used in dressing their wounds," a Confederate soldier recounted.[9]

Besides the 21 Confederates left at Dranesville, Ord also captured 10 others that were brought back as prisoners of war. Four each came from the 1st Kentucky and 10th Alabama, and two from the 6th South Carolina. Among the prisoners, "Several were very sullen and dogged, refusing to give any account of themselves, and answering no questions whatever," a soldier from the 6th Reserves remembered. Others, though, were more communicative. An Alabamian "identified several of the bodies near him." The soldier, spotting the body of James B. Martin, said, "that is our Lieutenant Colonel." Martin's coat had been taken by some Pennsylvanians.[10]

Three of the Confederates Ord brought back did not live long. John Caruthers from the 6th South Carolina had his back broken and "was left on the field" a comrade wrote. Union soldiers found Caruthers and moved him to the front porch of the Thornton House. He gave a Pennsylvanian "his watch and some mementoes to send to his mother." Transported to Camp Pierpont, Caruthers died the next day.[11] Likewise, Pvt. Ira. S. Chaney from the 10th Alabama was transported back to Camp Pierpont where he died the day after Christmas.[12] Private F. G. Alexander, from the 1st Kentucky, did not even make it to Camp Pierpont; shot through the abdomen, he died in an ambulance on the way.[13]

While the Confederate wounded were being recovered, other Federals searched for one of their own. Since the battle's opening shots, no one had seen 21-year-old Alexander B. Smith from the Pittsburgh Rifles. The soldiers "collected a party, and . . . went in search of him." They found the young man lying among the pines

7 *Wellsboro Agitator*, Jan. 8, 1862.

8 *OR* 5, 479.

9 *Richmond Dispatch*, Dec. 30, 1861.

10 *Wellsboro Agitator*, Jan. 8, 1862.

11 John M. Brice to his father, Dec. 21, 1861, VMHC; John Caruthers CSR, Company F, 6th SC Infantry, NARA, *Philadelphia Inquirer*, Dec. 23, 1861

12 Ira S. Chaney CSR, Company I, 10th AL Infantry, NARA.

13 F. G. Alexander, 1st KY, Compiled Service Record.

where he had fallen. "He was lying for three hours where he fell," one wrote, "shot in the side of the neck, still able to speak, though unable to move." Smith told his rescuers that the Confederates had given him water, but had taken his rifle and cartridge box, although the Sharps Rifle was soon found among debris of the battlefield. The soldiers brought Smith back to Camp Pierpont where he lingered for close to two weeks, dying on January 14, 1862. His comrades brought the casket to Washington and "served as a body-guard with reversed arms," remembered George Dean. Back in Pittsburgh, Smith's mother posted in a local newspaper, "The friends of the family are respectfully invited to attend the funeral from the residence at his mother, Greenwood st., West Manchester." Smith was buried in Pittsburgh's Allegheny Cemetery.[14]

By the time Ord's men tended to their wounded and gathered the Confederates, "it was almost dark," remembered John Bard, 1st Pennsylvania Rifles. McCall feared a stronger Confederate force coming out of Centreville and decided it was best to return to Langley. With his dead, wounded, and prisoners in tow, McCall turned his division around and began the long trek back.[15]

"Our march home that night about thirteen . . . miles was very trying on me and on all our boys," Sgt. A. P. Morrison, 9th Reserves, wrote. "We started back at dark—we had done hard work through the day we had been most intensely excited—we were hungry and shivering in the cold frosty air—the excitement was all over—our muscles were relaxed." The adrenaline that had carried the Pennsylvanians through the day ebbed. They dragged themselves back to camp, arriving close to 10:00 p.m., nearly 17 hours after they had left. The soldiers barely had enough energy to describe the fight to those who had been left behind before crawling into bed and falling fast asleep. "We were completely exhausted, and it was with difficulty that some of us could reach camp, for we were foot sore and lame," Sgt. John Lewis, 6th Reserves, wrote. Ord noted that he had been in the saddle "15 hours continuously."[16]

The march was a near-nightmare for the wounded. McCall now realized he did not have a viable plan to transport all the wounded, both his own and Stuart's. "The want of ambulances was felt on this occasion," McCall wrote in his report. "I would respectfully suggest that a few more be ordered to each regiment of my

14 *Pittsburgh Gazette*, Dec. 27, 1861; John McQuaide to William McQuaide, Dec. 23, 1861, *Civil War Times Illustrated Collection*, USAHEC; Dean, "Battle of Dranesville," 3; *Pittsburgh Daily Gazette and Advertiser*, Jan. 18, 1862.

15 Bard, *John Bard's History of the Old Bucktails*, 19.

16 A. P. Morrison to friend, Dec. 26, 1861, Author's Collection; James Chadwick to his mother, Dec. 20, 1861, Allegheny College; *Honesdale Democrat*, Jan. 9, 1862; Edward Ord to his wife, Dec. 24, 1861, Edward Ord Papers, Box 1, Folder 3, Item 12, Stanford University.

The grave of Alexander Smith, 9th Pennsylvania Reserves, in Pittsburgh's Union Dale Cemetery. *Courtesy of Jim DiNucci*

division."[17] Except, according to the army's high command, McCall did have enough ambulances.

"Upon the inspection of General McCall's division . . . on the 5th of December, they had 22 two-wheeled and 2 four-wheeled ambulances and 1 transport cart," wrote Charles Tripler, medical director of the Army of the Potomac. "Four of the two-wheeled are reported broken at this date, but as fifteen days elapsed before they were wanted, they must have been repaired if proper attention was given to their condition." Implying that McCall had not properly seen to his division's medical transport, Tripler finished, "There was then in General McCall's camp sufficient transportation for the wounded. Why it was not sent to the battle-field I don't know."[18]

To put it bluntly, the Army of the Potomac's medical transportation system was a mess. During its march to Manassas, the army relied on civilian contractors to drive ambulances and wagons for their wounded, but in the great retreat to Washington, many abandoned their vehicles. Wounded men were left on the battlefield for days. Now, months later, the army could claim each division had an allotment of ambulances, but the quality of those transports left much to be desired. The army bought hundreds of two-wheeled ambulances, known as Finleys, and a small scattering of four-wheeled transports, but soon found the two-wheeled vehicles "utterly unfit" for their designed use. As part of the *Medical and Surgical History of the War of the Rebellion,* the Surgeon General's office researched the use of the Finley ambulance early in the war and concluded that "experience soon proved them useless; their motion was intolerable and excruciating; wounded men begged to be taken out." Even if McCall's two-wheeled Finley carriages were in working order at Dranesville, they still likely would not have been of much help.[19]

17 *OR* 5, 476.

18 Ibid., 97.

19 Ibid., 87; *The Medical and Surgical History of the War of the Rebellion, 1861-1865*, Pt. 3, Vol. 2 (Washington, D.C., 1870-1883), 948. See Hennessy, *The First Battle of Manassas*, 148, for treatment of wounded at First Manassas.

The unpopular two-wheeled Finley ambulance. *Medical and Surgical History of the War of the Rebellion*

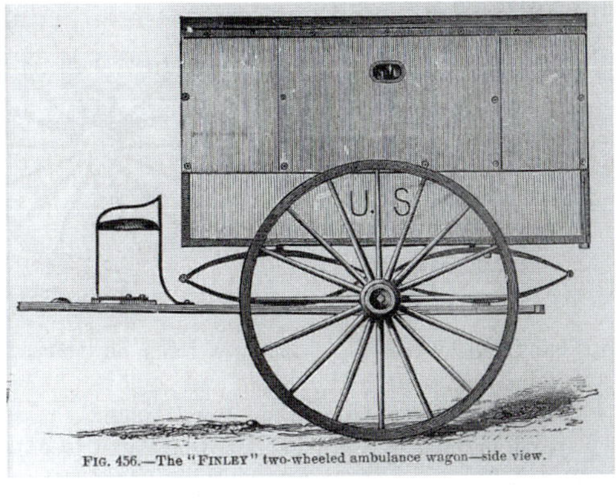

FIG. 456.—The "FINLEY" two-wheeled ambulance wagon—side view.

In the wake of the ambulance shortage, the soldiers improvised. "I saw others carried from the field, some on a comrade's back some borne along between two men—some carried on litters all pale, and blood stained," Sgt. Morrison wrote.[20]

Blood-covered and exhausted, the Federals dragged themselves back to Camp Pierpont. The Pennsylvanians brought the wounded and their own dead with them, but they left behind the Confederate corpses. Those bodies were someone else's problem.

*   *   *

Edwin Gaillard knew he needed to find as many ambulances and surgeons as he could as soon as possible. Gaillard was the medical director for the Second Corps, Confederate Army of the Potomac, and for the past couple of hours, plainly audible from Centreville, was the sound of battle. It rolled and crackled and boomed and snapped, and as Confederate soldiers streamed out of the town and towards the sound of gunfire, Gaillard made his own preparations. No one quite knew what was going on, but there was one certainty: there would be casualties. Gaillard wrote to the surgeons of six regiments, "You will repair immediately to Col. Radford's Cavalry Camp (on the Frying Pan Road) prepared with instruments and the requisite surgical appliances to move, with an escort, to the battle ground. You will take with you the ambulances of your Regiment." He ordered two other surgeons to send their ambulances to help pick up the wounded. Above all, he stressed, "You are instructed after having reached Col. Radford's Cavalry Camp not to await the ambulances of your respective Regiments, but to proceed, with the escort provided, to the temporary Hospital for the wounded."[21]

The convoy of surgeons and ambulances left Centreville, following the same route that Stuart's convoy had nearly twelve hours earlier. Their destination was the Frying Pan Baptist Meetinghouse, which, following the battle, was converted

20 A. P. Morrison to friend, Dec. 26, 1861, Author's Collection.

21 Dispatches of E. S. Gaillard, Dec. 20, 1861, William Sylvanus Morris Papers, 1854-1865, Section 5, VMHC.

into a field hospital. As Stuart's regiments retreated, they brought "with them all the wounded that could be found," Stuart wrote. The Confederate general stopped at the Loudoun & Hampshire Railroad and turned to ensure they were not being pursued any further. Stuart then "proceeded to Fryingpan Church, where the wounded were cared for."[22]

The Frying Pan Meetinghouse took its name from the nearby Frying Pan Run, which itself got its unusual name in the 18th century, when, according to legend, some American Indians had left behind their cookware.[23] Built on two acres of land in 1791, the church became a place local Baptists convened to conduct their religious services. Altogether, the building was a simple, square, one-and-a-half-story structure, with 29 pews arranged in two aisles.[24]

Before the war, the church housed a healthy-sized congregation that included not only whites but also free blacks and enslaved people. Outside sat a small cemetery. Now, late in the afternoon of December 20, 1861, it became a field hospital for the bleeding, broken bodies brought back from Dranesville.

In addition to the regimental surgeons, some of the locals went to the church to help. They found about 140 wounded Confederate soldiers with gunshot and shrapnel wounds. One woman arriving was 25-year-old Laura Ratcliffe, who lived nearby. She jumped to work and caught the eye of J. E. B. Stuart. He later wrote her a poem of his impressions, penning, "I saw thy beauteous image bending o'er/The prostrate form of one . . . I saw thee soothe the soldier's aching brow." Watching Ratcliffe treat the wounded soldier, Stuart even included in his poem the distasteful line, "And ardent wished his lot were mine-/To be carressed with care like thine."[25]

Among the wounded was Col. John Forney. With the Alabamian's arm shattered, it appeared the only cure would be to cut it off, but "the pleas of a young surgeon saved the arm from amputation." Though the arm was saved, "the wound was the source of much discomfort and suffering the remainder of his life."[26]

Frying Pan was only a hospital for a week or so at most. Being close to Centreville, the wounded were soon evacuated via rail to Richmond or other

---

22 *OR* 5, 492.

23 Mary McCutchen Kell and Richard Sacchi, "National Register of Historical Places—Nomination Form: Frying Pan Church," Fairfax County Park Authority, (1990), 2.

24 Ibid.

25 J. E. B. Stuart poem addressed to Laura Ratcliffe, quoted in Thomas Low, "Letters to Laura," *Civil War Times Illustrated* (Jul./Aug. 1992): 61. Stuart misspelled the word 'caressed.'

26 Daugette, "Life of Major General John H. Forney", 371.

Frying Pan Church, where Confederate wounded were treated after the battle of Dranesville.
Author

permanent establishments. Many wound up in Danville's General Hospital No. 1. Others were sent home to recuperate.[27]

There were some who never made it home. As recounted in the previous chapter, Capt. Obadiah Harden was shot carrying the 6th South Carolina's flag. He made it back to Centreville before dying. Private William Phelps from the 1st Kentucky also did not make it past Centreville. Shot in the wrist, Phelps's injury required amputation. Word spread to his family, including his mother, all the way back in Covington, Kentucky. She tried to make her way to Centreville, but had to pass through Pittsburgh, Washington, and Baltimore. At every turn she met roadblocks and hindrances, unable to get a pass through the lines by Federal officers who learned that the wounded son she sought was a rebel. Finally diverted through Fort Monroe and Norfolk, Phelps's mother arrived in Richmond, where she took a train up to Manassas Junction with her sister. But as the women arrived, they learned the news. "Her child had died that morning, just ten hours before," Phelps's aunt wrote. A comrade of Phelps's told both his mother and aunt the circumstances of his death. "Who can describe that night of horrors?" the aunt wrote.[28]

The story repeated itself as families learned of their loved ones' wounding, or worse. They rushed to Centreville and Manassas. Other families, though, had

27 For example, Pvt. Henry Harless from the 10th AL was admitted to the hospital in Danville on Jan. 9, 1862. Henry Harless, CSR, Company C, 10th AL Infantry, NARA.

28 Judith W. McGuire, *Diary of a Southern Refugee During the War* (New York, 1868), 82-86.

Laura Ratcliffe helped the wounded at Frying Pan and caught the eye of J. E. B. Stuart. *Library of Virginia*

nothing but questions with no answers. Those questions haunted them for decades—and it haunted the soldiers too. In their retreat, the Confederates could not take all their wounded.

Leaving comrades plagued the memories of soldiers for years. Private William Clinkinbeard of the 1st Kentucky wrote to the *Confederate Veteran* magazine in 1909, 48 years after the battle. "While falling back through the woods he caught up with a young soldier wounded in the arm and bleeding dreadfully," Clinkinbeard wrote in the third person. "He stanched the flow as best he could with a handkerchief about the arm and helped the soldier to a small branch of water; but as the enemy was pressing close, he had to leave him, and is now anxious to learn his fate." The fear and anxiety of a half-century of worrying comes through Clinkinbeard's plea for information. "The young soldier belonged to the 6th South Carolina, but he did not learn his name."[29]

In the wake of removing the wounded to Frying Pan, and eventually to more permanent hospitals, Stuart knew he needed to go back to Dranesville, if for nothing else than to collect his dead soldiers. But he also wanted to fight again. He had been defeated, and now he wanted the Federals to come again so that he might return the favor. He made plans to return to Dranesville the very next day.

Stuart could not take the same regiments. They were exhausted and ripped to shreds. With the four regiments of infantry, contingent of cavalry, and artillery battery he had taken, Stuart suffered 203 casualties. It was roughly 10 percent of his force: the losses had been heaviest in the 10th Alabama, with 67, and the 6th South Carolina, with 63 casualties. The 1st Kentucky suffered 27 killed and wounded, while the 11th Virginia lost 21. In terms of percentages, the Sumter Flying Artillery's 17 casualties nearly accounted for half of its strength, whereas the 6th South Carolina, having gone into battle with 334 rank and file, had 20% of

29 John M. Brice to his father, Dec. 21, 1861, VMHC; *Confederate Veteran* XVII, No. 1, Jan. 1909. No further information is available about Clinkinbeard's request for information, and it is not clear if any reply was made.

its force knocked out. It was a brutal reality check. The soldiers returned to their camps and took stock of what they had just experienced.[30]

On December 21, Stuart returned to Dranesville with two new regiments. The 9th Georgia and the 18th Virginia shuffled up from Centreville and with some cavalry in tow, again from the 1st North Carolina and 2nd Virginia, Stuart repeated the march to Dranesville. He once again brought wagons with him, this time not for forage, but for the bodies he knew still lay on the battlefield.[31]

Stuart's column returned to Dranesville around noontime, essentially twenty-fours after the battle began. "We [were] suspecting the enemy every moment," Pvt. Thomas Spencer, 18th Virginia, wrote to a friend. North Carolinian D. H. Gettys wanted to fight again, and wrote to his brother, "We expected to get another fight but were disappointed. The Cowards were satisfied with a meagre victory." No Federals were coming to interrupt Stuart's objective of gathering his dead.[32] The Confederates spread out on their grisly task.

Soldiers picking up the dead on December 21 were met by the horrific sights left behind by the Federals. The dead "were lying in heaps covered with their own and fellow's frozen gore," D. H. Gettys wrote. The beheaded bodies of John McGarrah and Washington F. Williams proved particularly gruesome, and soldiers continued to mention their corpses in letters home.[33]

Throughout the day the Georgians and Virginians stacked the dead in the back of the wagons. "Oh it was a sickening sight to see brave Southern men lying stiff in death's cold embrace scattered over acres of ground," Thomas Spencer wrote. "Then saw them picked up + placed on waggons to be taken to Centreville for internment, to see them piled in waggons like slaughter[ed] pork."[34]

As the Confederate dead were picked up, other soldiers played tourist. William T. Conn, from the 9th Georgia, came across Robert Coleman's house. "I counted twelve places where cannon balls struck it," he wrote, "some going through." Others tracked through the woods, finding more debris from the battle.[35]

And some, including J. E. B. Stuart, flirted with women from the Day family. "The Gen. & myself rode up to where there were several very pretty young ladies

---

30 See Appendix One for tabulated losses of each regiment and see Appendix Three for the names of the casualties.

31 *OR* 5, 491-492.

32 Thomas J. Spencer to unidentified friend, Dec. 23, 1861, VMHC; D. H. Gettys to his brother, Dec. 27, 1861, Western Carolina University (WCU).

33 D. H. Gettys to his brother, Dec. 27, 1861, WCU.

34 Thomas J. Spencer to unidentified friend, Dec. 23, 1861, VMHC.

35 William T. Conn to his brother, Dec. 22, 1861, Author's Collection.

& commenced talking with them," Lt. Chiswell Dabney, serving on Stuart's staff, wrote to his mother. "They admired my horse very much."[36]

Other Confederates also talked to the Days. The women had attended to eight wounded men in their home, and now those soldiers were removed for transportation back to Centreville. Ord had left the wounded Confederates in the Thornton House, and the Day women, including William's teenage daughter Emma, "had come up from their comfortable homes, bringing with them beds and bed clothes," a soldier with the 18th Virginia recounted. "They also prepared soups and such like delicacies suited to the conditions of the wounded."[37] Georgian William Conn said, "The people seemed glad to see us. Twice I had my haversack filled for which they would receive nothing."[38]

In those hectic, bloody days, Emma Day even fell in love with one of the wounded soldiers. Zebulon Mobley, a private in the 6th South Carolina, was shot in the leg on December 20. One of his comrades, John Brice, wrote, "I didn't see him or would have carried him, if possible." The Pennsylvania Reserves treated Mobley, and then left him behind when they returned to Camp Pierpont. That is how he met Emma Day. She "was his nurse during the entire time that his life was despaired of," and as the Virginians loaded Mobley into a wagon on December 22, it was Emma who told one of the soldiers, "that was her patient." The soldier replied, "I told her I prophecied for him a speedy recovery, having been nursed under such favorable auspices." Amputation of Mobley's leg followed, and he was sent to Chimborazo Hospital to recover. Emma followed, continuing to help. And after, once he had recovered, they got married. Emma Day Mobley died in 1868 and was remembered by veterans of the 6th South Carolina for her "true patriotic pride and womanly devotion." Zebulon Mobley lived another 44 years, dying in 1912.[39]

With the wounded and dead all secured in the back of his wagons, Stuart returned to Centreville. The grueling march taxed the soldiers. Stuart's column did not arrive back at Centreville until close to 11:00 p.m. By the time the soldiers reached their winter quarters, another couple of miles from Centreville, it was nearly 2:00 a.m.[40]

36 Trout, *With Pen and Saber*, 52.

37 *Richmond Dispatch*, Dec. 30, 1861.

38 William T. Conn to his brother Dec. 22, 1861, Author's Collection.

39 John M. Brice to his father, Dec. 21, 1861, VMHC; William Woodward Dixon, *The Mobleys and their Descendants* (Privately Published, 1915), 52; *Richmond Dispatch*, Dec. 30, 1861; *Alexandria Gazette and Virginia Advertiser*, May 17, 1868; *The Fairfield News and Herald*, Aug. 8, 1888.

40 *Richmond Dispatch*, Dec. 30, 1861; William T. Conn to his brother Dec. 22, 1861, Author's Collection.

Others were waiting for them. Felix Callaway, the man who had ridden all night to Joseph Johnston's headquarters, was now sent to transfer the bodies of the dead artillerists. "I found that our dead were in one of the wagons," he wrote. "It was standing there with no mules to it and the dead piled in like so many dead hogs on a wild hunt. I removed the tarpaulin and saw a man's hand with a red stripe on his sleeve, which I knew to be one of our men, as that red stripe indicated artillery, and we were the only command of the kind in the fight."[41]

The funerals started on December 22. With reversed arms and muffled drums, the regiments buried the dead. A soldier in the 4th South Carolina, in the same brigade as the 6th, wrote, "I hear them playing the dead march at the cemetery. Oh, how lonesome!"[42] Callaway oversaw the burial of the dead artillerists, remembering, "We buried the five with one who died at the hospital, in the same grave at Centerville, placing a headboard at each coffin. There they are to this day, and will remain until the resurrection."[43]

Some regiments, like the 10th Alabama, already had small cemeteries. The Alabamians had lost dozens to camp diseases earlier in the year and buried them at Bristoe Station. Now, at least three more soldiers from the regiment—Sidney Coleman, Robert Dunlap, and John F. Martin—were interred with their comrades.[44]

The 11th Virginia buried its dead, too. As part of the same brigade, Col. Montgomery Corse's 17th Virginia joined the funeral parade, which tugged at the heartstrings of the 11th's field officers. Colonel Samuel Garland wrote to Corse, "I desire to express, on my own behalf and on behalf of the officers and men of the 11th Virginia Volunteers, our grateful appreciation of the soldierly friendship which induced your command to unite in paying the last tribute of respect to those of our gallant comrades whom we buried on yesterday."[45]

Others were sent home for burial. Both Harden brothers, from the 6th South Carolina, shot within moments of each other, were shipped home. Lieutenant John Bratton telegraphed his cousins, "The body of Franklin English on the road home." His family buried him in the churchyard of Columbia's First Presbyterian Church. Lieutenant Colonel James B. Martin, the Confederates' highest-ranking fatality, was sent back to Alabama to be buried. One newspaper correspondent wrote, "Christmas week has been a sad week in this part of the State."[46]

---

41 Callaway, *The Bloody Links*, 31-32.

42 J. W. Reid, *History of the Fourth Regiment of South Carolina Volunteers* (Greenville, SC, 1892), 62.

43 Callaway, *The Bloody Links*, 32.

44 *Jacksonville Republican*, Nov. 10, 1883.

45 George Wise, *Campaigns and Battles of the Army of Northern Virginia* (New York, 1916), 47.

46 *Bratton Telegram*, Dec. 24, 1861, Frank English Letters; *South Western Baptist*, Jan. 9, 1862.

* * *

The dead were buried, and the wounded were being tended. With the onset of winter, both armies hunkered down to wait for spring. For the Federals, that gave them plenty of time to celebrate their victory. And for the Confederates, it gave them all the time in the world to find a scapegoat.

That search did not take any time at all. J. E. B. Stuart immediately came under harsh criticism. On December 22, D. H. Hill wrote from Leesburg, chastising Stuart, "From what I have been able to learn, the enemy knew your strength and destination before you started." Hill continued, "I would therefore respectfully suggest that when you start again, you should disguise your strength and give out a different locality from that actually taken." The letter, though mild in its language, got under Stuart's skin.[47]

Other writers were more severe. "Although the 'boys' fought finely, the little affair should teach our generals not to despise the enemy as supremely as some do," one newspaper editorialized. "Although our men are willing to 'do or die,' when called upon, I cannot see that any general should lose fifty or sixty men, simply from his own carelessness in not providing against a surprise."[48]

The *Selma Reporter* republished an especially harsh attack against Stuart. "There is such a thing, however, as foolishness. . . . A daring that is reckless of human life and unmindful of the best interests of the cause in which it is enlisted, is not patriotism, but folly." The editorial went on, "General Stewart, we are reliably informed, is but twenty-six years of age, with all the ardor and impetuosity of youth, and none of the experience and discretion of maturer years. . . . He has evidently risen to a post above his merit, and is but an additional instance of the unfortunate appointments that have come from the government at Richmond."[49]

Even the soldiers Stuart commanded at Dranesville thought he did a poor job. "Stuart's comb is cut," an officer in the 11th Virginia wrote. "If these useless forays he is so fond of getting up and which Johnston shows him such partiality in authorizing, are made less frequent by this partial disaster, it may be the means of preventing something worse hereafter."[50] Major Thomas Woodward, who in time recovered from his wound, later said he believed Stuart "allowed himself to be lured into this fight without due reconnaissance and proper arrangements."[51] Thomas

---

47 D. H. Hill to J. E. B. Stuart, Dec. 22, 1861, J. E. B. Stuart Collection, Huntington Library, CA.

48 *Daily Appeal*, Jan. 3, 1862.

49 *Selma Reporter*, Jan. 1, 1862. Stuart was twenty-eight when he commanded at Dranesville.

50 Kean, *Inside the Confederate Government*, 21.

51 Woodward, *From Fort Sumter to Dranesville*, 29.

Hobbs visited his friend, Capt. William Forney, 10th Alabama, still recuperating from his leg wound in Centreville. Hobbs wrote that Forney "describes the fight as a blunder on the part of Gen. Stuart . . . who was surprised by finding the enemy where he did not expect them." Forney later said that Stuart's report about the battle was "generally correct, but 'highly colored.'"[52] Brigadier General Cadmus Wilcox, who commanded the brigade to which the 10th Alabama was usually attached, snapped, "By God sir Gen. S[tuart] has no wright to lead my people into Battle. If they have to be cut to pieces I want to see it done myself."[53]

Jefferson Davis provided the coup de grâce. After reading through reports and a letter from Hill, Davis wrote that it all "painfully impresses upon me with that which has heretofore been indicated—a want of vigilance and intelligent observation on the part of General Stuart."[54]

Stuart was pained, embarrassed, and increasingly angry at what he saw as unfair criticism. "I notice that Congress voted thanks to all who have been engaged with the enemy except the brave men who were with me at Dranesville," he griped to his brother William in January 1862. "Have I no friends in Congress?"[55]

It fell to Pvt. John Brice from the 6th South Carolina to sum up the failures at Dranesville. "It was all the work of General Stuart, a cavalry general of distinction, but I think a very poor infantry officer, if I may judge by this affair." Brice wrote. "I don't see what we could have gained if we had won the field as it would have been worth nothing to us, except a few loads of corn & hay." Many of the Confederates, having lost family and friends, demanded to know what it was all for.[56]

Stuart had made a name for himself with his daring exploits on the outposts through the summer and fall. But those exploits had been done with his mounted troopers. Stuart would become one of the finest cavalry commanders of the war, but his infantry leadership left much to be desired in the winter of 1861. Nothing up to that point in his life had prepared him for what happened on December 20. At the beginning of the battle, Stuart performed his role as a cavalryman to a tee; though some of his critics accused him of not deploying skirmishers, he, in fact, did exactly that. It was his screening force of cavalrymen from the 1st North Carolina and 2nd Virginia that spotted the Federals in Dranesville and allowed Stuart to

52 Thomas Hubbard Hobbs, *The Journals of Thomas Hubbard Hobbs*, ed. Faye Acton Axford (Tuscaloosa, AL, 1976), 250-251.

53 William C. McClellan, *Welcome the Hour of Conflict: William Cowan McClellan and the 9th Alabama*, ed. John C. Carter (Tuscaloosa, AL, 2007), 117.

54 *OR* 5, 1063.

55 Stuart quoted in Thomason, *Jeb Stuart*, 128.

56 John M. Brice to his father, Dec. 21, 1861, VMHC.

escape what could have been a significantly worse situation. What Stuart needed next was a strong infantry commander to take the situation from there, and an equally capable artillery officer to oversee the placement of his guns. Captain Allen Cutts, though experienced from the Mexican War, had his hands tied because of the unforgiving terrain of thick pine trees in which Stuart was trapped. As a result, Cutts's battery was entirely ineffective over the course of the battle.

As Confederate sources pondered what had happened, the date of the battle did not go unnoticed. "Friday last, the anniversary of our secession, was signalized by a disaster to our arms," one South Carolinian wrote.[57]

Stuart ultimately had no other option but to weather the storm of criticism leveled at him in Dranesville's wake. His opponent, meanwhile, was being lauded as the next hero of the Republic.

*   *   *

George McCall heaped praise on Edward Ord, "for whose able disposition of his regiments and battery and personal exertions to encourage and urge on his men too much credit cannot be accorded him."[58]

Acclaim also came from Washington. Secretary of War Simon Cameron wrote in flowery praise: "I cannot refrain from expressing to you my admiration of the gallant conduct displayed by both officers and men in this their first contest with the enemy. . . . It is one of the bright spots that give assurance of the success of coming events, and its effect must be to inspire confidence in the belief that hereafter, as heretofore, the cause of our country will triumph." The Secretary finished his letter, "Other portions of the Army will be stimulated by their brave deeds, and men will be proud to say that at Dranesville they served under McCall and Ord."[59]

Ord deserved the praise. In his very first engagement commanding a substantial number of troops, he showed a coolness under fire that helped shape the victory. Ord's greatest tactical contribution to the battle was the active role he took in the deployment of Easton's battery. Years later, Ord gave credit to his posting at Fort Monroe's School of Artillery. "My being fresh from the school with practice in elevating at any range help'd me to win the little fight at Dranesville," he told his close friend William Sherman in 1882.[60] Additionally, Ord's rapid deployment of infantry along the Leesburg Turnpike prevented Stuart from occupying the crossroads. With George McCall not arriving until the closing stages of the battle,

---

57 *Yorkville Enquirer*, Jan. 2, 1862.

58 OR 5, 476.

59 Ibid., 476-477.

60 Ord to Sherman, Apr. 18, 1882, William T. Sherman Papers, LOC.

Dranesville was Edward Ord's battle to win or lose, and his command and control remained solid throughout the two-hour engagement.

"All is excitement in camp on account of the battle yesterday," Vernon Henderson, 6th Reserves, wrote. A newspaper correspondent added from Langley, "They are in great glee, and are full of narratives of the day, its dangers, disasters, and glory." The soldiers swapped stories around their fires and showed off their trophies. "The camps are filled with trophies of the field—knapsacks, cartridge-boxes, cartridges, bullets, canteens, bayonets, letters, diaries, coats, clothing, buttons, caps, guns, fragments of a gun carriage . . . pieces of shell, and in fact every possible object which could be converted into a memento."[61]

The soldiers also expressed adulation for their brigade commander. Ord, in the words of his brother Placidus, was "the idol of his men."[62] Hearing that Ord, in the process of "jumping my horse around [and] through woods & over fences [had] thrown my sword out of the scabbard," the Pennsylvanian soldiers raised enough money to buy Ord a new blade. They presented it to him on New Year's Day, with a silver engraving bearing the words, "Presented to Brig. General E. O. C. Ord by the Officers and Men engaged under him at Drainsville 20th Decr. 1861."[63]

One of Ord's fellow brigade commanders was jealous of the praise. Having missed all but the very end of the engagement, John Reynolds said, "Confound that fellow! I knew, if there was a fight to be scared up, Ord would find it."[64]

Newspapers across the North picked up the story and exulted in the Federal success. The *New York Herald* led the way, calling Dranesville, "a splendid little affair." Victory at Dranesville "gives great elation to all classes here," the *New York Times* added. Horace Greeley, editor of the *New York Daily Tribune*, wrote to his friend, the wounded Thomas Kane, offering his congratulations, and later wrote that the victory, "diffused an immense exhilaration throughout the Union ranks." Greeley continued, "It was a fitting and conclusive answer to every open assertion or whispered insinuation impeaching the courage or the steadiness of our raw Northern volunteers."[65]

Unsurprisingly, it was Pennsylvania newspapers that shouted loudest from the rooftops. Papers ranging from Philadelphia to Pittsburgh and further afield

---

61 Vernon Henderson, Dec. 21, 1861, Diary Entry, USAHEC; *Philadelphia Press*, Dec. 27, 1861.

62 Placidus Ord quoted in Cresap, *Appomattox Commander*, 73.

63 Edward Ord to his wife, Jan. 1, 1862, Edward Ord Papers, Box 1, Folder 3, Item 14, Sanford University.

64 Henry Coppee, *Grant and His Campaigns: A Military Biography* (New York, 1866), 133.

65 *New York Herald*, Dec. 21, 1861; *New York Times*, Dec. 21, 1861; Horace Greeley to Thomas Kane, Jan. 16, 1862, Kane Papers, Box 18, Folder 31, Item 18, BYU; Horace Greeley, *The American Conflict: A History of the Great Rebellion*, Vol. I (Hartford, 1864), 626.

all trumpeted the success. Bloomsburg's *Star of the North* published a poem sent in by a soldier:

> "Bully For All
>
> We whip[p]ed the rebels at Drainsville,
>
> Bully for us, Bully for us.
>
> We drove them back to Centerville,
>
> Bully for us, Bully for us.
>
> They say they want to try us again,
>
> Bully for them, Bully for them.
>
> But if they do we will whip them again,
>
> Bully for us, Bully for us.
>
> The Kentucky boys can run quite smart,
>
> Bully for them, Bully for them.
>
> After the reserves gave them a start,
>
> Bully for us, Bully for us."[66]

Here, finally, was a victory that the Northern press could praise after months of almost nothing but bad news. The small battle of Dranesville garnered column after column in papers throughout the North. While the newspapers filled pages with patriotic prose, officers filled out reports highlighting their soldiers. Ord required all his regimental commanders to submit names of soldiers "to do justice to all cases of individual bravery, as such can not be included in the report of a battle." The battle of Dranesville was fought before the creation of the Medal of Honor, and thus the army's system of commendation instead rewarded enlisted personnel mentioned in such reports with a two-dollar increase in pay per month, and brevets, or honorary promotions, for commissioned officers.[67]

As the newspapers and the officers' reports spread through the North, many flocked to Camp Pierpont. "The battle of Dranesville with its victory gave to the Pennsylvania Reserve Corps an honor and a name, which extended throughout the country, and were reported in every household," the Pennsylvanians' historian wrote. "The camps at Langley were visited by distinguished citizens and public

---

66 *Star of the North*, Jan. 22, 1862.

67 Thomas Kane Papers, Subseries 3, Box 23, Folder 1, Item 2, Dec. 27, 1861, Circular, BYU.

officers at Washington; and great numbers of people from Pennsylvania made the journey to Camp Pierpont."[68]

Most prominent of those visitors was Gov. Andrew Curtin, who arrived at Langley a week after the battle. Back in April, Abraham Lincoln pled with Curtin and begged to know, "What will Pennsylvania do?" Now, Lincoln had his answer. Pennsylvania's sons had stood at Dranesville, and Curtin came to camp to congratulate them.

Curtin joined Secretary of War Cameron, the two putting their political differences aside to visit the Reserves' hospital. They "spoke a kind word to each of the soldiers wounded in the recent engagement," before attending a review of the entire division. Afterwards, Curtin praised them and their victory: "You cannot imagine what a thrill of pleasure and of pride was felt in Pennsylvania, and how the great heart of your native State palpitated with joy when the telegraph first announced that a part of the Reserve Corps was engaged, and afterwards . . . that their battle was crowned with victory."[69]

Pennsylvania's governor went further than just giving speeches. He was enormously proud of his Reserve Corps, an organization that, at first, the Federal government had not even wanted. On Curtin's orders, the flags of Edward Ord's brigade, as well as the Bucktails, were sent to Washington to be painted in commemoration. On January 11, 1862, the flags were returned to the division in another elaborate ceremony. As the other two brigades watched, Ord's regiments were given their flags back. On a red stripe, each flag now had in gold lettering, "Dranesville, December 20, 1861." The Pennsylvanians would never forget the date. [70]

While J. E. B. Stuart endured criticism, Curtin pontificated, and the Reserves admired their new gold-lettered flags, there were some to whom the battle of Dranesville did not matter at all. The Dranesville men, still in jail at the Old Capitol, were wondering what lay in store for them.

<hr>

68 Sypher, *Pennsylvania Reserve Corps*, 142-143.

69 *Philadelphia Press*, Dec. 30, 1861.

70 Rufus Read Diary, Jan. 11, 1862, Special Collections, College of William & Mary; Sypher, *Pennsylvania Reserve Corps*, 141.

Chapter Thirteen

"Be Careful to Whom You Talk and What You Say"

Dranesville's Men Stand Trial

The inmates could hear carpenters outside, banging away at something. As the days passed with no news, paranoia took hold and "Rumor had it that a gallows was being constructed to execute several of the men from Dranesville." For John Day, it was too much. He "was quite excitable," and "prayed often and loud upon his knees to be spared such a fate." Day's tearful praying went on as each day passed and still no answer came to their question: why were they there?[1]

The families back in Dranesville had no answers either. "We are all at home except poor Phil," Kate Carper wrote on Christmas Day. Her brother had been captured during the ambush against Bayard's cavalry, and he was still, as she wrote sarcastically, "imprisoned in that Temple of Liberty, the Capitol at Washington."[2] Kate's mother sent money, clothing, and food to Philip but, for the time being at least, there was little information to be had about the situation in Washington.[3]

But the Dranesville men were not sitting idly by. As the rest of the country flocked to newspapers to read about the battle in their hometown, the prisoners sought redress with the Federal government. Having never received an answer to his December 3 letter asking for an explanation, Charles Coleman wrote another on New Year's Day, 1862. "Whoever reported me it has been guess work with them, and nothing would give me more pleasure than to meet them on trial," he

---

1 Cole, *Our Day Family*, 85-86.

2 Kate Carper Diary, Dec. 25, 1861, Virginia Room, Fairfax Regional Library.

3 Cordelia Grantham Sansone, *Journey To Bloomfield: Lives and Letters of 19th Century Virginia Families* (Fairfax, VA, 2012), 158.

wrote to Secretary of State William Seward. "If you will grant me the liberty of taking the oath of allegiance to the United States and to remain in the lines I will do it until my home is in the Union again."[4]

Coleman was not the only one writing. Kate Farr, daughter of imprisoned John B. Farr, and Charles's sister-in-law, lived in Washington and visited her father in prison. After returning from the jail she wrote to Seward, begging for his release. She called her father "a good and loyal citizen of the United States" and wrote, "his sentiments have always been those of loyalty to the Government, and his feelings are sorely wounded to think that he should thus suffer upon a false accusation." Kate finished her letter, "Now, sir, with these facts I beg and implore that you will give speedy attention to his case; and for the sake of humanity, for the sake of the cause of the Union, for the sake of his health which is declining from confinement and grief, for the sake of his helpless and unprotected family, for the sake of God, I trust your honor will grant him an immediate release."[5]

Rounding out the trio of letters came a note from William Day. Attempting to curry favor with Federal officials, Day claimed he had given aid to both Confederate and Union wounded soldiers at Manassas the previous July. Day claimed he was serving on the regimental staff of the 60th Virginia as the battalion's surgeon, but there is no evidence to corroborate that.[6]

The letters ended up on the desk of Erastus D. Webster, Seward's secretary. Webster's job was "to handle correspondence relating to political prisoners and 'rebels.'" But now, as he read the letters coming out of the Old Capitol, Webster did not fully understand the situation.[7]

Since their arrests in November by the Pennsylvania Cavalry, the prisoners were technically in the army's custody, and thus were the War Department's responsibility. As a secretary in the State Department, Webster really had no idea why or for what reason the Dranesville men were imprisoned. As the trio of letters sat on his desk, Webster reached out to Brig. Gen. Andrew Porter, the provost marshal in Washington. Referring to Kate Farr's letter, Webster wrote to Porter that, "Unless there are well-founded reasons to the contrary the prisoner may be released upon the usual conditions." Forwarding William Day's note, Webster

---

4 *OR* 2, Series 2, 1287-1288.

5 Ibid., 1288.

6 Ibid.; William P. Johnson II, *Brothers and Cousins: Confederate Soldiers & Sailors of Fairfax County, VA* (Athens, GA, 1995), 43.

7 Kenneth W. Munden and Henry Putney Beers, eds., *Guide to Federal Archives Relating to the Civil War* (Washington, D.C., 1962), 137.

added, "Report whether there is any well-founded reason why the prisoner should not be released upon taking the oath and making the usual stipulations."[8]

Those usual stipulations consisted of the person swearing their oath of allegiance to the United States and promising not to give aid to the rebel forces. It was a process with which Webster was familiar, having overseen dozens of such cases already. Perhaps he figured that by deferring to Porter, the Dranesville cases would go much the same way and he could move on to other matters. But that's not what happened.[9]

When Porter got Webster's request for information, he looked to an investigator who had been helping the army gather evidence. The investigator, who signed his correspondence "E. J. Allen," was in fact the famed detective Allan Pinkerton.

Born in Scotland, Pinkerton immigrated to the United States in 1842. He settled in Chicago and formed his Pinkerton Agency there in 1850. In early 1861, Pinkerton escorted President-elect Lincoln to Washington, having caught word of would-be assassins in Baltimore. He had worked closely with George McClellan during the general's western Virginia campaigns in the summer of 1861, and it was during those months that Pinkerton picked up his alias, which he used for the rest of the war. By the time Pinkerton moved to Washington to continue his work, "E. J. Allen" routinely appeared in correspondence between the Army and the State Department.[10]

Given the task of looking into the Dranesville matter, Pinkerton began interviewing witnesses. On January 13, he sent in his response. Over nearly three pages, Pinkerton laid out his evidence against John Farr, and by extension the rest of the imprisoned Dranesville men. He paraphrased the testimonies of Unionists driven out of the area in the wake of Virginia's secession, including Nelson Voorhees, Nathaniel Hanna, Daniel Borden, Henry Bishop, and others. With each testimony that claimed Farr was a secessionist and had taken part in persecuting the Unionists, Pinkerton built up to his conclusion. He finished with a flourish, "Such in brief is the evidence against Farr, the mere recital of which is sufficient to establish the groundlessness of his pretension to be a good and loyal citizen of the United States." Pinkerton, though, was not done. Beyond just persecuting the Unionists, Pinkerton also pointed to Farr as part of the group that shot at the Federal soldiers on Lowe's Island the previous fall. In pages of biting

---

8 *OR 2*, Series 2, 1288-1289.

9 For more information about prisoners being released on paroles or oaths of allegiances, see *OR 2*, Series 2, 226. For more about such cases in Fairfax County specifically, see Harrison, "Atop an Anvil."

10 Allan Pinkerton, *The Spy of the Rebellion* (New York, 1883), 156; Douglas Waller, *Lincoln's Spies: Their Secret War to Save a Nation* (New York, 2019), 3-23; See *OR 2*, Series 2, 1607 for an index of all of Pinkerton's correspondence during this time period.

Spy and detective Allan Pinkerton
LOC

narrative, Pinkerton wrote that had the New Yorkers been ambushed by opposing forces in the Confederate army, perhaps that would have been a different situation. But Farr was not a soldier and was "animated alone by his own brutal instincts, to gratify which he marked out voluntarily his own pathway of cruelty and crime, continuing to follow it until arrested by the strong arm of military power." In his concluding sentence, Pinkerton advised that Farr "be held until a military court can afford him trial for his manifold crimes." In the days to come, Pinkerton drafted similar reports for every Dranesville man confined in the Old Capitol Prison.[11]

George McClellan had taken a keen interest in the case back in November. Just two days after their incarceration, McClellan wrote to Porter that he "desires the circumstances investigated as far as the men now in custody . . . are connected with the alleged murder [of Oliver Darling], and if the matter of allegation can be proved he desires the men brought to trial for murder." Two months later, Porter began to connect the dots. He wrote to Seward on January 17 that he had in fact forgotten McClellan's directive and returned the three requests by Charles Coleman, Kate Farr, and William Day for release back to Seward without further comment.[12]

At this point, McClellan decided to reimpose himself into the situation. Still in his position as general-in-chief, McClellan's days were filled with logistical concerns and communicating with officers all over the country. President Lincoln and his cabinet put continuous pressure on the general to come up with plans for the coming spring campaign and bemoaned how slow the progress on that front was going. But alongside all those duties, McClellan made sure to have his input regarding Dranesville. On January 30, he ordered that the prisoners "who stand charged with the murder of Federal pickets . . . and with persecuting Union men in and near Dranesville be each and all of them kept in close confinement until such

11 *OR* 2, Series 2, 1289-1291, 1292.

12 Ibid., 1286, 1292.

time as they can be tried by a military commission for the crimes with which they stand charged."[13] As far as McClellan was concerned, the Dranesville civilians had shot his soldiers, and they would pay for it.

Another month passed. While Webster kept up with his mound of paperwork, and McClellan continued planning what would become the Peninsula Campaign, Lincoln transformed his cabinet. As evidence mounted that Secretary of War Cameron had engaged in a plethora of corrupt activities, Lincoln replaced him with acerbic Edwin Stanton. Now the prisoners, still in the custody of the army, were Stanton's problem.[14]

It is unclear whether any of the Dranesville men demanded a writ of *habeas corpus* during their imprisonment, though even if they had, it would not have done them much good. Back in April 1861, Lincoln suspended *habeas corpus* from Washington to Philadelphia. When a Marylander, John Merryman, was arrested for secessionist activities and subsequently demanded such a writ, Lincoln's government simply ignored the order. Even when Roger Taney, operating in a capacity as a circuit court judge of appeals, demanded Merryman's release, Lincoln refused.[15] Lincoln firmly believed he had every right as president to suspend the writ, based on the Constitution's Article I, Section 9. In a message to Congress, Lincoln explained his belief that the Constitution was silent on whether the power to suspend the writ was Congress's or the President's. At a time when Congress was not in session, Lincoln thought that the provision for public safety demanded he make the decision. He defended his actions against those who claimed he was violating the Constitution: "To state the question more directly, are all the laws, *but one*, to go unexecuted, and the government itself go to pieces, lest that one be violated?"[16] That message, given to Congress on July 4, 1861, still represented Lincoln's thoughts on the matter in the winter of 1861-62, and left the Dranesville men with little course of action other than to wait.

Then, on February 27, 1862, came Executive Order No. 2, a two-paragraph document simply titled, "Relating to Political Prisoners." The first paragraph created "a special commission of two persons, one of military rank and the other in civil life," who would "examine the cases of the state prisoners remaining in the military custody of the United States." The two-person panel was tasked then to decide whether the prisoners "should be discharged or remain in military

---

13 Ibid., 1292-1293.

14 William Marvel, *Lincoln's Autocrat: The Life of Edwin Stanton* (Chapel Hill, 2015), 148-150.

15 Michael Burlingame, *Abraham Lincoln: A Life*, Vol. 2 (Baltimore, 2008), 151-152.

16 Lincoln, *Collected Works*: Vol. 4, 430.

Major General John A. Dix
LOC

custody or be remitted to the civil tribunals for trial."[17]

Paragraph two appointed the commissioners. The first was Maj. Gen. John Adams Dix, then in command of the forces around Baltimore. Appointed as a major general of volunteers in the spring of 1861, Dix assumed command of the Department of Maryland on July 24. He famously arrested members of Maryland's legislature who threatened secession in September—a controversial move, approved by Lincoln and McClellan. He now became the army's representative on the commission.[18]

New York lawyer Edwards Pierrepont (not to be confused with Virginian politician Francis Pierpont) joined Dix as the civilian commissioner. Pierrepont was born in 1817 and graduated from New Haven Law School. Though a Democrat, Pierrepont supported Lincoln and served in the Union Defense League of New York, which fundraised for the Union war effort.[19]

To assist both Dix and Pierrepont, Erastus Webster reported to the commission as its clerk. Webster wrote to Dix on March 8, asking where and when to meet. He also opined, "It seems to me that it is desirable to dispose of all these cases as soon as possible," because "their cases are familiar to Mr. E. J. Allen . . . who I am informed intends to leave the city in a short time." Pinkerton was readying to leave for Fort Monroe alongside George McClellan for the Peninsula Campaign. If Dix

17 *OR* 2, Series 2, 249.

18 Warner, *Generals in Blue*, 125-126; Morgan Dix, *Memoirs of John Adams Dix*: Vol. 2 (New York, 1883), 25; David K. Graham, *Loyalty on the Line: Civil War Maryland in American Memory* (Athens, GA, 2018), 20-21; Rafuse, *McClellan's War*, 133-134.

19 Dumas Malone, ed., *Dictionary of American Biography*, Vol. 14 (New York, 1934), 587; *New York Times*, Mar. 7, 1892; New Haven Law School was an affiliate of Yale, but retained its name at the time.

Judge Edwards Pierrepont
LOC

and Pierrepont wanted Pinkerton's help, they needed to move quickly.[20]

But getting everything in order and relocated to Washington took time. Stanton, an impatient man, had the Assistant Secretary of War wire Pierrepont on March 11: "The Secretary of War directs me to inquire how soon the commission consisting of General Dix and yourself . . . will be ready to hear and determine cases and at what place it is proposed to sit first?"[21]

The Commission oversaw similar tribunals in Washington, New York, and Boston. Because of Webster's suggestion that the commissioners meet in the capital first to have the aid of Pinkerton, Dix wrote to Stanton on March 15: "I propose to be in Washington on Monday to meet Judge Pierrepont and take up the cases of political prisoners there."[22]

True to their word, the commissioners met on March 18, 1862, to begin the proceedings. The record is unclear where specifically the commission met, but when they reconvened in New York City in early April they sat in the Grand Jury room of the United States Court, so perhaps they assembled somewhere similar in the nation's capital.[23]

The following days and weeks fell into a similar pattern. Prisoners and witnesses were brought forward for questioning by the commission, and depositions read. Proceedings went quickly, with the *Philadelphia Inquirer* writing, "The commission to examine political prisoners are disposing of about twenty cases per day."[24] Per one historian, the commission's work went so quickly because, "When a civilian

20 *OR* 2, Series 2, 257; See Stephen W Sears, *To the Gates of Richmond: The Peninsula Campaign* (Boston, 1992).

21 *OR* 2, Series 2, 259.

22 Ibid., 263.

23 *New York Times*, Apr. 8, 1862.

24 *Philadelphia Inquirer*, Mar. 21, 1862.

prisoner was willing to take the oath of future loyalty to the Union, his release was usually rapid."[25]

Of course, some of the Dranesville men in the Old Capitol had tried just that. Charles Coleman and John B. Farr had both expressed a willingness to pledge allegiance to the Federal government well before the commission had even been created. But Pinkerton, in his scathing reports on their actions, had essentially said only a trial would be suitable. Just shy of four months since their arrests, the Dranesville men faced Dix and Pierrepont.

Seven of the men were officially charged with "Murdering and robbing Federal soldiers at Lowes Island, Va." George Coleman was charged with a lesser "Aiding and comforting the Insurgents, + oppressing Union men," while his cousin Richard faced charges of "Procuring recruits for Insurgent army," though Richard's case was soon thrown out due to his mistaken identity.[26]

William Day was the first to face the commission on March 21.[27] Day's first time in front of the commission consisted of 20 different statements and depositions against him being read into the record. The statements totaled about 36 pages, all neatly inscribed into a hardback book by the clerk Webster. Many of those statements have been previously quoted in this book, consisting of depositions by many Unionists that Day had helped run out of town. The statements had been recorded back in November and early December, right after the arrests, but were now finally entered into the record. Whereas the commission usually moved rapidly onto other cases, they paused with William Day. The allegations they heard about firing on Federal pickets, leaving corpses to be consumed by hogs, putting decapitated heads on wooden posts, and running Unionist neighbors out of town far surpassed the stories they had been hearing for the past few days.

Day's defense focused on 1) that he had nothing to do with the ambush at Lowe's Island and 2) that he had in fact helped the wounded soldier brought into town.[28] Day's testimony flew in the face of what Robert Gracey had told his comrades back in the fall when he escaped; that, in fact, Day had refused to provide any treatment. But the commission probably never knew Gracey's identity—his name appears nowhere in their papers. After reading the statements and listening to Day's side of the story, the commission decided it needed more

25 Harold M. Hyman, *Era of the Oath: Northern Loyalty Tests During the Civil War and Reconstruction* (Philadelphia, 1954), 34.

26 Charges from Untitled Packet in *Proceedings of the Commission Relating to State Prisoners*, Vol. 1, RG 59, NARA. See Chapter Nine for a discussion of Richard Coleman.

27 "Cases Examined by Commission Relating to State Prisoners" *Proceedings of the Commission*, Vol. 1, RG 59, NARA.

28 William B. Day Case File, 46-47.

time to deliberate on the case. In the meantime, William Day was shuffled back to the confines of the Old Capitol.[29]

Three days later, on March 24, the commission investigated six more Dranesville cases. Charles, George, and Richard Coleman, as well as John Day, and the Farr brothers— James and John—all had their time in front of Dix and Pierrepont. A similar pattern followed as with William Day, but the commissioners found far less nuance to most of the cases on the 24th. All except Charles Coleman and John Day were allowed to go home after giving their oath of allegiance. The next day, Richard Gunnell and John DeBell were also released from the Old Capitol.[30]

Just a week after they had started reviewing the Dranesville cases, the commissioners had overseen every case except for Philip Carper. Realizing his time would be soon, he wrote to his sister on March 27, "There are detectives now in your vicinity trying to find evidence against all the prisoners from Dranesville. Be careful to whom you talk and what you say." Alluding to Lowe's Island, Carper advised his sister to keep close-lipped: "Don't tell if you know who was in the fight on the river."[31]

The commission heard the case on March 28. Carper testified that he knew nothing about the ambush, nor about its participants. During the whole ambush, Carper claimed he was at home with his mother, and had nothing to do with the episode. That contradicted the testimonies of the enslaved people who swore that Carper bragged about his role in killing Oliver Darling. And if that was not complicated enough for Dix and Pierrepont, Carper claimed to have joined the Confederate army in September. If Carper was in the army at the time of the fight, whatever role he had taken part in on Lowe's Island would have been as a soldier, not a civilian engaged in irregular warfare. At least that was how Carper saw it. The commission sent Carper back to jail to wait alongside Charles Coleman and the Day brothers while they contemplated what to do.[32]

Carper wrote to his mother on April 3, six days after his first hearing with the commission: "I have hoped that I would be exchanged or paroled, but it seems I am here for the war." Yet, Carper told his mother not to worry. "The officers here are very kind, giving us all the liberty they can that does not transcend their

---

29 Ibid., 48.

30 *OR 2*, Series 2, 1293-1294.

31 Sansone, *Journey to Bloomfield*, 157-158.

32 *Proceedings of the Commission Relating to State Prisoners*, 1862, Vol. 1, Philip Carper Case File, RG 59, NARA (Hereafter cited as Philip Carper Case Files), 49-51.

authority." Prisoners were given supplemental food from sympathizing civilians who visited the jail.[33]

By the last days of March, the commission had investigated the cases of every Dranesville prisoner. Trying to reach through the web of entangled stories, the commission subpoenaed several Unionists. Nelson Voorhees, Jane Crippen, and several formerly enslaved people were all brought before the court. They did not have much new to say, at least not anything new from the depositions they had already given numerous times; it did not make anything easier for Dix or Pierrepont to decide.[34]

To pass the time, Carper kept writing to his sister and mother. In one letter he noted that he had sent "more than 30 letters to Dranesville," though not all of them got to their destination. Kate Carper and her mother sent equal amounts of letters back, with Philip thanking them after, "The eatables you sent me came safely & were very acceptable." The presents certainly made up for the prisoners' usual fare. "We are very tired of wheat-bran, that is, such as we get here, and would esteem a nice corn cake the greatest of luxuries."[35]

April became May. While the commissioners had not settled on what to do with the prisoners, they were at least sure they did not want to release them. Andrew Porter had left Washington with the Army of the Potomac, taking part in the Peninsula Campaign. The new provost marshal, Maj. W. E. Doster, reported to his superiors on May 5, "Dr. William B. Day . . . is confined in the Old Capitol Prison and is held to answer very serious charges, and his release was refused by the commission . . . on any terms."[36]

With each repeated refusal to let the four men go, their spirits sagged. John Day continued praying inside his cell. Philip Carper kept writing to the War Department, trying to convince them that, as a soldier in the Confederate army, he had no business being tried as a civilian. The War Department disagreed. "Your case has not been considered either with reference to an exchange or to a discharge from the military custody of the United States for the reason that you are held in confinement on the charge of having engaged in an irregular or guerrilla mode of warfare," Assistant Secretary of War P. H. Watson wrote. "Under these circumstances your application to be released on parole to return to your home . . . or for any other purpose cannot be granted."[37] In response, Carper again

---

33 Sansone, *Journey to Bloomfield*, 158-159.

34 Dranesville Murder Cases, Mar. 31, 1862, 3.

35 Sansone, *Journey to Bloomfield*, 160.

36 *OR* 2, Series 2, 1294.

37 Ibid.

wrote to his sister, "Everything here remains the same in respect to myself." He continued that "No chance of being released has yet presented itself, and never will, I fear, if some friend does not take my case in hand."[38]

"Some friend" is what the imprisoned men lacked. Besides their families, the prisoners had no one to speak on their behalf. Throughout the first six months of their imprisonment, there is nothing to indicate the prisoners enjoyed legal counsel of any kind. But then came an unusual communique to the Assistant Secretary of War on June 4, 1862. "Dr. John Day, William Day and Charles Coleman have at your suggestion and upon the advice of Mr. Mackall and myself consented to take the oath of allegiance to the United States," it read. "I respectfully ask that you order the release of John Day and Charles Coleman upon their taking the oath above stated." Continuing on in regard to William Day, "he has left the matter entirely with Mr. Mackall and myself; he is willing to take the oath at our request, and we will give bond in the sum of $20,000 that the said Dr. Day will observe all his obligations."[39]

The note was signed by John S. Hollingshead, a notary public and justice of the peace who lived in Washington.[40] "Mr. Mackall" is not identified in any other correspondence, though it can be assumed he was a partner of Hollingshead. Acting as a go-between for the prisoners and the War Department, Hollingshead's offer to pay the bail bond finally got the wheel moving. No correspondence has surfaced between the Dranesville prisoners and Hollingshead, so it remains unclear how they got into contact with one another or how Day arranged for the bond payment.

Things finally moved quickly for Charles Coleman and John Day after Hollingshead's note. Assistant Secretary of War Watson wrote to the Old Capitol's Superintendent William Wood on the same day, June 4, ordering the release of both Coleman and Day. If the two men pledged their allegiance, they were free to go.[41]

From the original ten prisoners arrested at Dranesville, all that remained in custody were William Day and Philip Carper. Why were those two not released at the same time? The answer seems to be because both claimed military service within the Confederacy's armed forces, Day as a surgeon and Carper as a scout. Though the War Department vehemently disagreed that either were serving in the

---

38 Sansone, *Journey to Bloomfield*, 162.

39 *OR* 2, Series 2, 1294.

40 1860 Census, Hollingshead, Washington, D.C.; *Boyd's Washington and Georgetown Directory: Containing a Business Directory of Washington, Georgetown and Alexandria* (Washington, D.C., 1860), 198.

41 *OR* 2, Series 2, 1295.

Confederate forces at the time of the ambush, it finally gave way in the face of Hollingshead's letters. Rather than being released after taking an oath of allegiance, Day and Carper instead were looked upon as prisoners of war and were processed through the prisoner exchange between Washington and Richmond.

That did not stop Carper's family from trying to get him released. Kate Carper and her mother continued to make repeated trips through the revolving door of commanders in charge of Washington's military district, including Brig. Gen. James Wadsworth. On July 15, their work finally paid off. "Go to see Wadsworth on [Philip's] behalf and to our surprise and joy succeed in getting him paroled for two weeks and bring him home with us. The Doctor's exchange is affected [*sic*] today and he and Phil come up with us," Kate wrote in her diary.[42]

When William Day and Philip Carper left the Old Capitol, they had been imprisoned for 230 days. Though out of prison, their story was not over. They returned to Dranesville, but in two weeks' time, travelled to Richmond, and then onto Fort Monroe, to take part in the official exchange. Within two days, Day and Carper arrived at Fort Monroe, and were soon after exchanged.[43]

Based on the number of accounts and depositions the commission had taken from local Unionists and escaped enslaved people, it seems the Federal government viewed Thomas Coleman, Philip Carper, and William Day as bearing the preponderance of guilt for what transpired at Lowe's Island, and its aftermath. Thomas Coleman's death prevented him from ever sharing the fate of staying at the Old Capitol, and with Carper and Day's release, the government closed its books on the Dranesville saga.

What had started with the civilians ended with the civilians. Dranesville's storied 1861 was over.

---

42 Kate Carper Diary, Jul. 15, 1862.

43 Sansone, *Journey to Bloomfield*, 168.

Chapter Fourteen

"A Proud Lot of Boys We Were"

Conclusion

For the town of Dranesville, 1861 produced a whirlwind of activity that included secession, violence, and warfare. But by the time William Day and Philip Carper were released from jail, the war had moved on. George McClellan's spring campaign shifted the epicenter of fighting from Fairfax County to the Virginia Peninsula. The soldiers who first experienced combat at Dranesville now found themselves engaged in battles at places like Williamsburg and Seven Pines. While the armies threw themselves at each other, Dranesville's populace tried to go back to their lives. Philip Carper immediately rejoined the Confederate army. William Day became an assistant surgeon at a hospital in Winchester. Others, like the Colemans and Farrs, kept their heads down.[1]

It soon became apparent, however, that the war was not finished with Dranesville. Because of its location directly on the turnpikes, soldiers constantly passed through. In the fall of 1862, as the Army of Northern Virginia marched north to invade Maryland, thousands of Confederates poured through the town on their way to the fords across the Potomac. J. E. B. Stuart, now a major general and commanding all the army's cavalry, also made his return to Dranesville, covering the army's rear.[2]

Nine months later the process repeated itself as the armies again moved north on their march to Gettysburg. Through the middle of June, multiple Federal

---

1 William P. Johnson, II, *Brothers and Cousins: Confederate Soldiers & Sailors of Fairfax County, VA* (Athens, GA, 1995), 24, 43.

2 Ezra A. Carman, *The Maryland Campaign of September 1862, Vol. I: South Mountain*, ed. Thomas G. Clemens (El Dorado Hills, CA, 2010), 82, 86.

corps passed through the town, leading Kate Carper to write in her diary, "Part of Hooker's army encamps around us." Stuart came hard on its heels, riding through town. It was from Dranesville that Stuart turned north, embarking on his famous ride into Pennsylvania that many blamed for the Confederate defeat at Gettysburg. The withering criticism Stuart received for that ride made what he endured after Dranesville pale by comparison.[3]

And yet, for all the forces marching through the town, the two armies never pitched a full fight at Dranesville again. Throughout the remaining years of the war, only the occasional skirmish broke the monotony of day-to-day life. In fact, if it wasn't for John Singleton Mosby, the town's only fighting would have been on December 20, 1861.

Mosby, who had served with Stuart at the battle of Lewinsville, raised his famed 43rd Battalion Virginia Cavalry in the winter of 1862-63. Rather than operate as traditional cavalry, Mosby's soldiers waged a guerrilla war against their Federal foes.[4] By the end of the war, the partisans so dominated the counties of Fairfax, Fauquier, Loudoun, and Prince William that the whole area came to be known as "Mosby's Confederacy." That, of course, included Dranesville.[5]

Even before the creation of Mosby's partisan unit, Federal cavalry had encamped at Dranesville during the winter of 1862-63, lodging themselves within various public and private buildings. The damaged Coleman house was even used as material for soldiers' huts. After the war, Ann Coleman petitioned the government for damages as the soldiers "took the house all to pieces and built huts out of it." Her petition was denied.[6]

Kate Carper wrote in late March 1863, "For four months we have the miserable yankees around us." Their mere presence deeply offended her, and, in another entry, she bemoaned, "Oh! that we had some protection against such insults."[7] And then Mosby came to town.

Mosby's men closed on the town on the last day of March. By then, however, the Federals had broken camp and withdrawn back across Difficult Run, closer to Washington. Mosby, with about 70 other troopers, turned around and rode west

---

3 Kate Carper Diary, Jun. 26, 1863; Edwin B. Coddington, *The Gettysburg Campaign: A Study in Command* (1968; repr., New York, 1979) 113, 119; See Eric J. Wittenberg and J. David Petruzzi, *Plenty of Blame to Go Around: Jeb Stuart's Controversial Ride to Gettysburg* (New York, 2006).

4 Hugh C. Keen and Horace Mewborn, *43rd Battalion Virginia Cavalry Mosby's Command* (Lynchburg, VA, 1993), 1.

5 Jeffry D. Wert, *Mosby's Rangers* (New York, 1990), 116.

6 Ann Coleman Southern Claims File, NARA.

7 Kate Carper Diary, Mar. 25 and Mar. 29, 1863.

Colonel John Mosby

LOC

a few miles into Loudoun County, bedding for the night at Thomas Miskel's farm.[8]

That same day, a Unionist sympathizer reported Mosby's presence. Major Charles Taggart ordered 150 troopers from the 1st Vermont Cavalry to capture or destroy Mosby's force. The Federals rode through the night, closing on Mosby's men sleeping at Miskel's.[9]

As the Vermonters approached the farmhouse early on the morning of April 1, an alert lookout raised the alarm. In a flash, Mosby's men were ready, and the skirmish of Miskel's Farm began. Ordering a saber charge, Capt. Henry Flint led the Vermonters up Miskel's lane, but soon dropped dead out of the saddle.[10] Mosby ordered a counter-attack, which shattered the Vermonters' will to fight. They retreated at a mad gallop back down the Leesburg Turnpike and through Dranesville. Kate Carper happily wrote, "We have the pleasure of seeing the yankees flying down the road with Moseby's men at their heels." In the quick skirmish, Mosby lost one killed and three wounded. The Vermonters, though, suffered seven killed, 22 wounded and 82 captured— nearly 75% of the 150 troopers that Maj. Taggart had sent.[11]

Mosby again fought near Dranesville a year later. On February 21, 1864, Mosby got word that a Union cavalry column planned to raid from Leesburg east towards Dranesville. He mounted his partisans and rode to intercept them. Camping near the town, Mosby planned an ambush the next day, about two miles

8 Wert, *Mosby's Rangers*, 52.

9 *OR* 25, pt. 1, 77.

10 George G. Benedict, *Vermont in the Civil War*: Vol. 2 (Burlington, VT, 1888) 586.

11 Kate Carper, Apr. 1, 1863, Diary Entry; Keen and Mewborn, *43rd Battalion Virginia Cavalry*, 47-48; Benedict, *Vermont in the Civil War*: Vol. 2, 587.

west of Dranesville along the Leesburg Pike near a blacksmith's shop owned by Samuel Ankers.[12]

The Federal cavalry, about 160 troopers from the 2nd Massachusetts and 16th New York, soon came into view. Seizing the moment, Mosby blew a whistle which unleashed a torrent of small arms fire. By the time the shooting stopped, Mosby's troopers had killed 10, wounded seven, and captured 56 prisoners, in exchange for six of their own losses.[13]

The fighting at Ankers's Shop was quick and decisive, and some of Mosby's men came to call it the Second Battle of Dranesville. The skirmishing on Feb. 22, 1864, was the last time there was fighting in Dranesville.

When the war's end finally came a little a year later, the town returned to a semblance of peace and normalcy. Kate Carper now devoted her diary passages to the mundane comings and goings of peacetime. The Day brothers resumed their doctoring to the locals, and Charles Coleman became postmaster.

Some of the Unionists who fled town in 1861 returned to live once again among their neighbors. Henry Bishop, who had sworn that William Day was responsible for his father's death, moved back to Dranesville, as did Minor Crippen and Nelson Voorhees.[14] The historical record is silent as to whether there was any ill-will between the inhabitants of Dranesville, but it appears that they let bygones be bygones.

Even Robert Dickey, who had stabbed Henry St. Clair to death in 1854, returned to Dranesville. Though sentenced to 18 years in prison for his crime, the Civil War had given Dickey a way out. In 1862, as George McClellan's army marched closer to Richmond, Dickey petitioned Virginia's governor for a release, so that he could, "enter the service in defence of his native state and her institutions."[15] The governor approved, and Dickey served as an artillerist, earning a commutation of his sentence. Returning home to Dranesville, Dickey lived until 1905.[16] Life in all forms was returning to normal.

* * *

---

12 James McLean, *California Sabers: The 2nd Massachusetts Cavalry in the Civil War* (Bloomington, IN, 2000), 71.

13 Ibid., 71; Wert, *Mosby's Rangers*, 147; Keen and Mewborn, *43rd Battalion Virginia Cavalry*, 113.

14 See 1870 Census for Fairfax County for evidence that Unionists such as Bishop, Voorhees, and Crippen had returned to Dranesville.

15 *Message of the Governor of Virginia and Accompanying Documents* (Richmond, 1862), 114; Robert Dickey Compiled Service Record.

16 Hofer, "Murder Most Foul," 4.

The battle of Dranesville catapulted Edward Ord's career. His first promotion had come from influential friends, but his next one came as a direct result of his military success on December 20, 1861. First, he received a brevet promotion to lieutenant colonel in the Regular Army, then in May 1862, a second star to become a major general of volunteers. "Ord has been made a major general for his Dranesville fight," George Meade wrote, and added, "I think the promotion of Ord just and deserved." Now in charge of a division, Ord bid farewell to the brigade he had led to victory at Dranesville with one final review. "Their enthusiasm and cheers were complimentary and indeed I could hardly restrain my tears," Ord wrote to his wife. "They were a fine set of men."[17]

With his new rank, Ord was sent to the Western Theatre, where he served under the rising figure of Ulysses S. Grant. Ord became one of Grant's close confidantes during their time together. Over and over, when Grant needed a man, he found Ord: he commanded a corps during the Siege of Vicksburg, and ultimately led the Army of the James at the war's conclusion. On April 9, 1865, when Grant met with Robert E. Lee at Appomattox, Edward Ord was in the room, too. The long road was at its end, and for Edward Ord, that journey had started at Dranesville.[18]

The experience at Dranesville had not been nearly as positive for J. E. B. Stuart, but it proved surprisingly beneficial for him. He received his drubbings and then some, but Stuart seems to have taken the bloody lessons to heart. Though one of the Civil War's most famous cavaliers, Stuart would be called on to command infantry and artillery again—perhaps most famously on May 3, 1863, during the battle of Chancellorsville.

After Stonewall Jackson's wounding, Stuart raced to the front to assume command of Jackson's corps. The Army of Northern Virginia was in a precarious position, split into two wings, heavily outnumbered with the bulk of the Army of the Potomac between Stuart and the rest of the Confederate Army. As the sun rose above the woods, Stuart led infantry forward.[19] At Dranesville, Stuart had struggled with close to 2,000 infantrymen. At Chancellorsville, he was tasked with commanding almost 20,000. Out of the pan and into the fire, Stuart rose to the occasion. Edward Porter Alexander, who had observed Federal positions from Mason's Hill in 1861, and was now an accomplished artillery officer, remembered that, "Stuart never seemed to hesitate or to doubt for one moment that he could

17 Meade, *Life and Letters of George Gordon Meade*: Vol. 1, 265; Edward Ord to his wife, May 18, 1862, in Edward Ord Papers, Box 1, Folder 3, Item 24, Stanford University.

18 William B. Feiss, "Grant's Relief Man: Edward O. C. Ord," in *Grant's Lieutenants: From Chattanooga to Appomattox*, ed. Steven E. Woodworth (Lawrence, KS 2008), 173.

19 Bigelow, *The Campaign of Chancellorsville*, 339.

just crash his way wherever he chose to strike."[20] After five hours of incredibly bloody and close fighting, Stuart accomplished his mission, driving the Federals away from the Chancellor house site and linking back up with Robert E. Lee.[21] Alexander summarized: "Altogether, I do not think there was a more brilliant thing done in the war than Stuart's extricating that command from the extremely critical position in which he found it as promptly and as boldly as he did."[22]

If the battle of Chancellorsville had not provided Stuart with enough chances at commanding infantry, he would have another opportunity just a year later. After the tactically indecisive two-day battle of the Wilderness, both armies raced to the important crossroads town of Spotsylvania Court House on May 8, 1864. Stuart's tired and worn-out cavalry brigades contested the Federal army's advance, delaying and fighting from roadblocks hour after hour. The time Stuart's men bought with their lives allowed Confederate infantry to rush to Laurel Hill, a prominent ridge outside of the town. Whomever controlled Laurel Hill controlled the approach to Spotsylvania Court House. It was a race that came down to mere minutes, with the exhausted rebel troopers giving way in the presence of overwhelming numbers of Federal infantry. There, at the crest of Laurel Hill, was Stuart, guiding the vanguard of Confederate infantry into position.[23]

One of the Confederate infantrymen, John Coxe, remembered that Stuart, "was all action." Stuart had shown the same instinct at Dranesville but had soon thereafter lost control of the situation. He would not at Spotsylvania. "Stuart was the only Confederate general officer in sight and . . . just as cool as a piece of ice," Coxe wrote. "He rode right along the lines and with the help of his staff personally posted all the regiments of the brigade."[24] Another soldier said, "General Stuart remained with our regiment during the entire action, sitting on his horse amidst a storm of bullets, laughing and joking with the men and commending them highly for their courage and for the rapidity and accuracy of their fire."[25] The Confederate line held, setting up the grueling battle of Spotsylvania that would last for nearly two weeks.

---

20 E. P. Alexander quoted in McClellan, *I Rode with Jeb Stuart*, 255.

21 John Bigelow, *The Campaign of Chancellorsville: A Strategic and Tactical Study* (New Haven, 1910), 372.

22 Alexander quoted in McClellan, *I Rode with Jeb Stuart*, 255.

23 Gordon C. Rhea, *The Battles for Spotsylvania Court House and the Road to Yellow Tavern, May 7-12, 1864* (Baton Rouge, 2005), 30-50.

24 John Coxe, "Last Struggles and Successes of Lee," in *Confederate Veteran* 22, No. 8 (Aug. 1914): 357.

25 William Wallace, "Operations of Second South Carolina Regiment in Campaigns of 1864 and 1865," in *Southern Historical Society Papers* 7: 129.

Four days after his stand at Laurel Hill, Stuart was dead. Felled as he led his soldiers during the battle of Yellow Tavern, Stuart died in Richmond on May 12. In the wake of Dranesville, John M. Brice from the 6th South Carolina had written that Stuart was, "a cavalry general of distinction, but I think a very poor infantry officer." That may have been the case in 1861, but it certainly was not by 1864. Stuart carried the lessons of Dranesville with him until the day he died.

*   *   *

Why, in the grand scheme of things, is a book about the battle of Dranesville necessary? It was not a large battle, it did not produce tens of thousands of casualties, and it did not materially impact the war. But that does not mean it did not matter.

The Federal victory there, albeit small, lifted the morale of a Northern public that had very little to cheer. Hoping that Dranesville gave confidence to the army and its commanders, a pro-Union paper out of Wheeling, Virginia, wrote that it could "prove one of the most fortunate occurrences of the war."[26] Or, as New York editor Horace Greeley put it later, "The victory at Dranesville, unimportant as it may now seem, diffused an immense exhilaration throughout the Union ranks. It was a fitting and conclusive answer to every open assertion or whispered insinuation impeaching the courage or the steadiness of our raw Northern volunteers."[27]

Specifically, Dranesville boosted the confidence of the Pennsylvania Reserve Corps and started them down the road to becoming one of the best fighting units of the entire war. While the Federal forces had won other victories before Dranesville, as one soldier in the 9th Reserves wrote, "This battle was the first Younnion victory that has been won on the Potomic River."[28] Their victory was something the Pennsylvanians never forgot. Nearly fifty years later, reflecting on the battle, one veteran wrote in its aftermath, "A proud lot of boys we were."[29]

For the next three years, until they disbanded in 1864, the Reserves fought and bled during the Seven Days, Second Bull Run, Antietam, Fredericksburg, Gettysburg, and the Overland Campaign. Yet, in later years, the Reserves chose Dranesville's anniversary to host reunions around. In 1889, the veterans congregated in Pittsburgh "in celebration of the twenty-eighth anniversary of the Battle of Dranesville." They sang "some of the old campaign songs" and departed after a "very pleasant evening was spent."[30] Two years later, to remember

26 *Wheeling Daily Intelligencer*, Dec. 28, 1861.

27 Greeley, *The American Conflict*, Vol. 1, 626.

28 William Leslie to friend Emma, Jan. 17, 1862, Library of Virginia

29 *The National Tribune*, Apr. 4, 1907.

30 *The Pittsburg Dispatch*, Dec. 21, 1889.

the 30th anniversary of the battle, the Pennsylvanians held "a banquet, speech-making, and other entertainment," using it as "an occasion when the members scattered all over the country get together and renew their wartime friendships and acquaintances."[31] The meetings continued into the early 1900s, when a paper noted sadly, "The membership of the association is being reduced by natural causes, and the attendance was below average for December meetings."[32] John McCalmont, who had led the 10th Reserves into combat at Dranesville, attended every single meeting for a decade until frail health finally forced him to stay home.[33] When it came time to dedicate their monuments at Gettysburg, veterans spoke of their success at Dranesville over and over again.[34] Until their dying days, the men of the Pennsylvania Reserves remembered what they had accomplished on December 20, 1861.

Confederate soldiers, on the other hand, talked little of the battle. In its immediate aftermath, they wrote letters and newspaper editorials home, but it soon passed out of their collective thought, replaced by grander tales of victory outside Richmond or at Manassas. As veterans, when they held their reunions, they occasionally talked about Dranesville, as Maj. Thomas Woodward did in 1883. But for the most part it seems former Confederates were happy to forget the battle ever happened. Even the burial grounds of their former comrades were sometimes forgotten. In 1909, James Coleman wrote to surviving members of the 10th Alabama that he had recently returned from a pilgrimage to their former camp at Bristoe Station. He visited their old cemetery there and reported, "The cedar posts that were placed there as a directory of each grave were so badly obliterated that I was unable to make out the names. A number of cedar trees have grown up over the graves, the largest being about the size of a man's thigh." For James, this was more than a sight-seeing trip. "I wanted this spot especially to show the respect I have for my brother, Sidney L. Coleman, who was killed at Dranesville."[35]

For some, whether they wanted to remember or not, Dranesville was a constant reminder of what had happened, and what had been lost. During the battle, Capt. Robert Galway, 9th Reserves, was shot in the left leg. He resigned from the army in 1862. The wound continued to plague him, and Galway found solace in the

31 *The Pittsburg Dispatch*, Dec. 4, 1891.

32 *The Evening Star*, Dec. 21, 1901.

33 Ibid.

34 John P. Nicholson, ed. *Pennsylvania at Gettysburg: Ceremonies at the Dedication of the Monuments Erected by the Commonwealth of Pennsylvania to Mark the Positions of the Pennsylvania Commands Engaged in the Battle* (Harrisburg, 1904), 74, 82, 99, 226, 234, 238, 248, 255, 262.

35 James Coleman, "To Survivors of the Tenth Alabama Regiment," in *Confederate Veteran* 17 (1909): 233.

only cure he could find— morphine. Galway became addicted to the opiate, and he died in 1864 from what was styled a "disease of the brain."[36]

On the opposite side of the battle line, Pvt. James Spence, in the 10th Alabama's Company E, was shot in the leg during the fighting. The wound proved bad enough that his war experience ended then and there, with him sent home after his first battle. In a newspaper article published in 1904, hidden away in the paper's sixth page, is a small blurb. "James Spence, a member of the Tenth Ala. Regiment . . . had a minnie ball extracted from his leg at Tuscaloosa last week," the blurb reads. "The ball had been embedded in his flesh for forty-two years and four months and at times gave him much trouble."[37] It posed as a daily reminder of the battle, even 40 years later.

In the battle's wake, families tried to recover. When Cpl. Samuel Galbraith, 1st Pennsylvania Rifles, died at Dranesville, he left behind his wife of 13 years, Elizabeth, and his two children, nine-year-old Mary and eight-year-old Charles. Petitioning the government, Elizabeth filed for a pension. Illiterate, Elizabeth left an X on the signature line. The government paid Elizabeth $12 a month for her and her young children. She died sometime after 1880, having worked as a housekeeper in Harrisburg and never remarrying. Samuel Galbraith was killed instantly, but the ramifications of his death, like all those who died on December 20, 1861, reverberated for years.[38]

*   *   *

Life went on, and the years began to pass. As they did, preservation, or more accurately, a lack thereof, also played a role in why the fighting at Dranesville was largely forgotten. Dranesville's proximity to Washington, D.C., meant it was only a matter of time before urban sprawl overtook the town. It was far too small a battle to be preserved in the 1890s when Congress first started to appropriate land for national battlefield parks, and no other park, state or otherwise, was dedicated to the battle. The only green space set aside— the Dranesville Tavern—is nearly a mile away from where any of the fighting took place.[39]

36 Julia Galway Widow Application, NARA.

37 *Daily Mountain Eagle*, May 18, 1904.

38 Elizabeth Galbraith Widow Pension, NARA; Elizabeth Galbraith in 1880 Dauphin County, Pennsylvania Census.

39 The Dranesville Tavern is sometimes confused for the tavern that Washington Drane built, but in actuality is a tavern owned by George Jackson that operated at its height in the second half of the 19th century. Ross De Witt Netherton and Nan Netherton, *The Dranesville Tavern: An Historic Landmarks Research Report* (Fairfax, VA, 1966), 1.

The 19th century gave way to the 20th century. Dranesville's turnpikes were paved over and became major state highways, including Virginia Route 7, designated in 1933.[40] Thousands of cars turned into tens of thousands of cars driving down the corridor from Leesburg to Washington every day. Those cars needed gas stations, and rest stops, and mechanics. The pine trees and dirt roads that J. E. B. Stuart's men fought through became housing developments and convenience stores. The development exploded again with the dedication of Dulles International Airport in 1962, only ten miles away from Dranesville. One newspaper touted the airport as a "New Gateway to the U.S."[41] A new gateway meant more paving over of the old. Fairfax County and its environs were now covered in asphalt.

Some held out hope for Dranesville. As late as the 1980s, there were advocates for a small county park, and others who fought steadfastly just to keep a simple Virginia Department of Transportation sign detailing the battle. But in the end, no park came to be. One county official claimed in 1989, "If we tried to preserve all the historical sites in the County, we would be preserving the entire county."[42]

In a strange twist, the only thing that one could consider truly memorialized is the site of the September 16 ambush at Lowe's Island. The ground where Pvt. Oliver Darling was shot and killed by the Dranesville Home Guard became a multi-million-dollar golf club. In 2009, Donald Trump bought the course, and soon paid to have a monument put in. The monument, standing only a few feet tall, has the inscription, "Many great American soldiers, both of the North and South, died at this spot. The casualties were so great that the water would turn red and thus became known as 'The River of Blood.'"[43] The monument came to light during the 2016 presidential campaign, and historians scoffed at the sensational plaque. Of course, no major battle was ever fought at Lowe's Island, and the Potomac River was never known as the River of Blood, but in the most circular, round-about way, that monument is the only testament to what happened on the evening of September 16, 1861.

Despite the loss of the Dranesville battlefield, the battle is not totally forgotten, however. In the early 20th century, a congregation built a simple church atop Drane Hill, where Hezekiah Easton had unlimbered his cannon during the battle. The Dranesville Church of the Brethren is an unassuming white building. Inside, the congregation's core values include pacifism and preaching the horror and

40 *The Times Dispatch*, May 10, 1933.

41 *The Daily Times* (New Philadelphia, Ohio), Nov. 24, 1962.

42 *Herndon Times*, Oct. 4, 1989; *McLean Providence Journal*, Sep. 7, 1989.

43 *Washington Post*, Feb. 14, 2009; *New York Times*, Nov. 24, 2015.

A 2019 photograph looking over the area where the battle of Dranesville was fought. Compare to the *Harper's Weekly* sketch printed in Chapter 10. Easton's battery unlimbered in the grassy foreground. The site of the Thornton House is now a convenience store, and the site of the Robert Coleman House is now a fire station. The Dranesville Church of the Brethren stands behind the camera's viewpoint. *Author*

futility of war. Even though the battlefield is gone, covered in multi-lane highways and convenience stores, the Brethren remember the battle.

Every December, the congregants meet in their small sanctuary for a peace service. In a corner sits a table, covered in candles with wicks slowly burning down. The congregation's peace service offers a chance to reflect on what happened outside their doors more than 160 years ago. Hymns are sung, and selections read. With a final hymn, "Amazing Grace," the lights are turned off. In the darkness of the sanctuary, the only light remaining is that of the candles. The reflections flicker off the walls like bouncing spirits. In the darkness, the names of the dead of Dranesville are read, one by one. The names of young men whose lives came to violent ends over the space of two hours on a chilly Friday afternoon. With each name read, a candle is extinguished. Alexander Smith. George Cook. Samuel Galbraith. The room grows darker. Thomas Harden. James Martin. Franklin English. Before long, the candles are all out, and total darkness envelops the church. It is a somber reminder of the lives dashed to pieces.

So, the questions deserve to be asked again: why is a study about the battle of Dranesville necessary? Why does it matter? And the simplest answer is because the civilians and soldiers of Dranesville mattered. Their lives, no matter where they started, collided in a panorama of noise, smoke, and blood. While history may seem to have passed them by, their names endure.

Appendix One

Fates After Dranesville

George D. Bayard received a promotion to brigadier general of cavalry. He commanded a brigade in the Shenandoah Valley and during the battle of Second Manassas in August 1862. Appointed as chief of cavalry for the Left Grand Division during the Fredericksburg Campaign, Bayard was resting at headquarters on December 13, 1862, when a shell fragment struck him in the thigh. He died a day later, five days shy of his 27th birthday.[1]

Though only a lieutenant at Dranesville, **John Bratton** rose through the ranks and commanded the 6th South Carolina during the battle of Williamsburg on May 5, 1862. Wounded and captured at Seven Pines, Bratton missed most of the fighting in 1862, but returned in time for Fredericksburg. He led his regiment into combat during the fighting around Chattanooga in the fall of 1863, and again in the opening stages of the bloody Overland Campaign. When his brigade commander was killed at the Wilderness, Bratton received a promotion to brigadier general and assumed command, leading the brigade through the rest of the war. Bratton returned to South Carolina and found it devastated. He threw himself into farming and politics, serving as a representative of South Carolina's Constitutional Convention in 1865. Continuing in politics, Bratton supported Gov. Wade Hampton's Redemption policies as South Carolina's Comptroller

---

1 Warner, *Generals in Blue*, 26; *New York Daily Herald*, Dec. 22, 1862, 5.

General, and as a member of the U.S. House of Representatives. Though he ran for governor twice, Bratton did not win, and he died in 1898.[2]

After his release from the Old Capitol Prison, **Philip Carper** rejoined the Confederate army, enlisting in the 35th Battalion, Virginia Cavalry. He was wounded at Brandy Station and subsequently captured, earning him a second stay at the Old Capitol. Released again, Carper was captured a third time in January 1864, near his home at Dranesville. His incarceration at Point Lookout, Maryland lasted until February 1865. He married in 1865, and then, after his first wife's death in 1869, wed again in 1878. Carper died in 1918, just shy of his 77th birthday.[3]

Charles W. Coleman avoided the rest of the war. There are no further indications that he had any other run-ins with the Federal government during the war. In December 1865, he became the postmaster of Dranesville. Married twice, Coleman had a total of ten children before his death in 1897.[4]

Allen S. Cutts commanded the Sumter Flying Artillery until his promotion to lieutenant colonel in May 1862. In charge of a battalion of artillery, Cutts took part in many of the Army of Northern Virginia's campaigns. In 1864 he received a promotion to colonel, a rank he held until the end of the war. Cutts returned to Georgia and served as mayor of Americus for six years. From 1890-1891 he served as a state representative. He died in 1896.[5]

John T. Day, once released from the Old Capitol Prison, stayed out of the war. Though one of the loudest voices of the Home Guard, his introduction to the realities of the war and his anxiety inside the jail seem to have softened his ardor. Back in Dranesville, he returned to his role as a doctor. Kitty Hanna later remembered, after the war, "Doctor Jack, so tall an' redfaced, with long gray beard and flowin' locks, drivin' so fas' 'round the country, in a two horse buggy, his dogs followin' him a-barkin' an' racin.'" A devout Episcopalian, Day became a trustee of St. Timothy's Church in Herndon, Virginia. After his death in 1893, the congregation put up a stained-glass window dedicated to his memory.[6]

2 Bratton, *General John Bratton*, 269-272.

3 Philip Carper, CSR, Company A, 35th Battalion, Virginia Cavalry; Poland, *Dunbarton and Dranesville*, 54n104.

4 *Alexandria Gazette and Advertiser*, Dec. 12, 1865, 3; *Poland, Dunbarton, Dranesville*, 83n49.

5 Speicher, *The Sumter Flying Artillery*, 267.

6 Castleman, *Reminiscences of an Oldest Inhabitant*, 33; "Mayfield and Ivy Chimney," 14.

Unlike his brother John, who stayed out of the rest of the war, **William B. Day** was just getting started. In the fall of 1862, he was appointed as an assistant surgeon at a hospital in Winchester, Virginia, before becoming a surgeon at Camp Winder, in Richmond. In the fall of 1863, Day was reassigned to a hospital in Georgia, but resigned his position in early 1864 to return home. He resumed his role as a doctor for Dranesville and the outlying area until his death in 1886.[7]

Captain **Hezekiah Easton** commanded Battery A, 1st Pennsylvania Artillery until his death at the battle of Gaines's Mill on June 27, 1862. Moments before he was killed, Easton called out, "The enemy shall never take this battery but over my dead body."[8]

William D. Farley joined J. E. B. Stuart's staff after his release from the Old Capitol Prison. He served in almost every major battle in which the Army of Northern Virginia fought until he was mortally wounded at the battle of Brandy Station on June 9, 1863. Originally buried in Culpeper County, Virginia, his remains were moved to South Carolina in 2002.[9]

John Forney, 10th Alabama, recovered from his arm wound. Promoted to brigadier general in the spring of 1862, Forney served in the Gulf Department before another promotion to major general. Commanding a division outside Vicksburg, Forney's men participated in some of the heaviest fighting of the siege. Returning to duty after his capture and exchange, Forney spent the rest of the war jumping among various departments. After the war, he oversaw civil engineering projects before his death in 1902. His funeral procession extended over a mile.[10]

Samuel Garland, colonel of the 11th Virginia at Dranesville, continued to command into 1862. At Williamsburg, a musket ball hit Garland in the elbow, but he refused to leave the field. His tenacity and combat skills earned him a promotion to brigadier general. Garland again earned praise for his actions at Seven Pines. On September 14, 1862, Garland was ordered to hold Fox's Gap during the battle of South Mountain. Killed in the subsequent fighting, his body was brought back for burial in Lynchburg, Virginia.[11]

---

7 Johnson, *Brothers and Cousins*, 43; Sprouse, Volume 2, 505.

8 *OR* 11, pt. 2, 408.

9 Trout, *They Followed the Plume*, 106-114; *The Washington Post*, Apr. 7, 2002.

10 Daugette, "Life of Major General John H. Forney", 382.

11 Warner, *Generals in Gray*, 98-99.

Conrad F. Jackson commanded the 9th Pennsylvania Reserves through the Peninsula Campaign, Seven Days, and the battle of Second Manassas. The busy summer's actions won him acclaim, earning him a promotion to brigadier general. But that same constant fighting wore him down, and he missed the Antietam Campaign. Returning in time for the Fredericksburg Campaign, Jackson led his brigade into action on December 13. As Jackson went forward, a bullet struck him in the side of the head, killing him instantly. His body was returned to Pittsburgh and buried in the city's Allegheny Cemetery.[12]

Thomas L. Kane eventually recovered from his facial wound and returned to the Bucktails. His wife made him promise to drop his challenge against his one-time antagonist Charles Biddle, and the gentlemen's contest never happened. He was with the Bucktails when the regiment fought in the Shenandoah Valley in the spring of 1862, where he was wounded again. Promoted to brigadier general, Kane led a brigade at Gettysburg, where it fought in the defense of Culp's Hill. Due to his numerous wounds and ill-health, Kane resigned from the army in the fall of 1863. He and his wife Elizabeth settled in western Pennsylvania, where they helped create the town of Kane. They fell victim to a fraud that emptied their bank accounts but were saved when oil was discovered on their property. Kane remained close friends with Brigham Young and a supporter of the Mormons. He died in 1883, just a year after the government started paying him $30 a month for near total disability caused by his war injuries.[13]

Edward O. C. Ord was wounded twice during the Civil War—once at the battle of Hatchie's Bridge and again at Fort Harrison in 1864. Neither wound proved serious, and Ord, through his connections with Ulysses S. Grant, received promotions and accolade. At war's end he commanded the Army of the James and helped block Lee's escape at Appomattox. Ord was in the parlor of Wilmer McLean's house when the surrender negotiations were reached, and he quickly bought the table at which Lee had sat for $40. He mustered out of the volunteer service and returned to the Regular Army as a brigadier general. Ord served for another 15 years before he retired in 1881. While on a ship Ord contracted yellow fever and died in Cuba on July 22, 1883. He is buried in Arlington National Cemetery. In a General Orders published to the army, Ord's closest friend since

---

12 Warner, *Generals in Blue*, 247.

13 Elizabeth Kane Diary, Dec. 26, 1861, BYU; Warner, *Generals in Blue*, 257; Grow, *"Liberty to the Downtrodden,"* 254; Thomas L. Kane Pension, NARA.

West Point, William T. Sherman, eulogized that "a more unselfish, manly and patriotic person never lived."[14]

Major General **George A. McCall's** fighting came to an end when he was captured at the battle of Glendale on June 30, 1862. Once exchanged, he retired to Pennsylvania. When McCall died in 1868, Col. John Taggart—commander of the 12th Reserves at Dranesville—eulogized him: "We have assembled together to-day to pay our tribute of sincere respect to his memory, and to testify our unfeigned and hearty admiration for his sterling worth, his manly and noble qualities, both as a soldier and a gentleman."[15]

J. E. B. Stuart became one of the Confederacy's everlasting heroes. Though heavily criticized for his defeat at Dranesville, Stuart made a name for himself when he and his cavalry rode around the Army of the Potomac in the spring of 1862. He was promoted to major general and became one of Robert E. Lee's most trusted subordinates. Stuart led the Army of Northern Virginia's cavalry and again weathered the storm of controversy after his controversial ride to Gettysburg in 1863. On May 11, 1864, Stuart was shot below the ribs during the battle of Yellow Tavern. He died the next day and was buried in Richmond's Hollywood Cemetery. One of his staff officers wrote, "I cannot realize that he is gone, that I am to see his gallant figure nor hear his cheering voice, no more." Stuart was 31-years-old when he died.[16]

Thomas Taylor served as the 1st Kentucky's colonel until it was disbanded in the spring of 1862. He subsequently served as a brigade commander in Tennessee and Kentucky, before transferring to serve on Lt. Gen. John Pemberton's staff during the Vicksburg Campaign. Exchanged after the city's fall, Taylor spent the rest of the war serving in various capacities in Mobile, Alabama. He ended the conflict as a brigadier general, and returned home to Kentucky where he worked as a U.S. Marshal and the chief of police in Louisville. Taylor died in 1901 and is buried in Frankfort, Kentucky.[17]

---

14 Cresap, *Appomattox Commander*, 214, 341-343; General Orders No. 54 in Index of General Orders and Circulars, Adjutant General's Office, 1883 (Washington, D.C., 1884), 25.

15 Warner, *Generals in Blue*, 289; *Tribute of Respect to the Memory of Maj.-Gen. Geo. A. McCall*, 7-8.

16 Thomas, *Bold Dragoon*, 292; Trout, *With Pen and Saber*, 254.

17 Allardice and Hewitt, *Kentuckians in Gray*, 260-263.

Appendix Two

Dranesville Order of Battle

United States of America

Pennsylvania Volunteer Reserve Corps
Maj. Gen. George A. McCall (Personally arrived at the end of the battle)
Third Brigade: Brig. Gen. Edward O. C. Ord
10 Killed, 63 Wounded: 73 Total

Lt. Col. Thomas Kane (w): 1st Pennsylvania Rifles (13th Pennsylvania Reserve)
[42nd Pennsylvania Infantry]
3 Killed, 31 Wounded: 34 Total

Lt. Col. William Penrose: 6th Pennsylvania Reserves [35th Pennsylvania Infantry]
3 Killed, 13 Wounded: 16 Total

Col. Conrad F. Jackson: 9th Pennsylvania Reserves [38th Pennsylvania Infantry]
4 Killed, 18 Wounded: 22 Total

Col. John McCalmont: 10th Pennsylvania Reserves [39th Pennsylvania Infantry]
0 Casualties

Col. John Taggart: 12th Pennsylvania Reserves [41st Pennsylvania Infantry]
0 Killed, 1 Wounded: 1 Total

Lt. Col. Jacob Higgins: 1st Pennsylvania Reserve Cavalry
0 Casualties

Capt. Hezekiah Easton: Battery A, 1st Pennsylvania Light Artillery
0 Casualties

Confederate States of America

Confederate Army of the Potomac Outposts
Brig. Gen. J. E. B. Stuart
65 Killed, 125 Wounded, 5 Captured: 195 Total[1]

Col. Thomas H. Taylor: 1st Kentucky Infantry
5 Killed, 20 Wounded, 2 Captured: 27 Total

Lt. Col. Andrew Secrest: 6th South Carolina Infantry
24 Killed, 39 Wounded: 63 Total

Col. John Forney (w): 10th Alabama Infantry
Lt. Col. James B. Martin (k)
Maj. John Woodward
24 Killed, 40 Wounded, 3 Captured: 67 Total

Col. Samuel Garland: 11th Virginia Infantry
6 Killed, 15 Wounded: 21 Total

Maj. James Gordon: 1st North Carolina Cavalry (100 Troopers)
0 Casualties

Capt. Andrew Pitzer: 2nd Virginia Cavalry (50 Troopers)
0 Casualties

Capt. Allen S. Cutts: Sumter Flying Artillery [Battery A, 11th Georgia Artillery]
6 Killed, 11 Wounded: 17 Total

(k): Killed
(w): Wounded

---

1 A total of 10 Confederates were captured because of the battle of Dranesville. However, five of them were wounded and thus have been counted elsewhere.

Appendix Three

Names of Casualties at the Battle of Dranesville

As mentioned in the Acknowledgments, this list is the result of research by several people. It has been compiled by combing through service records, official reports, newspaper articles, and unit histories. Several names had wide varieties of spelling; I have gone with the spelling printed on service records or in unit musters. Any omissions are accidental, and any errors are entirely my own. (c) = captured; (k) = killed; (mw) = mortally wounded; (w) = wounded.

United States of America

1st Pennsylvania Rifles
Pvt. Fidel Ambruster, Co. F: (w)
Pvt. John F. Barnes, Co. K: (w)
Cpl. Enoch Barnum, Co. C: (w)
Pvt. John P. Blair, Co. C: (w)
Pvt. George Bott, Co. F: (w)
Pvt. John B. Brink, Co. H: (w)
Pvt. Taylor Brink, Co. H: (w)
Pvt. Samuel W. Campbell, Co. E: (w)
Pvt. Myron C. Cobb, Co. D: (w)
Pvt. George Cook, Co. E: (k)
Pvt. George W. Cook, Co. C: (w)
Pvt. Brazilla Dewey, Co. E: (w)
Pvt. Ferdinand Eickhoff, Co. F: (w)
Cpl. George W. Fine, Co. C: (w)
Pvt. Francis A. Foster, Co. B: (w)
Pvt. James Freel, Co. H: (w)
Pvt. Thomas Furlong, Co. G: (w)
Cpl. Samuel Galbraith, Co. B: (k)
Pvt. Nelson Geer, Co. D: (w)
Pvt. James Glenn, Co. K: (w)

Lt. Col. Thomas L. Kane: (w)
Pvt. Robert T. Lane, Co. I: (w)
Pvt. George A. Ludlow, Co. E: (w)
Pvt. George W. McGowen, Co. C: (w)
Pvt. Lewis McGraff, Co. E: (w)
Pvt. Charles Meddler, Co. F: (w)
Pvt. Parish Mosier, Co. E: (w)
Capt. Alanson E. Niles, Co. E: (w)
Pvt. Edward Osborn, Co. E: (w)
Pvt. John Pennell, Co. B: (w)
Pvt. Benjamin B. Potter, Co. E: (w)
Pvt. George Raup, Co. B: (k)
Pvt. Absalom Sweger, Co. B: (w)
Pvt. Hiram G. Wolf, Co. B: (w)

6th Pennsylvania Reserves
Capt. Daniel Bradbury, Co. F: (w)
Pvt. George Brower, Co. K: (w)
Pvt. John W. Brown, Co. K: (w)
Pvt. Thomas Conway, Co. H: (w)
Pvt. Daniel Darling, Co. C: (k)

Pvt. Edwin Demander, Co. K: (w)

Pvt. W. H. Densmore, Co. F: (w)

Capt. William D. Dixon, Co. D: (w)

Pvt. William H. Jayne, Co. C: (w)

Pvt. Halsey Lathrop, Co. C: (w)

Pvt. Benjamin Seeley, Co. G: (w)

Pvt. Edgar Smith, Co. G: (w)

Pvt. James Surrine, Co. C: (w)

Pvt. William R. Van Dyke, Co. D: (k)

Pvt. Samuel C. Walter, Co. A: (k)

Pvt. Charles Yahn, Co. H: (w)

9th Pennsylvania Reserves

Pvt. Edward K. Davis, Co. H: (w)

Capt. Samuel B. Dick, Co. F: (w)

Pvt. William Earnest, Co. C: (w)

Capt. Robert Galway, Co. D: (w)

Pvt. John Hatch, Co. F: (w)

Pvt. John T. Henon, Co. D: (w)

Pvt. William Lindsay, Co. D: (w)

Pvt. William McGill, Co. F: (w)

Pvt. Joshua McMaster, Co. D: (w)

Pvt. William Milliron, Co. F: (w)

Pvt. George Moter, Co. D: (w)

Pvt. Silas B. Newell, Co. H: (mw);
died Dec. 22, 1861

Pvt. William Oberthur, Co. D: (w)

Pvt. Cadwallader Patton, Co. D: (w)

Cpl. Francis Pearsol, Co. D: (w)

Pvt. John Raymond, Co. D: (w)

Pvt. John Schmidt, Co. D: (w)

Pvt. John Sexton, Co. E: (k)

Pvt. Alexander B. Smith, Co. A: (mw);
died Jan. 14, 1862

Pvt. Joseph Stockdale, Co. F: (k)

Pvt. John Weber, Co. I: (w)

Pvt. Ralph White, Co. E: (w)

12th Pennsylvania Reserves

Pvt. William R. Fox, Co. K: (w)

Confederate States of America

1st Kentucky Infantry

Pvt. Frederick G. Alexander, Co. C:
(mw and captured)
died Dec. 21, 1861

Pvt. Marcus Asbury, Co. C: (w)

Pvt. John L. Barbee, Co. C: (mw)
died. Dec. 23, 1861

Cpl. J. M. Bean, Co. C: (w)

Pvt. James Brown, Co. C: (w)

Pvt. James Burham, Co. I: (w)

Pvt. Josephus Cummins, Co. C: (w)

Capt. Joseph Desha, Co. C: (w)

Cpl. W. N. Fishback, Co. C: (w)

Cpl. John Horine, Co. D: (w)

Pvt. Patrick Hughes, Co. D: (w); (c)

Cpl. John M. Johnson, Co. E: (k)

Cpl. George W. Lail, Co. C: (w)

Pvt. J. W. Lair, Co. C: (w)

Pvt. Richard Lennard, Co. K: (w)

Cpl. F. E. Long, Co. A: (c)

Pvt. John Mullen, Co. C: (w)

Pvt. William Nelson, Co. H: (c)

Pvt. Noah Parsons, Co. E: (mw);
died Jan. 6, 1862

Pvt. William B. Phelps, Co. C: (mw);
died Jan. 9, 1862

Pvt. George P. Simms, Co. C: (w)

Pvt. George W. Simpson, Co. C: (w)

Pvt. James W. Smith, Co. D: (w)

Pvt. Charles H. Stoner, Co. C: (w)

Pvt. George Stump, Co. C: (w)

Pvt. A. J. Thompson, Co. C: (w)

Pvt. Johnson West, Co. K: (w)

6th South Carolina

Pvt. William H. Abell, Co. F: (w)
Cpl. Alston P. Butler, Co. C: (w)
Pvt. Ira C. Atkinson, Co. K: (w)
Pvt. John G. Barber, Co. B: (k)
Pvt. Andrew J. Barnes, Co. B: (w)
Pvt. David W. Blassingame, Co. K: (w)
Pvt. Charles A. Boyd, Co. B: (w)
Pvt. George W. Brakefield, Co. E:
    (mw); died c. Dec. 20, 1861
Pvt. A. F. Branch, Co. H: (w)
Pvt. R. Wade Brice, Co. C: (w)
Cpl. William C. Byers, Co. C: (mw);
    died Jan. 15, 1862
Pvt. Joseph T. Caldwell, Co. G: (k)
Sgt. William J. Campbell, Co. H: (w)
Sgt. John N. Caruthers, Co. F: (mw);
    (c); died Dec. 21, 1861
Pvt. William Crosby, Co. H: (w)
Pvt. Theodore Cunningham,
    Co. K: (w)
Cpl. L. S. Douglass, Co. G: (w)
Pvt. Major R. Dye, Co. G: (w)
Pvt. J. M. Elliot, Co. D: (mw);
    died Dec. 27, 1861
Sgt. John T. Elliot, Co. F: (w)
Pvt. Franklin English, Co. C: (k)
Sgt. John N. Faris, Co. H: (mw);
    died Dec. 25, 1861
Pvt. James Gladden, Co. B: (w)
Pvt. James L. Griffith, Co. K: (w)
Pvt. William Hamilton, Co. H: (mw);
    died Mar. 20, 1862
Capt. Obadiah Harden, Co. E: (mw);
    died Jan. 1, 1862
Pvt. Thomas Harden, Co. E: (k)
Pvt. Samuel Hoffman, Co. H: (k)
Pvt. Daniel Hollis, Co. C: (w)

Pvt. J. W. Holtzclaw, Co. K: (w)
Pvt. John Honey, Co. H: (w)
Pvt. John M. Jackson, Co. K: (w)
Pvt. R. T. Johnston, Co. F: (k)
Cpl. W. F. Knox, Co. B: (w)
Pvt. Reese B. Latham, Co. K: (mw);
    died Dec. 26, 1861
Pvt. Lawrence Lenhardt, Co. K: (k)
Pvt. Robert Lipsey, Co. F: (w)
Pvt. John Lucas, Co. E: (w)
Pvt. A. P. Lyle, Co. C: (w)
Sgt. William McAiley, Co. F: (w)
Pvt. William S. McDill, Co. G: (k)
Pvt. William McFadden, Co. A: (mw);
    died Jan. 13, 1862
Pvt. James McKeown, Co. F: (k)
Capt. Edward J. Means, Co. C: (w)
Pvt. B.W. Means, Co. C: (w)
Pvt. Andrew Minter, Co. H: (w)
Pvt. Zebulon Mobley, Co. C: (w)
1st Lt. Frederick Moore, Co. H: (k)
Sgt. Robert Morris, Co. C: (k)
Pvt. Thomas J. Parks, Co. H: (w); (c)
Pvt. Ira Patterson, Co. H: (w)
Pvt. Henry P. Price, Co. H: (k)
Cpl. W. T. Robinson, Co. H: (k)
Pvt. James Rowan, Co. K: (k)
Pvt. K. H. Sadler, Co. H: (w)
Sgt. J. A. Sanders, Co. E: (w)
Pvt. James P. Scates, Co. I: (w)
Pvt. S. M. Shuler, Co. G: (w)
Pvt. Charles Sibley, Co. B: (w)
Pvt. Jeremiah W. Smith, Co. F: (k)
Pvt. William W. Whiteside, Co. H: (w)
Pvt. Robert S. Wylie, Co. A: (w)
Maj. Thomas W. Woodward: (w)

10th Alabama

Pvt. Henry Alexander, Co. C: (mw); died Jan. 2, 1862

Pvt. James O. Bloxton, Co. E: (k)

Pvt. Thornwell Brownlee, Co. H: (k)

Pvt. Stephen J. Bryant, Co. H: (k)

Pvt. William N. Caldwell, Co. H: (w)

Pvt. John Calahan, Co. K: (k)

Pvt. Henry H. Cates, Co. C: (w)

Pvt. Ira Chaney, Co. I: (mw); (c); died Dec. 26, 1861

Pvt. Alexander Cheatwood, Co. H: (w)

Pvt. M. T. Christian, Co. E: (w)

Pvt. Obal Christopher, Co. I: (w)

Pvt. James B. Churchill, Co. B: (w)

Pvt. B. F. Coker, Co. H: (w)

Sgt. Sidney Coleman, Co. F: (k)

Pvt. Thomas Cook, Co. H: (w)

Pvt. Berryman H. Corley, Co. F: (mw); died c. Jan. 27, 1862

Pvt. Andrew J. Cost, Co. C: (w)

Pvt. George W. Cowley, Co. B: (w)

Pvt. James Crook, Co. D: (w)

Pvt. George S. Dannelly, Co. A: (mw); died Dec. 21, 1861.

Pvt. Columbus De Shazo, Co. C: (w)

Pvt. Robert G. Dunlap, Co. F: (k)

Pvt. Thomas Ferguson, Co. I: (mw); died Jan. 20, 1862

Col. John Forney: (w)

Capt. William Forney, Co. G: (w)

Pvt. John G. Francis, Co. G: (w)

Pvt. Benjamin Fry, Co. I: (w)

Pvt. Sanford M. Fulton, Co. C: (k)

Pvt. James W. Glover, Co. E: (w)

Pvt. William Goodwin, Co. E: (w)

Pvt. James Graves, Co. E: (k)

Pvt. Merry J. Hall, Co. I: (w)

2nd Lt. Lemuel Hamlin, Co. I: (w)

Pvt. Alexander Hanna, Co. H: (k)

Pvt. Henry Harless, Co. C: (w)

Pvt. Jesse Harris, Co. G: (w)

Pvt. Philip A. Harris, Co. A: (w)

Pvt. Herman Herzberg, Co. I: (w)

Pvt. Bannister Jennings, Co. D: (w)

Cpl. George L. Johnson, Co. I: (w)

Pvt. William A. Jones, Co. I: (w)

Pvt. John W. Lindsey, Co. K: (w)

Pvt. Napoleon B. Lyon, Co. H: (k)

Pvt. George S. Lytton, Co. C: (k)

Pvt. John P. Manning, Co. H: (mw); died Feb. 8, 1862

Lt. Col. James B. Martin: (k)

Pvt. John F. Martin, Co. F: (k)

Pvt. Allious McAdory, Co. B: (k)

Pvt. Lafayette McClendon, Co. C: (w)

Pvt. William W. Mohon, Co. G: (w)

Pvt. William Morris, Co. H: (c)

Pvt. Bushrod Moss, Co. K: (mw); died Dec. 28, 1861

Pvt. Robert Moss, Co. K: (c)

Pvt. Calvin Owens, Co. D: (w)

Pvt. James Partain, Co. B: (w)

Pvt. Lewis Reynolds, Co. D: (w)

Pvt. Benjamin F. Sides, Co. E: (w)

Pvt. Jesse Sims, Co. D: (w)

Pvt. R. M. Smith, Co. E: (w)

Pvt. James Spence, Co. E: (w)

Pvt. William H. Sprinkles, Co. H: (mw); died Jan. 16, 1862

Pvt. James S. Walden, Co. H: (k)

Cpl. Charles A. Webb, Co. I: (k)

Pvt. Samuel Whaling, Co. H: (w)

Pvt. Ransom A. Wiley, Co. G: (w)

Pvt. James Williamson, Co. F: (c)

Pvt. George T. Wilson, Co. C: (w)

11th Virginia Infantry

Pvt. Lucian J. Black, Co. K: (w)

Pvt. Robert Burton, Co. F: (w)

Pvt. William Campbell, Co. K: (k)

Pvt. Peter Coyle, Co. K: (w)

Pvt. Judson J. Embrey, Co. I: (w)

Pvt. John Flowers, Co. H: (w)

Pvt. Samuel T. Franklin, Co. C: (w)

Pvt. Melvin Gibbs, Co. D: (k)

Pvt. Henry Goulden, Co. H: (k)

Pvt. John Henry, Co. A: (k)

Pvt. William H. Hobson, Co. C: (mw); died Dec. 21, 1861

2nd Lt. Thomas B. Horton, Co. B: (w)

Capt. James H. Jameson, Co. I: (w)

Pvt. James D. Johnson, Co. K: (w)

Cpl. James McDowell, Co. D: (w)

Pvt. James N. Painter, Co. K: (k)

Pvt. Joseph E. Rice, Co. C: (w)

Pvt. George W. Rogers, Co. H: (w)

Pvt. Walker Thurmond, Co. B: (w)

Pvt. John B. Wood, Co. C: (w)

Capt. Albert A. Yeatman, Co. K: (w)

Sumter Flying Artillery

Pvt. Thomas J. Calhoun: (w)

Pvt. John H. Capps: (mw); died Dec. 21, 1861

Pvt. James M. Conner: (w)

Pvt. Jasper N. English: (w)

Sgt. William H. Fletcher: (w)

Pvt. Simeon D. Frazier: (w)

Pvt. Lewis P. Haines: (w)

Pvt. William P. Long: (k)

Pvt. John L. McGarrah: (k)

Pvt. Thomas Mills: (mw); died Dec. 27, 1861

Pvt. John Murphy: (w)

Pvt. James S. Proctor: (mw); died Dec. 21, 1861

Pvt. William F. Richards: (w)

1st Lt. George F. Smith: (w)

Pvt. Griffin L. Smith: (w)

Pvt. Charles H. Varner, (w)

Pvt. Washington F. Williams: (k)

Bibliography

Primary Sources

Unpublished

Manuscripts

Alabama Department of Archives & History, Montgomery, AL

    Confederate Regimental History Files

        10th Alabama Infantry

            "Confederate Deaths Near Bristow Station, Virginia, Prince William County, 10th Alabama"

            McClelen, Bailey George. Diary

            Whatley, George C. Letters

Allegheny College, Meadville, PA

    Chadwick, James D. Letters (10th Pennsylvania Reserves)

American Civil War Museum, Richmond, VA

    Photo Record of Oakley Farm

Author's Collection

    Conn, William T. Letter (9th Georgia Infantry)

    King, Francis J. Letter (1st Pennsylvania Rifles)

    Morrison, A.P. Letter (9th Pennsylvania Reserve Infantry)

    Prall, Lewis. Letter (1st Pennsylvania Reserve Infantry)

Brigham Young University, Provo, UT

    Kane Family Papers

Kane, Elizabeth W. Diary
Kane, Thomas L. Papers (1st Pennsylvania Rifles)
College of William & Mary, Williamsburg, VA
Austin-Twyman Papers
Benson, A. H. Letter (11th Virginia)
Read, Rufus. Diary (2nd Pennsylvania Reserves)
Fairfax County Courthouse Historical Records Room, Fairfax, VA
1860 Fairfax County Maps
Henry Clay St. Clair Coroner's Inquest
Fredericksburg & Spotsylvania National Military Park, Fredericksburg, VA
Snyder, Thompson. "Recollections of Four Years with the Union Cavalry," Bound Vol. 42 (1st Pennsylvania Reserve Cavalry)
Taylor, J. R. "Report of J. R. Taylor, 1st Penn. Volunteer Cavalry," Bound Vol. 42.
Fairfax County Regional Library, Virginia Room, Fairfax, VA
Carper, Kate. Diary
Huntington Library, San Marino, CA
Stuart, J. E. B. Papers
Hill, D. H. Letter
Jones Memorial Library Manuscript Collection, Lynchburg, VA
Beardsworth, Susan R. "Three Lynchburg Generals of 1861-1865."
Wiley, Aubrey. "Garland's Men: Lynchburg's Home Guard." (11th Virginia Infantry)
Library of Congress, Washington, D.C.
Bourne, William O. Papers
Moore, Wallace M. Letter (1st Pennsylvania Rifles)
Buchanan, James and Harriet Lane Johnston. Papers
Lincoln, Abraham. Papers
McClellan, George B. Papers
Sherman, William T. Papers
Library of Virginia, Richmond, VA
Owen, Henry T. Papers and Letters
Leslie, William. Letter (9th Pennsylvania Reserves)
Minnesota Historical Society, Saint Paul, MN
Dean, William Blake. Papers
Dean, George. "The Battle of Dranesville, VA." (9th Pennsylvania Reserves)
National Archives of the United States of America
Washington, D.C., Location
Compiled Service Records
Davis, Jefferson. Papers
Regimental Letter and Order Book, 6th Pennsylvania Reserves

Regimental Letter and Order Book, Vol. 2, 12th Pennsylvania Reserves

1st Pennsylvania Light Artillery, Morning Reports, Companies A to H and Recruits, Vol. 6

Letters Received by the Office of the Adjutant General, Main Series, 1861-1870.

Southern Claims Files

Biggs, Henry.

Cockrell, Joseph.

Coleman, Ann.

Crocker, Lott W.

Crippen, Minor.

Voorhees, Nelson.

Widow's Pension Applications

Darling, Amanda.

Galbraith, Elizabeth.

Galway, Julia.

College Park, MD Location

Record Group 59

Proceedings of the Commission Relating to State Prisoners, 1862. Vol. 1.

"Cases Examined by Commission Relating to State Prisoners"

Carper, Philip Case File

Coleman, Charles W. Case File

Coleman, George Case File

Day, John T. Case File

Day, William B. Case File

Dranesville Murder Cases

Farr, John B. Case File

Gunnell, R.H. Case File

Untitled Packet

New York State Library, Albany, NY

O'Keeffe Family Papers

O'Keeffe, Arthur. Letters (34th New York)

O'Brien, J. Michael. Letter (34th New York Infantry)

North Carolina State Archives, Raleigh, NC

Gordon, James B. Papers (1st North Carolina Cavalry)

Stanford University, Stanford, CA

Ord, Edward Otho Cresap. Papers

South Carolina Historical Society, Charleston, SC

Blackwell, Thomas. Letters (6th South Carolina Infantry)

United States of America Censuses

Georgia. Sumter County. 1860 Census.

Georgia. Sumter County. 1860 Slave Schedule Census.

Missouri. Cooper. 1850 Census.

New York. Herkimer County. 1860 Census.

Pennsylvania. Dauphin County. 1880 Census.

South Carolina. Chester County. 1860 Census.

South Carolina. Chester County. 1860 Slave Schedule Census.

South Carolina. Fairfield County. 1860 Census.

South Carolina. Richland County. 1860 Census

South Carolina. Richland County. 1860 Slave Schedule Census.

Virginia. Fairfax County. 1860 Census.

Virginia. Fairfax County. 1870 Census.

Washington, D.C. 1860 Census.

United States Army Heritage and Education Center, Carlisle, PA

Civil War Times Illustrated Collection

Henderson, Vernon. Diary (6th Pennsylvania Reserves)

McQuaide, John. Letter (9th Pennsylvania Reserves)

Harrisburg Civil War Round Table Collection

Ashenfelter, Benjamin. Diary and Letters (6th Pennsylvania Reserves)

Lewis Leigh Collection

Helmer, William H. Letter (34th New York Infantry)

University of South Carolina, Columbia, SC

Brice, R. Wade. Letter (6th South Carolina Infantry)

Coleman, William. Letters (6th South Carolina Infantry)

"History of the Means Family," Vol. 3.

"Letters and Genealogy of the Means-English Families, 1828-1950."

English, Franklin. Letters (6th South Carolina Infantry)

University of Virginia, Charlottesville, VA

King, William. Letters (11th Virginia Infantry)

Valdosta State University Archives and Special Collections, Valdosta, GA

McConnell, Andrew. Diary. (6th South Carolina)

Virginia Museum of History & Culture, Richmond, VA

Brice, Walter. Letters

Brice, John Moore. Letter (6th South Carolina Infantry)

Franklin, Philip. Letter (11th Virginia Infantry)

Morris, William Sylvanus. Papers

Gaillard, E.S. Dispatches, Section 5

Old, James. (11th Virginia Infantry)

Spencer, Thomas. Letter (18th Virginia Infantry)

Stuart, J. E. B. Papers

Stuart, William Alexander. Papers

Virginia Polytechnic Institute and State University, Blacksburg, VA

Burgess, William. Letter (6th Pennsylvania Reserves)

Western Carolina University, Cullowhee, NC

Gettys, D. H. Letter (1st North Carolina Cavalry)

Wisconsin Historical Society, Madison, WI

Edwin B. Quiner "Scrapbooks: Correspondence of the Wisconsin Volunteers, 1861-1865, Volume 1." (5th Wisconsin Infantry)

Published

Books

Alexander, Edward P. *Fighting for the Confederacy: The Personal Recollections of General Edward Porter Alexander*. Edited by Gary Gallagher. Chapel Hill: University of North Carolina Press, 1989.

Bard, John. *John Bard's History of the Old Bucktails*. West Conshohocken, PA: Infinity Publishing, 2013.

Bates, Samuel P. *History of Pennsylvania Volunteers, 1861-65*: Vol. 1. Harrisburg, PA: B. Singerly, State Printer, 1869.

______. *Martial Deeds of Pennsylvania*. Philadelphia: T. H. Davis & Co., 1876.

Bayard, Samuel. *The Life of George Dashiell Bayard*. New York: G. P. Putnam's Sons, 1874.

Blackford, W. W. *War Years with Jeb Stuart*. 1945. Reprint Baton Rouge: Louisiana State University Press, 1993.

Boyd's Washington and Georgetown Directory: Containing a Business Directory of Washington, Georgetown and Alexandria. Washington, D.C.: Taylor and Murray, 1860.

Brandt, Dennis, ed. *Pathway to Hell: A Tragedy of the American Civil War*. Lincoln: University of Nebraska Press, 2010. (1st Pennsylvania Rifles)

Bratton, John. *General John Bratton, Sumter to Appomattox: In Letters to his Wife*. Edited by J. Luke Austin. Sewanee, TN: Proctor's Hall Press, 2003. (6th South Carolina Infantry)

______. *Letters of John Bratton to his Wife*. Edited by Elizabeth Porcher Bratton. Privately published, 1942. (6th South Carolina Infantry)

Brewer, W. *Alabama: Her History, Resources, War Record, and Public Men, From 1540 to 1872*. Montgomery, AL: Barrett & Brown, 1872.

Brewer, W. W. *Corporal Brewer: A Bucktail Survivor*, Vol. 1. Edited by William Means. Edmonton, ALB: Commonwealth Publications, 1997. (1st Pennsylvania Rifles)

Callaway, Felix. *The Bloody Links*. No Publisher: Shreveport, LA, 1907. (Sumter Flying Artillery)

Carman, Ezra A. *The Maryland Campaign of September 1862*, Vol. 1: South Mountain. Edited by Thomas G. Clemens. El Dorado Hills, CA: Savas Beatie, 2010.

Castleman, Virginia Carter. *Reminiscences of an Oldest Inhabitant*. Herndon VA: Herndon Historical Society, 1976.

Chapin, Louis N. *A Brief History of the Thirty-Fourth Regiment N. Y. S. V.* Privately Published, 1903.

Chesnut, Mary B. *A Diary from Dixie.* Edited by Isabella D. Martin and Myrta Lockett Avary. New York: D. Appleton and Company, 1906.

________. *Mary Chesnut's Civil War.* Edited by C. Vann Woodward. New Haven: Yale University Press, 1981.

Cooke, John E. *Wearing of the Gray: Being Personal Portraits, Scenes and Adventures of the War.* New York: E. B. Treat & Co., 1867.

Crawford, Samuel W. *The Genesis of War: The Story of Sumter, 1860-1861.* New York: C. L. Webster & Company, 1887.

Cullum, George W. *Biographical Register of the Officers and Graduates of the U.S. Military Academy at West Point,* Vols. 1 & 2. New York: D. Van Nostrand, 1868.

Davis, Rodney O., and Douglas L. Wilson, eds. *Herndon's Informants: Letters, Interviews, and Statements about Abraham Lincoln.* Urbana: University of Illinois Press, 1998.

Dix, Morgan. *Memoirs of John Adams Dix:* Vol. 2. New York: Harper & Brothers, 1883.

Dixon, William Woodward. *The Mobleys and their Descendants.* Privately Published, 1915.

Doubleday, Abner. *Reminiscences of Forts Sumter and Moultrie in 1860-'61.* New York: Harper & Brothers, Publishers, 1876.

Duff, Levi B. *To Petersburg with the Army of the Potomac: The Civil War Letters of Levi Bird Duff, 105th Pennsylvania Volunteers.* Edited by Jonathan E. Helmreich. Jefferson, NC: McFarland & Company, Inc., 2009. (9th Pennsylvania Reserves)

Evans, Clement, ed. *Confederate Military History,* Vol. 9. Atlanta: Confederate Publishing Company, 1899.

Folsom, James M. *Heroes and Martyrs of Georgia: Georgia's Record in the Revolution of 1861.* Macon: Burke, Boykin & Company, 1864.

Garesché, Louis. *Biography of Lieut. Col. Julius P. Garesché, Assistant Adjutant-General, U. S. Army.* Philadelphia: J. B. Lippincott, 1887.

Goree, Thomas. *Longstreet's Aide: The Civil War Letters of Major Thomas Goree.* Edited by Thomas W. Cutrer. Charlottesville: University Press of Virginia, 1995.

Greeley, Horace. *The American Conflict: A History of the Great Rebellion,* Vol. I. Hartford: O. D. Case & Company, 1864.

Grow, Matthew J. and Ronald W. Walker, eds. *The Prophet and the Reformer: The Letters of Brigham Young and Thomas L. Kane.* Oxford: Oxford University Press, 2015.

Hardin, M. D. *History of the Twelfth Regiment Pennsylvania Reserve Corps.* New York: Privately Published, 1890.

Hewett, Janet B., ed. *Supplement to the Official Records of the Union and Confederate Armies,* 100 vols. Wilmington: Broadfoot Publishing Company, 1998.

Hill, A. F. *Our Boys: The Personal Experience of a Soldier in the Army of the Potomac.* Philadelphia: John E. Potter, 1865. (8th Pennsylvania Reserves)

Hobbs, Thomas Hubbard. *The Journals of Thomas Hubbard Hobbs.* Edited by Faye Acton Axford. Tuscaloosa: University of Alabama Press, 1976.

Holland, William P. *Recollections of a Private.* Rocky Mount, VA: Franklin County Historical Society, 2009. (11th Virginia Infantry)

Hopkins, Margaret Lail. *Dranesville Methodism.* Stephens City, VA: Commercial Press, 1984.

Howard, O. O. *Autobiography of Oliver Otis Howard,* Vol. 1. New York: Baker & Taylor Company, 1907.

Johnston, Joseph E. *A Memoir of the Life and Public Service of Joseph E. Johnston.* Edited by Bradley T. Johnson. Baltimore: R. H. Woodward & Company, 1891.

Jomini, Antoine Henri. *Summary of the Art of War.* Translated by G. H. Mendell and W.P. Craighill. Philadelphia: J. B. Lippincott & Co., 1862.

Jones, John B. *A Rebel War Clerk's Diary at the Confederate States Capital,* Vol. 1. Philadelphia: J. B. Lippincott & Co., 1866.

Kean, Robert G. H. *Inside the Confederate Government: The Diary of Robert Garlick Hill Kean.* Edited by Edward Younger. Oxford: Oxford University Press, 1957.

Kessler, Dorothy Sue Simmons, ed. *The Fincastle Rifles.* Fincastle, VA: Historic Fincastle, Inc., 1979.

Lee, J. Edward and Ron Chepesiuk, eds. *South Carolina in the Civil War: The Confederate Experience in Letters and Diaries.* Jefferson, NC: McFarland & Company, Inc., 2000.

Leeson, M. A. *History of the Counties of McKean, Elk, and Forest, Pennsylvania, with Biographical Selections Including Their Early Settlement and Development.* Chicago: J. H. Beers & Co., 1890.

Lincoln, Abraham. *Collected Works of Abraham Lincoln*: Vol. 4. Edited by Roy P. Basler, Marion Dolores Pratt, and Lloyd A. Dunlap. New Brunswick, NJ: Rutgers University Press, 1953.

Longstreet, James. *From Manassas to Appomattox: Memoirs of the Civil War in America.* Philadelphia: J. B. Lippincott, 1896.

Lucas, Thomas. *I Seat Myself to Write You a Few Lines: Civil War and Homestead Letters from Thomas Lucas and Family.* Edited by Dona B. Sauerburger and Thomas L. Bayard. Privately Published, 2002. (1st Pennsylvania Reserve Cavalry)

Lyman, Theodore. *Meade's Army: The Private Notebooks of Lt. Col. Theodore Lyman.* Edited by David W. Lowe. Kent, OH: The Kent State University Press, 2007.

Lyon, Henry. *Desolating This Fair Country: The Civil War Diary and Letters of Lt. Henry C. Lyon, 34th New York.* Edited by Emily N. Radigan. Jefferson, NC: McFarland & Co., 1999.

Marshal, John A. *American Bastille: A History of the Illegal Arrests and Imprisonment of American Citizens During the Late Civil War.* Philadelphia: Thomas W. Hartley & Co., 1881 Edition.

McClelen, Bailey George. *I Saw the Elephant: The Civil War Experiences of Bailey George McClelen Company D, 10th Alabama Infantry Regiment.* Edited by Norman E. Rourke. Shippensburg, PA: White Pane Publishing, 1994.

McClellan, George B. *The Civil War Papers of George B. McClellan: Selected Correspondence, 1860-1865.* Edited by Stephen W. Sears. New York: Ticknor & Fields, 1989.

McClellan, Henry B. *I Rode with Jeb Stuart: The Life and Campaigns of Major General J. E. B. Stuart.* 1885. Reprint, Bloomington: University of Indiana Press, 1994.

McClellan, William C. *Welcome the Hour of Conflict: William Cowan McClellan and the 9th Alabama.* Edited by John C. Carter. Tuscaloosa: University of Alabama Press, 2007.

McClendon, W. A. *Recollections of War Times By An Old Veteran While Under Stonewall Jackson and Lieutenant General James Longstreet.* Tuscaloosa: The University of Alabama Press, 2010. (15th Alabama Infantry)

McGuire. Judith W. *Diary of a Southern Refugee During the War.* New York: E. J. Hale & Son, 1868.

Meade, George G. *The Life and Letters of George Gordon Meade*: Vol. 1. Edited by George G. Meade. New York: Charles Scribner's Sons, 1913.

Miller, Maria. *The Old Capitol and Its Inmates.* New York: E. J. Hale & Son, 1867.

Minnigh, H. N. *History of Company K., 1st (Inft,) Penn'a Reserves.* Duncansville, PA: Home Print Publisher, 1891.

Moore, Frank, ed. *Rebellion Record: A Diary of American Events.* Vol. 3. New York: G. P. Putnam, 1864.

Mosby, John S. *The Memoirs of John S. Mosby.* Edited by Charles W. Russell. Boston: Little, Brown, and Company, 1917.

Nicholson, John P., ed. *Pennsylvania at Gettysburg: Ceremonies at the Dedication of the Monuments Erected by the Commonwealth of Pennsylvania to Mark the Positions of the Pennsylvania Commands Engaged in the Battle.* Harrisburg, PA: Wm Stanley Ray, 1904.

No Author, *Iron Age*, Vol. 62. New York: David Williams Company, 1898.

Parker, Robert W. *Lee's Last Casualty: The Life and Letters of Sgt. Robert W. Parker, Second Virginia Cavalry.* Edited by Catherine M. Wright. Knoxville: The University of Tennessee Press, 2008.

Pate, James P., ed. *When This Evil War Is Over: The Correspondence of the Francis Family, 1860-1865.* Tuscaloosa: The University of Alabama Press, 2006. (10th Alabama)

Patterson, Robert. *A Narrative of the Campaign in the Valley of the Shenandoah in 1861.* Philadelphia: Sherman & Co., 1865.

Peck, Rufus H. *Reminiscences of a Confederate Soldier of Co. C, 2nd Va. Cavalry.* Fincastle, PA: Privately Published, 1913.

Pinkerton, Allan. *The Spy of the Rebellion.* New York: G. W. Carleton & Co., 1883.

Rauch, William H., and O. R. Howard Thomson. *History of the "Bucktails."* Philadelphia: Electric Printing Company, 1906.

Reid, J. W. *History of the Fourth Regiment of South Carolina Volunteers.* Greenville, SC: Shannon & Co., 1892.

Rhett, Robert B. *A Fire-Eater Remembers: The Confederate Memoir of Robert Barnwell Rhett.* Edited by William C. Davis. Columbia: University of South Carolina Press, 2000.

Ruffin, Edmund. *The Diary of Edmund Ruffin*: Vol. 1. Edited by William Kauffman Scarborough. Baton Rouge: Louisiana State University Press, 1972.

Russell, William Howard. *My Diary North and South*, Vol. 1. Boston: T.O.H.P. Burnham, 1863.

Smith, Ernest A. *Allegheny—A Century of Education.* Meadville, PA: The Allegheny College History Company, 1916. (10th Pennsylvania Reserves)

Sprouse, Edith A., ed. *Fairfax County in 1860: A Collective Biography*, 7 vols. Privately Published, 1996.

Stuart, J. E. B. *Letters of General J. E. B. Stuart to his Wife, 1861.* Edited by Bingham Duncan. Atlanta: Emory University Press, 1943.

______. *The Letters of Major General James E. B. Stuart.* Edited by Adele H. Mitchell. Fairfax, VA: Stuart-Mosby Historical Society, 1990.

Styple, William B, ed. *Generals in Bronze: Interviewing the Commanders of the Civil War.* Kearny, NJ: Belle Grove Publishing Company, 2005.

Sypher, J. R. *History of the Pennsylvania Reserve Corps.* Lancaster, PA: Elias Barr & Co., 1865.

Todd, William. *The Seventy-Ninth Highlanders New York Volunteers in the War of Rebellion.* Albany: Press of Brandow, Barton & Co., 1886.

Townsend, George Alfred. *Campaigns of a Non-Combatant.* New York: Blelock & Company, 1866.

Tribute of Respect to the Memory of Maj.-Gen. Geo. A. McCall, Organizer and Original Commander of the Pennsylvania Reserve Volunteer Corps. Philadelphia: King & Baird, 1868.

Trout, Robert, ed. *With Pen and Saber: The Letters and Diaries of J. E. B. Stuart's Staff Officers.* Mechanicsburg, PA: Stackpole Books, 1995.

Veil, Charles H. *The Memoirs of Charles Henry Veil: A Soldier's Recollections of the Civil War and the Arizona Territory.* Edited by Herman J. Viola. Thorndike, ME: Thorndike Press, 1994. (9th Pennsylvania Reserves)

Wise, George. *Campaigns and Battles of the Army of Northern Virginia.* New York: The Neale Publishing Company, 1916. (17th Virginia Infantry)

Woodward, E. M. *Our Campaigns; Or, The Marches, Bivouacs, Battles, Incidents of Camp Life and History of Our Regiment During Its Three Years Term of Service.* Philadelphia: John E. Potter, 1865. (2nd Pennsylvania Reserves)

Woodward, Thomas W. *Address of Maj. Thomas W. Woodward: From Fort Sumter to Dranesville.* Columbia, SC: Presbyterian Publishing House, 1883. (6th South Carolina Infantry)

Government Documents

Acts of the General Assembly of Virginia Passed at the Session Commencing 2nd December 1839, and Ending 19th March 1840. Richmond: Samuel Shepherd, 1840.

Documents of the Assembly of the State of New York, Vol. 10. Albany, NY: Printing House of C. Van Benthuysen & Sons, 1867.

Executive Documents Printed by Order of the House of Representatives During the Second Session of the Thirty-Seventh Congress, Vol. 5. Washington, D.C.: Government Printing Office, 1862.

Index of General Orders and Circulars, Adjutant General's Office, 1883. Washington, D.C.: Government Printing Office, 1884.

Journal of the Convention of the People of South Carolina, Held in 1860, 1861 and 1862, Together With the Ordinances, Reports, Resolutions, etc. Pub. by Order of the Convention. Columbia, SC: R. W. Gibbs, 1862.

Journal of the Executive Proceedings of the Senate of the United States of America, Vol. 12. Washington, D.C.: Government Printing Office, 1887.

List of Post Offices in the United States, with the Names of the Post-Masters. Washington, D.C.: Way & Gideon, 1828.

Message of the Governor of Virginia and Accompanying Documents. Richmond: William F. Ritchie, 1861.

Message of the Governor of Virginia and Accompanying Documents. Richmond: William F. Ritchie, 1862.

Official Register of the Officers and Cadets of the U.S. Military Academy, 1818-1872. Washington, D.C.: U.S. Government Printing Press.

Report of the Joint Committee on the Conduct of the War, Vol. 1, Part 2: *Bull Run—Ball's Bluff*. Washington, D.C.: Government Printing Office, 1863.

The Medical and Surgical History of the War of the Rebellion, 1861-1865, 2 vols. Washington, D.C.: Government Printing Office, 1870-1883.

The Sixth, Seventh, and Eighth Annual Reports of the Board of Public Works to the General Assembly of Virginia: Vol. 3. Richmond: Shepherd & Pollard, 1824.

United States Army. *Revised United States Army Regulations of 1861*. Washington, D.C.: Government Printing Office, 1863.

United States War Department. *The War Of the Rebellion: A Compilation of the Official Records of the Union and Confederate Armies,* 128 vols. Washington, D.C.: U.S. Government Printing Press, 1894.

Periodicals and Journals

Barringer, Rufus. "First Cavalry." *Histories of the Several Regiments and Battalions from North Carolina, In the Great War 1861-'65* 1. Edited by Walter Clark. Raleigh: E. M. Uzzell, 1901.

Brackett Anna C. "Charleston, South Carolina (1861)." *Harper's New Monthly Magazine* 88, *December, 1893 to May 1894*. New York: Harper & Brothers, Publishers, 1894.

Clinkinbeard, William E. Untitled Article. *Confederate Veteran* 17, no. 1 (January 1909).

Coleman, James. "To Survivors of the Tenth Alabama Regiment." *Confederate Veteran* 17 (1909).

Cooke, John E. "Captain William D. Farley, The Partisan." *The Confederate Reader: How the South Saw the War.* Edited by Richard B. Harwell. New York: Dover Publications, Inc, 1989.

Coxe, John. "Last Struggles and Successes of Lee." *Confederate Veteran* 22, no. 8 (August 1914).

Daugette, Annie Forney. "The Life of Major General John H. Forney." *The Alabama Historical Quarterly* 9, no. 3 (Fall 1947).

Gunderson, Robert Gray. "Letters from the Washington Peace Conference of 1861." *The Journal of Southern History* 17, no. 3 (August 1951).

Hobson, Charles F. et al., "Colonel of the Bucktails: Civil War Letters of Charles Frederick Taylor." *The Pennsylvania Magazine of History and Biography* 97, no. 3 (July 1973).

Holsinger, Frank. "How Does One Feel Under Fire?" *War Talks in Kansas: A Series of Papers Read Before the Kansas Commandery of the Military Order of the Loyal Legion of the United States.* Kansas City: Franklin Hudson Publishing Company, 1906.

McClellan, H. B. "Gen'l J. E. B. Stuart." *Southern Historical Papers* 8. Edited by R. A. Brock. Richmond: Southern Historical Society, 1880.

Murdoch, Alexander. "The Pittsburgh Rifles and the Battle of Dranesville." *The Western Pennsylvania Historical Magazine* 53, no. 3 (July 1970). (9th Pennsylvania Reserves)

Peck, W. F. G. "Four Years Under Fire in Charleston." *Harper's New Monthly Magazine* 31, June to November 1865. New York: Harper & Brothers, Publishers, 1894.

Rogan, W. R. "Capt. Jo Desha." *Confederate Veteran* 10, no. 8 (1902)

Thomas, Emory M, editor. "'The Greatest Service I Rendered the State': J. E. B. Stuart's Account of the Capture of John Brown." *The Virginia Magazine of History and Biography* 94, no. 3, *Virginians at War, 1607-1865* (July 1986).

Torrance, Ell. "The Pennsylvania Reserves." *Glimpses of the Nation's Struggle: Papers Read Before the Minnesota Commandery of the Military Order of the Loyal Legion of the United States, 1889-1892.* New York: D. D. Merrill Company, 1893.

Wallace, William. "Operations of Second South Carolina Regiment in Campaigns of 1864 and 1865." *Southern Historical Society Papers*, Vol. 7. Edited by R. A. Brock. Richmond: Southern Historical Society, 1879.

Willoughby, Charles H. "Extracts from Journal of Charles H. Willoughby, Private Company C., Thirty-Fourth New York Volunteers." *Documents of the Assembly of the State of New York, Ninety-First Session*, Vol. 40. Albany, NY: Printing House of C. Van Benthuysen & Sons, 1868.

Newspapers

Alexandria Gazette (Alexandria, Virginia)

American Manufacturer and Iron World (Pittsburgh, Pennsylvania)

Atlanta Daily Constitution

Centre Democrat (Bellefonte, Pennsylvania)

Charleston Mercury

Daily Appeal (Memphis, Tennessee)

Daily Intelligencer (Wheeling, West Virginia)

Genius of Liberty (Leesburg, Virginia)

Harper's Weekly

Herndon Times (Herndon, Virginia)

Honesdale Democrat (Honesdale, Pennsylvania)

Jacksonville Republican (Jacksonville, Alabama)

Jamestown Journal (Jamestown, New York)

Lamoille Newsdealer (Hyde Park, Vermont)

Lebanon Evening Express (Lebanon, Pennsylvania)

Lewistown Gazette (Lewistown, Pennsylvania)

McLean Providence Journal (McLean, Virginia)

New York Herald

New York Tribune

Northumberland County Democrat (Sunbury, Pennsylvania)

Our Mountain Home (Talladega, Alabama)

Pennsylvania Daily Telegraph (Harrisburg, Pennsylvania)

Philadelphia Inquirer

Richmond Daily Dispatch

Richmond Whig

Selma Reporter (Selma, Alabama)

South Western Baptist (Marion, Alabama)

Star of the North (Bloomsburg, Pennsylvania)

The Agitator (Tioga County, Pennsylvania)

The Alleghanian (Ebensburg, Pennsylvania)

The Cecil Whig (Elkton, Maryland)

The Columbus Daily Sun (Columbus, Georgia)

The Daily Exchange (Baltimore, Maryland)

The Daily Express (Petersburg, Virginia)

The Daily Mountain Eagle (Jasper, Alabama)

The Daily Picayune (New Orleans, Louisiana)

The Daily Times (New Philadelphia, Ohio)

The Evening Star (Washington, D.C.)

The Fairfield News and Herald (Fairfield, South Carolina)

The Globe (Huntingdon, Pennsylvania)

The Intelligencer (Anderson, South Carolina)

The Middlebury Register (Middlebury, Vermont)

The National Tribune (Washington, D.C.)

The News and Herald (Winnsboro, South Carolina)

The New York Times

The Philadelphia Press

The *Pittsburg Dispatch*

The Pittsburgh Daily Gazette

The Press (Philadelphia, Pennsylvania)

The Times Dispatch (Richmond, Virginia)

Vermont Journal (Windsor, Vermont)

Warren Ledger (Warren, Pennsylvania)

Washington Evening Star (Washington, D.C.)

Washington Post

Weekly Mariettian (Marietta, Pennsylvania)

Weekly State Journal (Raleigh, North Carolina)

Wellsboro Agitator (Wellsboro, Pennsylvania)

Wisconsin State Journal (Madison, Wisconsin)

Yorkville Enquirer (York, South Carolina)

Secondary Sources

Books

Allardice, Bruce S. and Lawrence Lee Hewitt. *Kentuckians in Gray: Confederate Generals and Field Officers of the Bluegrass State.* Lexington: The University Press of Kentucky, 2015.

Bagley, Will and David L. Bigler. *The Mormon Rebellion: America's First Civil War, 1857–1858.* Norman: University of Oklahoma Press, 2012.

Baker, Norman L. *Braddock's Road: Mapping the British Expedition from Alexandria to the Monongahela.* Charleston, SC: The History Press, 2013.

Ballard, Ted. *Battle of Ball's Bluff: Staff Ride Guide.* Washington, D.C.: Center of Military History, 2001.

Beatie, Russel H. *Army of the Potomac*, Vol. II: *McClellan Takes Command, September 1861-February 1862.* Cambridge, MA: Da Capo Press, 2004.

Benedict, George C. *Vermont in the Civil War: A History*, 2 Vols. Burlington, VT: The Free Press Association, 1888.

Bigelow, John. *The Campaign of Chancellorsville: A Strategic and Tactical Study.* New Haven: Yale University Press, 1910.

Bridges, Hal. *Lee's Maverick General: Daniel Harvey Hill.* Lincoln: University of Nebraska Press, 1961.

Burlingame, Michael. *Abraham Lincoln: A Life*, Vol. 2. Baltimore: The Johns Hopkins University Press, 2008.

Coddington, Edwin B. *The Gettysburg Campaign: A Study in Command* 1968. Reprint, New York: Simon & Schuster, 1979.

Cole, Elisabeth Alice Gibbens. *An Account of Our Day Family of Calvert County, Maryland.* Lettsworth, MD: Privately Published, 1982.

Conley, Brian A. *Fractured Land: Fairfax County's Role in the Vote for Secession, May 23, 1861.* Fairfax Court House: Fairfax County Public Library, 2001.

Connery, William S. *Civil War Northern Virginia 1861.* Charleston, SC: The History Press, 2011.

Coppee, Henry. *Grant and His Campaigns: A Military Biography.* New York: Charles B. Richardson, 1866.

Coski, John M. *The Confederate Battle Flag: America's Most Embattled Emblem.* Cambridge: Harvard University Press, 2005.

Cresap, Bernard. *Appomattox Commander: The Story of General E. O. C. Ord.* London: The Tantivy Press, 1981.

David, Saul. *Prince of Pleasure: The Prince of Wales and the Making of the Regency.* New York: Grove Press, 1998.

Davis, Burke. *Jeb Stuart: The Last Cavalier.* New York: Rinehart, 1957.

Davis, William C. *A Government of Our Own: The Making of the Confederacy.* New York: The Free Press, 1994.

______. *Rhett: The Turbulent Life and Times of a Fire-Eater.* Columbia: University of South Carolina Press, 2001.

Detzer, Davis. *Allegiance: Fort Sumter, Charleston, And The Beginning Of The Civil War.* Orlando: Harcourt Books, 2001.

Dew, Charles. *Apostles of Disunion.* Charlottesville: University of Virginia Press, 2001.

Driver, Robert J. *1st Virginia Cavalry.* Lynchburg, VA: H. E. Howard, 1991.

Egle, William H, ed. *Andrew Gregg Curtin: His Life and Services.* Philadelphia: Avil Printing Company, 1895.

Engle, Stephen D. *Gathering to Save a Nation: Lincoln & the Union's War Governors.* Chapel Hill: University of North Carolina Press, 2016.

Ent, Uzal. *The Pennsylvania Reserves in the Civil War: A Comprehensive History.* Jefferson, NC: McFarland & Co. Inc., 2014.

Freeman, Douglas S. *R. E. Lee: A Biography*, Vol. 1. New York: Charles Scribner's Sons, 1934.

Gaff, Alan D. *On Many a Bloody Field: Four Years in the Iron Brigade.* Indianapolis: Indiana University Press, 1999.

Gernand, Bradley E. *A Virginia Village Goes to War: Falls Church During the Civil War.* Virginia Beach: Donning Co. Publishers, 2002.

Gibbs, Joseph. *Three Years in the Bloody Eleventh: The Campaigns of a Pennsylvania Reserve Regiment.* University Park: The Pennsylvania State University Press, 2002.

Glatthaar, Joseph T. *General Lee's Army: From Victory to Collapse.* New York: Free Press, 2008.

Glover, Edwin A. *Bucktailed Wildcats: A Regiment of Civil War Volunteers.* New York: Thomas Yoseloff, 1960.

Graham, David K. *Loyalty on the Line: Civil War Maryland in American Memory.* Athens: University of Georgia Press, 2018.

Greene, Jerome. *The Guns of Independence: The Siege of Yorktown, 1781.* New York: Savas Beatie, 2005.

Grimsley, Mark. *The Hard Hand of War: Union Military Policy Toward Southern Civilians, 1861-1865.* Cambridge: Cambridge University Press, 1997.

Grow, Matthew J. *"Liberty to the Downtrodden": Thomas L. Kane, Romantic Reformer.* New Haven: Yale University Press, 2009.

Gunderson, Robert G. *Old Gentlemen's Convention: The Washington Peace Conference of 1861.* Madison: University of Wisconsin Press, 1961.

Head, James W. *History and Comprehensive Description of Loudoun County, Virginia.* Washington, D.C.: Park View Press, 1908.

Hennessy, John H. *The First Battle of Manassas: An End to Innocence, July 18-21, 1861.* 2d. ed. Mechanicsburg, PA: Stackpole Books, 2015.

Herrick, Carole L. *Images of America: McLean.* Charleston, SC: Arcadia Publishing, 2011.

Holt, Michael F. *The Election of 1860: A Campaign Fraught with Consequences.* Lawrence: University Press of Kansas, 2017.

Holzer, Harold, ed. *Dear Mr. Lincoln: Letters to the President.* Carbondale: Southern Illinois University Press, 1993.

Hyman, Harold M. *Era of the Oath: Northern Loyalty Tests During the Civil War and Reconstruction.* Philadelphia: University of Pennsylvania Press, 1954.

Johnson, John L. *The University Memorial: Biographical Sketches of Alumni of the University of Virginia Who Fell in the Confederate War.* Baltimore: Turnbull Brothers, 1871.

Johnson, William P., II. *Brothers and Cousins: Confederate Soldiers & Sailors of Fairfax County, VA.* Athens, GA: Iberian Publishing Company, 1995.

Keen, Hugh C. and Horace Mewborn. *43rd Battalion Virginia Cavalry Mosby's Command.* Lynchburg, VA: H. E. Howard, 1993.

Kelsey, D. M. *Deeds of Daring by the American Soldier North and South.* Chicago: The Werner Company, 1897.

Klein, Maury. *Days of Defiance: Sumter, Secession, and the Coming of the Civil War.* New York: Knopf, 1997.

Krick, Robert K. *Civil War Weather in Virginia.* Tuscaloosa: The University of Alabama Press, 2007.

Laboda, Lawrence R. *From Selma to Appomattox: The History of the Jeff Davis Artillery.* New York: Oxford University Press, 1994.

Leslie, Shane. *George The Fourth.* London: Bouverie House, 1926.

Lockwood, Charles, and John Lockwood. *The Siege of Washington: The Untold Story of the Twelve Days that Shook the Union.* Oxford: Oxford University Press, 2011.

Longacre, Edward G. *The Early Morning of War: Bull Run, 1861.* Norman: University of Oklahoma Press, 2014.

Lopez, Mary Stachyra. *Centreville and Chantilly.* Charleston, SC: Arcadia Publishing, 2014.

Lowe, Richard. *Republicans and Reconstruction in Virginia, 1856-70.* Charlottesville: University Press of Virginia, 1991.

Malone, Dumas, ed. *Dictionary of American Biography*, Vol. 14. New York: Charles Scribner's Sons, 1934.

Martin, Jonathan. *Divided Mastery: Slave Hiring in the American South.* Cambridge: Harvard University Press, 2004.

Marvel, William. *Lincoln's Autocrat: The Life of Edwin Stanton.* Chapel Hill: The University of North Carolina Press, 2015.

McLean, James. *California Sabers: The 2nd Massachusetts Cavalry in the Civil War.* Bloomington: Indiana University Press, 2000.

McLean, Jess. N. Sr., ed. *The Official Records of the 13th Mississippi Infantry Regiment. . . As Told By Those Who Were There.* Privately Published, 2015 Edition.

McPherson, James M. *Battle Cry of Freedom: The Civil War Era.* Oxford: Oxford University Press, 2003 Edition.

Miller, William J. *The Training of an Army: Camp Curtin and the North's Civil War.* Shippensburg, PA: White Mane Publishing Co., 1990.

Morgan, James A., III. *A Little Short of Boats: The Battles of Ball's Bluff & Edwards Ferry, October 21-22, 1861.* El Dorado Hills, CA: Savas Beatie, 2011.

Mott, Hopper Striker, ed. *The New York Genealogical and Biographical Record*: Vol. 44. New York: The New York Genealogical and Biographical Society, 1913.

Munden, Kenneth W., and Henry Putney Beers, eds. *Guide to Federal Archives Relating to the Civil War.* Washington, D.C.: National Archives and Records Services, 1962.

Netherton, Ross De Witt and Nan Netherton. *The Dranesville Tavern: An Historic Landmarks Research Report*. Fairfax, VA: Fairfax Historical Landmarks Preservation Commission, 1966.

Newell, Clayton R. *The Regular Army Before the Civil War, 1845 – 1860*. Washington, D.C.: Center of Military History, 2014.

Nichols, Edward J. *Toward Gettysburg: A Biography of General John F. Reynolds*. Gaithersburg, MD: Butternut Press, 1986.

Niven, John. *John C. Calhoun and the Price of Union: A Biography*. Baton Rouge: Louisiana State University Press, 1988.

Oakes, James. *Freedom National: The Destruction of Slavery in the United States, 1861-1865*. New York: W. W. Norton & Company, 2013.

O'Harrow, Robert Jr., *The Quartermaster: Montgomery C. Meigs, Lincoln's General, Master Builder of the Union Army*. New York: Simon & Schuster, 2016.

O'Reilly, Francis A. *The Fredericksburg Campaign: Winter War on the Rappahannock*. Baton Rouge: LSU Press, 2003.

Poland, Charles Preston, Jr. *Dunbarton, Dranesville, Virginia*. Fairfax Court House: Fairfax County Office of Comprehensive Planning, 1974.

________. *The Glories of War*. Privately Published, 2006.

Rafuse, Ethan S. *McClellan's War: The Failure of Moderation in the Struggle for the Union*. Bloomington: Indiana University Press, 2005.

Reardon, Carol. *With a Sword in One Hand and Jomini in the Other: The Problem of Military Thought in the Civil War North*. Chapel Hill: UNC Press, 2012.

Rhea, Gordon C. *The Battles for Spotsylvania Court House and the Road to Yellow Tavern, May 7—12, 1864*. Baton Rouge: Louisiana State University Press, 2005.

Robertson, James I. Jr. *Stonewall Jackson: The Man, the Soldier, the Legend*. New York: Macmillan Publishing, 1997.

Roman, Alfred. *The Military Operations of General Beauregard in the War Between the States, 1861 to 1865*, Vol. 1. New York: Harper & Brothers, 1884.

Sansone, Cordelia Grantham. *Journey To Bloomfield: Lives and Letters of 19th Century Virginia Families*. Fairfax: Friends of the Virginia Room, 2012.

Sears, Stephen W. *George B. McClellan: The Young Napoleon*. Cambridge, MA: Da Capo Press, 1988.

______. *To the Gates of Richmond: The Peninsula Campaign*. Boston: Mariner Books, 1992.

Shanks, Henry T. *The Secession Movement in Virginia, 1847-1861*. Richmond: Garrett and Massie, 1934.

Smith, Timothy B. *Corinth 1862: Siege, Battle, Occupation*. Lawrence: University Press of Kansas, 2016.

Speicher, James L. *The Sumter Flying Artillery: A Civil War History of the Eleventh Battalion of Georgia Light Artillery*. Gretna, LA: Pelican Publishing Company, 2009.

Stephens, Gail. *Shadow of Shiloh: Major General Lew Wallace in the Civil War*. Indianapolis: Indiana Historical Society, 2010.

Stevens, Hazard. *The Life of Isaac Ingalls Stevens*, Vol. 2. Boston: Houghton, Mifflin and Company, 1900.

Stine, J. H. *A History of the Army of the Potomac.* Philadelphia: J. B. Rodgers Printing Co., 1892.

Taylor, Paul and Phil Shiman. *Orlando M. Poe: Civil War General and Great Lakes Engineer.* Kent, OH: The Kent State University Press, 2005.

Thomas, Emory M. *Bold Dragoon: The Life of J. E. B. Stuart.* New York: Harper & Row, 1986.

Thomason, John W. *Jeb Stuart.* Lincoln: University of Nebraska Press, 1930.

Thurston, George H. *Pittsburgh's Progress: Industries and Resources.* Pittsburgh: A. A. Anderson & Son, 1886.

Trout, Robert J. *Galloping Thunder: The Stuart Horse Artillery Battalion.* Mechanicsburg, PA: Stackpole Books, 2002.

_____. *They Followed the Plume: The Story of J. E. B. Stuart And His Staff.* Mechanicsburg, PA: Stackpole Books, 1993.

Unrau, Harlan D. *Historic Resource Study: Chesapeake & Ohio Canal.* Hagerstown, MD: United States Department of Interior, 2007.

Waller, Douglas. *Lincoln's Spies: Their Secret War to Save a Nation.* New York: Simon & Schuster, 2019.

Warner, Ezra. *Generals in Blue: Lives of the Union Commanders.* Baton Rouge: Louisiana State University Press, 1964.

_______. *Generals in Gray: Lives of the Confederate Commanders.* Baton Rouge: Louisiana State University Press, 1959.

Wert, Jeffry. *Cavalryman of the Lost Cause: A Biography of J. E. B. Stuart.* New York: Simon & Schuster, 2008.

_____. *General James Longstreet: The Confederacy's Most Controversial Soldier.* New York: Simon & Schuster, 1994.

_____. *Mosby's Rangers.* New York: Simon & Schuster, 1990.

Williams, T. Harry. *P. G. T. Beauregard: Napoleon in Gray.* Baton Rouge: Louisiana State University Press, Second Edition 1995.

Wilson, Harold S. *Confederate Industry: Manufacturers and Quartermasters in the Civil War.* Jackson: University Press of Mississippi, 2002.

Wittenberg, Eric J. and J. David Petruzzi. *Plenty of Blame to Go Around: Jeb Stuart's Controversial Ride to Gettysburg.* New York: Savas Beatie, 2006.

Zeller, Paul G. *The Second Vermont Volunteer Infantry Regiment, 1861-1865.* Jefferson, NC: McFarland & Company Inc., 2002.

Zobell, Albert L. *Sentinel in the East: A Biography of Thomas L. Kane.* Salt Lake City: Nicholas G. Morgan, 1965.

Articles, Journals, and Theses

Arrington, Leonard J. "'In Honorable Remembrance': Thomas L. Kane's Services to the Mormons." *Brigham Young University Studies* 21, no. 4 (Fall 1981).

Baumgarten, Ron. "A Splendid Little Affair: The Battle of Dranesville." *Civil War Trust* (December, 2011).

Beauchamp, Tanya Edwards and Karen Washburn. "National Register of Historical Places— Nomination Form: William Gunnell House." Tanya Edwards and Associates, 2002.

Bell, Robert Thomas. "The 11th Virginia Infantry Regiment, C.S.A." Master's Thesis. Virginia Polytechnic Institute, 1968.

Boeche, Thomas L. "Victory in Western Virginia: McClellan's First Campaign." *America's Civil War* 10, no. 6 (Jan. 1998)

Burton, Harold H., and Thomas E. Waggaman. "The Story of the Place: Where First and A Streets Formerly Met at What Is Now the Site of the Supreme Court Building." *Records of the Columbia Historical Society, Washington, D.C.* 51/52 (1951/1952).

David, Elizabeth. "National Register of Historic Places—Nomination Form: Langley Fork Historic District." Fairfax County Office of Comprehensive Planning, May 1980.

Davis, Curtis Carroll. "The 'Old Capitol' and Its Keeper: How William P. Wood Ran a Civil War Prison." *Records of the Columbia Historical Society, Washington, D.C.* 52 (1989).

East, Sherrod E. "Montgomery C. Meigs and the Quartermaster Department," *Military Affairs* 25, no. 4 (Winter 1961-1962).

Everett, Edward G. "Contraband and Rebel Sympathizers in Pennsylvania in 181." *Western Pennsylvania Magazine of History* 41, no. 1 (Spring 1958).

———. "Pennsylvania Raises an Army, 1861." *The Western Pennsylvania Historical Magazine* 39, no. 2 (Summer 1956).

Feiss, William B. "Grant's Relief Man: Edward O. C. Ord." *Grant's Lieutenants: From Chattanooga to Appomattox.* Edited by Steven E. Woodworth. Lawrence: University of Kansas Press, 2008.

Furniss, Jack. "Andrew Curtin and the Politics of Union." *The Pennsylvania Magazine of History and Biography* 141, no. 2 (April 2017).

Glatthaar, Joseph T. "Confederate Soldiers in Virginia, 1861." *Virginia at War, 1861.* Edited by William C. Davis and James I. Robertson, Jr. Lexington: University Press of Kentucky, 2005.

Hammond, William S. "The Battle of Dranesville." *Southern Historical Society Papers*, Vol. 35. Edited by R.A. Brock. Richmond: Southern Historical Society Papers, 1907.

Harrison, Noel G. "Atop an Anvil: The Civilians' War in Fairfax and Alexandria Counties, April 1861-April 1862." *The Virginia Magazine of History and Biography* 106, no. 2 (Spring 1998).

Henkle, Michael G. "The Botetourt Dragoons in War and Peace." Honors Thesis. University of Richmond, 2000.

Hofer, Janet. "A Most Foul Murder." *Great Falls Historical Society Reflections* (1984-1985).

Hon, Edgar R., "A Civil War Action at Lewinsville, Virginia, 11 September 1861." *The Historical Society of Fairfax County, Virginia Yearbook* 29 (2003-2004).

Hubbell, H. W. "The Organization and Use of Artillery in the War of the Rebellion." *Journal of the Military Service Institution of the United States*, Vol. 11. Governor's Island, NY: Military Service Institution, 1890.

Kell, Mary McCutchen and Richard Sacchi. "National Register of Historical Places—Nomination Form: Frying Pan Church." Fairfax County Park Authority, 1990.

King, Charles, "Rufus King: Soldier, Editor, and Statesman." *The Wisconsin Magazine of History* 4, no. 4 (June 1921).

Layne, J. Gregg. "Edward Otho Cresap Ord: Soldier and Surveyor." *Quarterly Publication Historical Society of Southern California* 17, no. 4 (December 1935).

Link, Kenneth A. "Courage and Betrayal: The Union Loyalists in Lewinsville." *Northern Virginia Heritage* VIII, no. 1 (February 1986).

Low, Thomas. "Letters to Laura." *Civil War Times Illustrated* (July/August 1992).

MacKinnon, William P. "'Full of Courage': Thomas L. Kane, the Utah War and BYU's Kane Collection as Lodestone." *Brigham Young University Studies* 48, no. 4 (2009).

McNeely, Gina. "Dranesville Tavern: The History of a Roadside Inn." *Virginia Cavalcade* 43, no. 2 (Autumn 1993).

Morgan, Jim. "Unintended Consequences: Ball's Bluff and the Rise of the Joint Committee on the Conduct of the War." *Turning Points of the Civil War.* Edited by Chris Mackowski and Kristopher D. White. Carbondale: Southern Illinois University Press, 2018.

Power, J. Tracy. "The Confederate as Gallant Knight: The Life and Death of William Downs Farley." *Civil War History* 37, no. 3 (September 1991).

Robertson, James I. Jr. "The Virginia State Convention of 1861." *Virginia at War, 1861.* Edited by William C. Davis and James I. Robertson, Jr. Lexington: University Press of Kentucky, 2005.

Rogers, William Warren and Jerrell H. Shofner. "Montgomery to Richmond: The Confederacy Selects a Capital." *Civil War History* 10, no. 2 (June 1964).

Sanderlin, Walter S. "A History of the Chesapeake & Ohio Canal." Ph.D. Dissertation, University of Maryland, 1945.

Scott, Joseph C. "The Infernal Balloon: Union Aeronautics During the American Civil War." *Army History* 93 (Fall 2014).

Wainwright, Nicholas B. "The Loyal Opposition in Civil War Philadelphia." *The Pennsylvania Magazine of History and Biography* 88, no. 3 (July 1964).

Walmsley, James Elliott. "The Change of Secession Sentiment in Virginia in 1861." In *The American Historical Review* 31, no. 1 (October 1925).

Weissinger, Ira Harrison Jr., "The Tenth Alabama Infantry Regiment in the Confederate States Army." Master's Thesis. Auburn University, 1961.

Whittaker, David J. "New Sources on Old Friends: The Thomas L. Kane and Elizabeth W. Kane Collection. *Journal of Mormon History* 27, no. 1 (Spring 2001).

Wooster Ralph. "Membership of the South Carolina Secession Convention." *The South Carolina Historical Magazine* 55, no. 4 (October 1954).

Online Sources

Boynton, Emerson A. Letter, August 17, 1861, Quoted on "Vermont Civil War." Accessed May 22, 2019. https://vermontcivilwar.org/get.php?input=643 (3rd Vermont Infantry).

Clarke, Lewis. "Leaves from a Slave's Journal of Life," *The Anti-Slavery Standard, 20 and 27 October 1842,* University of North Carolina, accessed January 4, 2020. https://docsouth.unc.edu/neh/clarke/support1.html#menu_links.

Hyde, Leo. Letter, September 20, 1861. Quoted on "Vermont Civil War." Accessed May 22, 2019. https://vermontcivilwar.org/get.php?input=3253 (3rd Vermont Infantry).

Moon Phases, September 16, 1861. Accessed June 1, 2019. https://www.moonpage.com/index.html?go=T&auto_dst=T&tzone=et&m=9&d=16&y=1861&hour=19&min=0&sec=1.

Reed, Carlos. Letter, August 30, 1861. Quoted on "Vermont Civil War." Accessed May 22, 2019. https://vermontcivilwar.org/get.php?input=27052 (3rd Vermont Infantry).

Roster of the 34th New York Infantry. Retrieved from the New York State Military Museum and Veterans Research Center. Accessed May 1, 2017. https://dmna.ny.gov/historic/reghist/civil/rosters/Infantry/34th_Infantry_CW_Roster.pdf.

The Papers of George Washington Digital Edition, ed. Theodore J. Crackel. Charlottesville: University of Virginia Press, Rotunda, 2008. Accessed May 7, 2017. http://financial.gwpapers.org/?q=content/colemans-ordinary-virginia.

"Map of N. Eastern Virginia and Vicinity of Washington." Library of Congress. Accessed March 1, 2017. https://www.loc.gov/resource/g3881s.cw0468000/.

"The Dead Alive, And The Lost Found", in Unknown Newspaper Publication, 34th Regiment New York Volunteers Civil War Newspaper Clippings, New York State Military Museum and Veterans Research Center. Accessed May 1, 2017. https://dmna.ny.gov/historic/reghist/civil/infantry/34thInf/34thInfCWN.htm.

Index

About the Author

Ryan Quint is a native of Maine and earned his degree in history from the University of Mary Washington in Fredericksburg, VA. He has worked in the field of public history, including at the George Washington Foundation, Colonial Williamsburg, and the National Park Service. Ryan has been involved with Emerging Civil War since 2013, and his first book, *Determined to Stand and Fight: The Battle of Monocacy*, was published by Savas Beatie in 2017 as part of the Emerging Civil War series (emergingcivilwar.com).